Education in the European Union
Post-2003 Member States

Education in the European Union Post-2003 Member States

Edited by Trevor Corner

Education Around the World

Bloomsbury Academic
An imprint of Bloomsbury Publishing Plc

B L O O M S B U R Y
LONDON · OXFORD · NEW YORK · NEW DELHI · SYDNEY

Bloomsbury Academic

An imprint of Bloomsbury Publishing Plc

50 Bedford Square	1385 Broadway
London	New York
WC1B 3DP	NY 10018
UK	USA

www.bloomsbury.com

BLOOMSBURY and the Diana logo are trademarks of Bloomsbury Publishing Plc

First published 2015
Paperback edition first published 2017

British Library Cataloguing-in-Publication Data
A catalogue record for this book is available from the British Library.

ISBN: HB: 978-1-4725-2331-0
PB: 978-1-3500-1678-1
ePDF: 978-1-4725-2448-5
ePub: 978-1-4725-2228-3

Library of Congress Cataloging-in-Publication Data
A catalog record for this book is available from the Library of Congress.

Series: Education Around the World

Typeset by Integra Software Services Pvt. Ltd.

Contents

Series Editor's Preface

This series will comprise nineteen volumes looking at education in virtually every territory in the world. The initial volume, *Education Around the World: A Comparative Introduction*, aims to provide an insight to the field of international and comparative education. It looks at its history and development and then examines a number of major themes at scales from local to regional, to global. It is important to bear such scales of observation in mind because the remainder of the series is inevitably regionally and nationally based.

The identification of the eighteen regions within which to group countries has sometimes been a very simple task, elsewhere less so. Europe, for example, has four volumes, and most of a fifth, and more than fifty countries overall. National statistics vary considerably in their availability and accuracy, and in any case date rapidly. Consequently, the editors of each volume point the reader towards access to regional and international datasets, available on line, that are regularly updated. A key purpose of the series is to give some visibility to a large number of countries that, for various reasons, rarely, if ever, have coverage in the literature of this field.

For this volume, *Education in the European Union: Post 2003 Member States*, Professor Trevor Corner has assembled a range of well-chosen authors, each an authority on his or her subject. The collection provides a clear overview of education in each respective country while also highlighting particular issues of contemporary import. Many of these countries figure much less in the literature of comparative and international education than their pre-2003 member counterparts. Professor Corner is to be warmly thanked for the considerable effort that this has entailed and the quality of the outcome, especially as at the same time compiling the other EU volume in this series. He is a long-standing and active member of the Comparative Education Society in Europe (CESE). His fellow members will find this book a valuable addition to their collections.

Colin Brock: Series Editor

Notes on Contributors

Kiril Bankov is Professor of Mathematics Education in the Faculty of Mathematics Education at the University of Sofia, Bulgaria. He has previously been senior researcher and visiting professor at the Department of Teacher Education at the Michigan State University (MSU), United States (2007–9), and National Science Coordinator for TIMMS in Bulgaria. He has worked for major international organizations including the World Bank and the Soros Foundation, and is a member of a number of national mathematics associations including the European Society for Research in Mathematics Education (ERME) and senior research coordinator for mathematics, mathematics pedagogy knowledge and curriculum analysis in FIRSTMATH in the International Study Centre at MSU.

Carmel Borg is Associate Professor in the Department of Education of the Faculty of Education at the University of Malta. He is a former head of the Department of Education and ex-Dean of Education. His lecturing and research interests include sociology of education, curriculum theory, development and design, critical pedagogy and adult education. He has worked as an educational expert for the European Commission's education agency and is currently a coordinator and leader of a number of European projects. He is founder-editor of the *Journal of Maltese Education Research*, now the *Malta Review of Educational Research* (MRER).

Trevor Corner is Emeritus Professor and Director of the Institute for Research and Postgraduate Studies at the University of Middlesex, London, UK. He has published widely in international and comparative studies and has taught in Universities in France, Denmark, Canada and the United States. His research interests include international trends in education, lifelong learning and adult education, and he has worked on a number of national and international programmes as well as the European Union programmes of Erasmus and FP7. He has been a member of the World Council of Comparative Education Societies British and European Comparative Education Societies and published widely on European secondary and higher education.

Vlatka Domović is Professor at the Faculty of Teacher Education, University of Zagreb, Croatia. She holds a master's degree in Adult Education and a PhD in Education (2000). Her research interests include teacher education and training, education administration, comparative education, school effectiveness, and vocational education and training. She has coordinated seven science projects supported by the Croatian Ministry for Science, Education and Sports and has been involved in numerous international projects (Tempus, ETF, CARDS). Since 2010, she has been Vice President of the Comparative Education Society in Europe (CESE) and has worked as a World Bank consultant. In 2013 she won the Croatian state award 'Ivan Filipovic' for contributions to Croatian higher education. She has published more than sixty research papers, co-authored two books and edited four others.

Danut Dumitrascu is Professor and Head of the Department of Business Development at the Lucien Blaga University, Sibiu, Romania. He is a specialist in business management and education and coordinator of PhD research and master's courses within the faculty. He has written widely in the fields of education and technical management, environment management, marketing and professional training.

Ewa Frankiewicz is a PhD student at the Opole University in Silesia, Poland. Previously, she taught in the Economy and Innovation College and Lublin Higher Education College, both in Poland. She is author of more than a dozen scholarly articles in the fields of elementary education, history of education and comparative education. She completed postgraduate courses in Preparation to Integrated Education (2010) and Pedagogic Therapy (2014) at the Rzeszów University, Poland. She holds degrees in Master of Arts in History (2004) and Master of Arts in Protective and Educational Pedagogy (2005) from the Maria Curie Skłodowska University, Poland.

David Greger is Director of the Institute for Research and Development of Education at the Faculty of Education, Charles University, Czech Republic. He holds a doctoral degree in education science from Charles University, and his research activities are orientated towards the fields of comparative education, educational policy and sociology of education. He was a coordinator and member of several national as well as international research projects: currently he leads the first large-scale longitudinal study in education in the Czech Republic (CLoSE—Czech Longitudinal Study in Education). His main research activities concern equity and quality in education, priority education policies, educational transitions and school choice, and the use of early tracking.

Eleftherios Klerides is Lecturer in Comparative Education and History of Education in the Department of Education at the University of Cyprus and Secretary-Treasurer of the Comparative Education Society in Europe (CESE). His degrees include an MA and PhD in Comparative Education (Institute of Education, University College London, UK, 2008). Before joining the University of Cyprus, he worked at the Institute of Education of University of London (2008), the Georg Eckert Institute for International Textbook Research in Germany (2009), the American University of Beirut in Lebanon (2009–12) and the European University of Cyprus (2009–12). Currently, he is working as a consultant for the World Bank. He has edited and guest-edited a number of comparative education international journals.

Ryszard Kucha is Head of the Faculty of Pedagogics and Psychology Branch at Deblin Higher Military Aviation School, Poland, and Head of the History of Education and Comparative Education Chair in the Institute of Pedagogics at the University of Social Sciences in Lodz, Poland. Previously, he was Vice Dean of Education and International Exchange Programmes (1984–90 and 1993–99); Head of the History of Education Department in the Faculty of Pedagogics and Psychology Faculty of Pedagogics and Psychology of Maria Curie Skłodowska University in Lublin, Poland. He has been Visiting Professor at many universities in Europe and is a member the European Association for International Education and the Polish Pedagogical Association. He has written over two hundred articles and twenty-five books in the fields of history of education and European integration.

Andrea Laczik is Research Fellow at the Centre for Education and Industry at the University of Warwick, UK. She studied for a DPhil in Comparative and International Education at the Department of Education, University of Oxford, UK. Her current research interests include Pre/post-16 VET, work-related learning, education reform processes and young people in jobs without training, and changes in the Eastern European education systems. Recent projects include comparative research–orientated curricula in IVET, work-based learning for low-skilled unemployed adults (funded by the European Centre for the Development of Vocational Training (CEDEFOP), and the under-utilization of Hungarian migrants in the UK (Skills, Knowledge and Organizational Performance/Economic and Social Research Council [SKOPE/ESRC]).

Peter Mayo is Professor in the Faculty of Education in the University of Malta. He has published on a wide and diverse range of educational research subjects, particularly in adult education and critical pedagogies, which include studies on Gramsci and Friere, as well as social movements through education in general. He edits a number of educational international journals, including *Post Colonial Studies in Education* and *International Issues in Education*. He recently published the book *Echoes from Friere for a Critically Engaged Pedagogy* (Bloomsbury, 2013).

Carmen Novac is a post-doctoral researcher in the Faulty of Engineering of Lucien Blaga University in Sibiu, Romania. Having obtained a Higher Diploma in European Institutions Management, she developed her PhD research in the area of higher educational financial management and how third stream activities could contribute to higher educational studies and research in a situation of transforming higher educational studies in Romania. She collaborated with the Institute of Education, University College London, UK, in the process of developing an international view of financial management in universities and third-level institutions. She has collaborated with a number of European Projects in the field of e-Learning.

Mojca Peček is Associate Professor in the Theory of Education, in the Pedagogical Faculty of the University of Ljubljana, Slovenia, having previously obtained his PhD in Pedagogical Studies with expertise in the theory of education, civic education, regulation policy of school systems, inclusive education and justice in educational systems. He is President of the Program Council for further education and training of professional staff with the Slovenian Ministry of Education and national representative in ENTEP (European Network on Teacher Education Policies. He has been active on a number of European programmes such as Tempus, Comenius and Socrates, and has published widely on developments in Slovenian education in Europe and the United States.

Stavroula Philippou is Lecturer in Curriculum and Instruction at the Department of Education, University of Cyprus. Her studies include an MEd in Curriculum Studies (University of Sydney, Australia, 1999) and a PhD in Education (University of Cambridge, UK, 2004). She has worked in a variety of educational contexts and as a consultant for UNESCO (United Nations Educational, Scientific and Cultural Organization) and the Council of Europe. She is currently the General Assembly Cyprus representative of the International Association for the Advancement of Curriculum Studies (IAACS) and the Cyprus Coordinator for CiCe (Children's Identity and Citizenship in Europe, Erasmus Thematic Network). Her research interests include theory, history and sociology of curriculum, curriculum reform, change and review; and curriculum development and design.

Iveta Silova is Associate Professor and Program Director of Comparative and International Education at LeHigh College of Education, Pennsylvania, United States. Her research and publications cover issues of critical understanding of globalization and post-socialist education transformation processes, including the professional development of teachers and teacher educators, gender equity in Eastern/Central Europe and Central Asia, and minority/multicultural education in the former Soviet Union, as well as the scope, nature and implications of private tutoring in cross-national perspective. Her recent publications include *Globalization on the Margins: Education and Post-Socialist Transformations in Central Asia* (2011), and she is the editor of *European Education: Issues and Studies*.

Doyle Stevick is Associate Professor of Educational Leadership and Policies, University of South Carolina, United States. He studied mathematics and classical studies at the University of Pennsylvania, United States, and completed his PhD on Civic Education: Policy and Practice in Estonia, in 2006 with Indiana University. He has been a recipient of a Fulbright Fellowship in 2003 and 2014 for studies in Estonia. He has written a wide range of publications on civic education and cultural diversity, with a focus on educational and social developments in Estonia over the past ten years. His research interests are Holocaust education, educational policy, comparative and international education, and civic education.

Eva Tandlichová is Professor in Educational Foundations, Leadership and Technology (EFLT) Methodology and Applied Linguistics at the Department of British and American Studies in the Faculty of Arts of Comenius University, Slovakia. She has worked extensively across Europe, including in the UK, Spain, Austria and the Czech Republic, and in the United States. She is a member of the Advisory Board at the Pedagogical Research Institute in Bratislava and a National Advisor in foreign language teaching and learning for the Slovakian Ministry of Education. She has been active in advising the Ministry of Education on the recent educational reforms. She has written many course books on language teaching and learning and on the evaluation of education as a foreign language (EFL) as well as being influential in the development of European projects such as Comenius; in recognition of her work in the field of EFL, she has been the recipient of a number of awards from Comenius University.

Vlasta Vizek Vidović is Senior Researcher at the Centre for Educational Research and Development in the Institute for Social Research in Zagreb, Croatia, and previously worked at the Department of Psychology at the University of Zagreb, Croatia. She was Head of the Chair of School of Psychology and Vice-Dean of the Faulty of Philosophy at the University of Zagreb and Head of the Accreditation Board for Croatia. Her main areas of research include work values, professional development, professional stress, motivation to learn and learning strategies. She has coordinated international education projects for UNESCO and SEE (Sharing Experience Europe) projects linking with the University of Georgia, United States. Author and co-author of ten monographs and handbooks, and eighty scientific and professional papers, she also has acted as translator for a number of English psychology textbooks into Croatian.

Rimantas Zelvys is Vice-Rector for Research, Lithuanian University of Educational Sciences, and Professor, Department of Education, Vilnius University, Lithuania. She graduated in Psychology from Vilnius University and obtained her PhD at the Bechterev Research Institute in St Petersburg, Russia. She became D.Habil. with Vilnius Pedagogical University in 2000. She has experience of many Central and Eastern European countries, with a high expertise in educational policy and management, and quality assessment and appraisal with the OECD, Soros Foundation, the World Bank and the United Nations Development Programme (UNDP).

She has published widely in English on topics of teacher education, national educational reforms, and management and change in the new millennium.

Introduction

Educational Change and Transformation in South and Central European Countries: A Regional Overview

Trevor Corner

Trends in European Education

The focus of this second book covering the member states of the European Union is on those that joined after 2003, which are predominantly those countries in the central and eastern parts of the subcontinent. Many of these countries have previously been under the educational and political influence of the Soviet Union and are now moving through a series of transitional phases towards more western models. The relatively small, yet complex, educational systems of the Mediterranean islands Cyprus and Malta, which also formally joined the European Union in 2004, illustrate some of the potential educational opportunities and problems that arise when joining the European integration process.

The two books on the EU area, covering twenty-seven of the twenty-eight EU countries, provide a concise analysis and overview of the major educational traditions and their recent evolution across Europe, while offering insights into the mosaic of schools and colleges, languages and social characteristics that each country exhibits through the education it provides for its citizens. The chapters are written by educational experts from each country, who have insights, experience and knowledge of the educational systems that have formed their country's citizens over the past half-century. These authors also shed light on the countervailing forces for integration towards a European identity and the yet enduring wish for regional autonomy and locally based school administrations.

Taking the long view, Ringer has made the point that the role of social and political conflict cannot be ignored in the history of educational development

(Ringer, 1979). The demand for increased opportunities, for 'democratization', has been an important factor in the enlargement of European education systems since 1918 and, more generally, in the growth of enrolments progressively through systems. A reform consensus emerged during the interwar years, the importance of which stemmed from the wide support it had from the centre and left of the political spectrum. Segmentation in education was generally disapproved of as tending to preserve privilege, whilst greater inclusiveness was seen as an aid to the economy and as a democratic measure. If the breakdown of class barriers, increase of educational opportunities for lower-class students and merit rather than family background determined access to education, then inclusiveness and progressiveness ensued.

During the Cold War, a social and economic revolution transformed the Balkans. The all-important shift to an urban, industrial—and now post-industrialized—society brought fundamental changes to the nature of daily life and new challenges to domestic political elites. The ending of the Cold War has allowed the Eastern European states to participate in a different Europe, whose values are inscribed in its dominant cross-national institutions—the European Union, North Atlantic Treaty Organization (NATO) and the Comparative Education Society in Europe (CESE). It has also transformed them geo-politically, because they now find themselves at the centre of a greatly expanded market which takes in the Black Sea, the former Soviet Union and Central Asia, offering possibilities for business across a vaster area than at any time since the Ottoman Empire. As well, therefore, as inheriting the educational patterns of the past, these Eastern European states have to take on dilemmas familiar to most of the European countries: how to reconcile older patterns of educational provision, absorb the competitive pressures of global capitalism and mould the output of educational systems to build prosperous economies and allow social democracy to flourish (Mazower, 2000).

Education and life chances

The role of education as a determinant of individual life chances and as a predictor of young peoples' chances in the labour market and society is the subject of continual discussion for teachers and educationalists. A central part of the professional educationalists' existence is to make the case for the importance of education 'from cradle to grave' and act as both a protagonist and critic. The writers of these thirteen chapters on the national education systems of eastern and southern members of the European Union have undertaken their task, for the most part, as both citizens and experts of their 'home' educational systems.

The power of a national state, and the extent to which each interacts with others, are expressions of the historic, political and economic strands which infuse and inform an education system. The Western European social democratic view has been to argue that by relieving the individual of the hazards of poverty; by providing more opportunity, not least by means of education, for self-development; and by limiting the arbitrary use of power by the holders of money and status, the margin of individual options has been widened. The liberal consensus is that perhaps the overriding purpose of the educational system should be to help the individual to realize his or her potentialities, abilities and interests as they develop from interaction among the agents of educational influences (Husen, 1979).

Writing in 1979, Grant interpreted the purpose of education in the USSR as primarily a political tool for the construction of a communist society, and he quotes the Basic Law on Education (1974): 'The goal of public education in the U.S.S.R. is the preparation of [sic] highly educated, well-rounded, physically healthy and active builders of communist society' (Grant, 1979). Was it the case that in gaining membership to the European Community in 2003/4, the governments of Bulgaria, Croatia, Czech Republic, Estonia, Hungary, Latvia, Lithuania, Poland, Romania, Slovakia and Slovenia (and coming from a different perspective, Cyprus and Malta) were taking on acceptance of Western European values of social solidarity which find political and legal expression in the welfare state and a programmatic commitment to free education from kindergarten through to university, irrespective of political ideology? The question perhaps, especially at the present time, is whether this rhetoric of social solidarity can be translated into constitutional guarantees which can allow the European Constitution to gain traction in identity and identification (Weiler et al., 2003).

The major trends examined here (and in the sister accompanying book *Education in the EU: Pre-2003 Member States*) are therefore the evolution of the school systems, the main factors that have shaped these systems in the past thirty years, the political changes during the late 1980s and the expansion of the European Union in May 2004, when it formally accepted a further ten member states (eight of the then Central and Eastern Europe (CEE) countries, with Bulgaria and Romania joining in January 2007). As consistently indicated by the writers of these chapters, the view of the European Commission in Brussels was that this rapid enlargement enhanced the prospects of embracing the cultural heritage of a 'greater Europe'; at the same time there was an increase in cultural heterogeneity, social disparities and economic imbalances and their ensuing influences.

Diversity, states and regions

Whilst following the Maritza River near Plovdiv in Bulgaria, Patrick Leigh Fermor relates some of the colours and complexities of cultures to be found in that region during the 1930s:

> There was a pinnacle mosque and suddenly Turks—sashed in red like the Bulgars, but they wore baggy black trousers and slippers and scarlet fezzes. I might also have seen some Kutzovlachs, or semi-nomadic Aruman shepherds speaking a low Latin Dialect laced with Slav and akin to Rumanian. The Pomaks are said to be Bulgarians converted to Islam after the Turkish conquest. On either side of the border live tiny pockets of Kizilbashi, red-headed and Shi'ite Muslims. A turn in the lane and all the shops would become Greek and the air would ring with this language. (Fermor, 2013)

Today, cultural and linguistic diversity persists in many of the CEE countries, but the major changes in educational provision have grown step by step with radical political and economic transformations; new patterns of education, new types of schools and new institutional structures have emerged. Whilst some changes have reached back to a pre-Communist era, others have adopted Western European trends. For example, the structure of post-secondary education has been diversified, both through the introduction of secondary vocational programmes and the appearance of private institutions. Hungary, the Czech Republic, Slovenia, Slovakia and Poland, having been part of the Austro-Hungarian Empire, inherited influences from the Austrian and German education and training systems, whilst Hungary, the Czech Republic and Slovakia also introduced early selection in prestigiously academic gymnasia, along with a dual system of vocational training (Graf, 2015).

The three Baltic states, Estonia, Latvia and Lithuania, have been influenced by both German and Russian education traditions and have significant Russian minority populations. Continuing links with the Scandinavian countries from the 1990s have encouraged secondary-based vocational education and enhanced social welfare initiatives. Significant increases in the tertiary and private sectors are also common to these countries.

Bulgaria has inherited a centralized economy and standardized education system from the Soviet era but has found difficulties in the transition to a market-based economy, especially during the 1960s. Whilst open to European integration, it has some reservation in fully exposing changes in general educational attainment to international gaze, as illustrated by its tentative adoption of international achievement tests such as TIMMS, and has lagged some other eastern countries, with vocational education at lower secondary level remaining low and ethnic groups achieving significantly lower educational levels (Kogan et al., 2008: 100–14). Romania too has had a relatively late education expansion, with continuing Soviet influences remaining into the 1990s. By the end of the Ceausescu period, less than 8 per cent of secondary students were enrolled in theoretical (academic) education (Mocanu, 2008).

Malta and Cyprus both officially joined the European Union in May 2004 as a part of the new enlargement. Malta, the smallest member of the community by size and population, continues to debate the benefits and drawbacks of membership; though educationalists see some benefits in the access to education in other European states, others conclude that Malta is becoming a staging post for refugees seeking access to the European continent, which membership has inadvertently encouraged. In their chapter on Maltese education, Borg and Mayo particularly examine the role that international influences have had on education, how achievement is seen as both passport and cogent element of life, and how the growth of adult and higher education has been emphasized as fundamental for a competent workforce.

The accession of the Republic of Cyprus was again part of the 2004 enlargement and had been anticipated as a potential force for the unification of the island (much in the same way as the potential for the alleviation of Belgian regionalism would be hopefully realized via the 1957 Treaty of Rome). In practice the negotiations between the Cypriot communities have been complicated by this accession, and whilst, legally at least, EU regulations cover the whole of the island, they are enforceable only in the southern part of the island. In Chapter 3, the authors point to the internationalization of Cyprus with regards to membership of the EU, United Nations Educational, Scientific and Cultural Organization (UNESCO) and the Organisation for Economic Cooperation and Development (OECD), whilst nonetheless, recent educational developments on the island are shaped by local, post-colonial anxieties, ideologies and histories as well as by Greek national culture and identity, which have become the dominant factors in the last 20 years.

Enlargement and integration or dissipation and confrontation

There are currently over 500 million people in the EU countries, compared to 320,000 million in the United States, frequently cited as a similar world region and friendly competitor. There will soon be over one billion teenagers on the planet, and, as James Martin has pointed out, this 'Transition Generation' will benefit from much 'free' education via internet forums as well as within formal schooling. This is an area where the EU countries have yet to make an impact. On a grander scale, much of future educational development should come from the deliberate transfer of knowledge of how to cure diseases, grow food and create employment; this process of educational transfer between the major regions of the world would enable populations to grow at a slower rate and reduce poverty (Martin, 2006). Writing in 2007, Symecki has pointed to political, economic and educational factors that drove the eastern and southern European countries to anticipate EU membership with enthusiasm.

> This enlargement must not be the last. It is difficult to define the limits to 'Europe'. And perhaps it is useless to discuss where Europe ends, while the new Member States are likely to become diligent and disciplined neophytes. If the old EU-15 becomes more active in fostering integration, the diligent converts will follow suit. If the path chosen by the EU is bold and far-reaching, then the marriage (of enlargement) could perhaps be stormy and adventurous, but not boring. (Symecki, 2007: 410)

The thirteen chapters that follow lead to equivocation on the direction of educational change and the role and functions of European integration for the countries concerned. To a certain extent, enthusiasm for integration has waned, and the sought-for economic drivers for monetary union remain elusive. Whilst the Lisbon-Copenhagen-Maastricht and Bologna processes have pushed educational integration a step further, particularly in vocational education and higher education, the sought-after marriage of the E-15 to the E-13 is turning out to be stormy and adventurous, but the overall direction of travel is not easy to discern.

Acknowledgement

Thanks are expressed to the Committee and members of the Comparative Education Society in Europe (CESE) for their helpful suggestions to the authors who have provided many of the chapters in this volume and its companion, *Education in the European Union: Pre-2003 Member States*.

References

Fermor, P.L. (2013). *The Broken Road: From the Iron Gates to Mount Athos*. London: John Murray, 28–29.

Grant, N. (1979). *Soviet Education*. Harmondsworth: Pelican Books, 25.

Graf, L. (2015). 'Germany: Stability and Change', in T. Corner (ed.), *Education in the European Union: Pre-2003 Member States*. London: Bloomsbury, 133–40.

Husen, T. (1979). *The School in Question: A Comparative Study of the School and its Future in Western Societies*. Oxford: Oxford University Press, 4–5.

Kogan, I., Gebel, M., and Noelke, C. (2008). *Europe Enlarged: A Handbook of Education, Labour and Welfare Regimes in Central and Eastern Europe*. Bristol: Policy Press.

Martin, J. (2006). *The Meaning of the 21st Century: A Vital Blueprint for Ensuring our Future*. London: Random House, 362–64.

Mazower, M. (2000). *The Balkans: From the End of Byzantium to the Present Day*. London: Orion, 150–51.

Mocanu, C. (2008). 'Romania', in I. Kogan, M. Gebel, C. Noelke (eds), *Europe Enlarged: A Handbook of Education, Labour and Welfare Regimes in Central and Eastern Europe*. Bristol: Policy Press, 295–304.

Ringer, F.K. (1979). *Education and Society in Modern Europe*. London: Indiana University Press, 200–2.

Symecki, P. (2007). 'Some Remarks on Poland's Membership of the EU: The qualities in demand', in J. Weiler, I. Begg and J. Petersen (eds), (2003) *Integration in an Expanding European Union: Reassessing the Fundamentals*. Oxford: Blackwell, 410.

Weiler, J. (2003). 'A constitution for Europe?: Some hard choices', in J. Weiler, I. Begg and J. Petersen (eds), (2003). *Integration in an Expanding European Union: Reassessing the Fundamentals*. Oxford: Blackwell, 17–33.

1

Bulgaria: An Overview

Kiril Bankov

Introduction

The territory of Bulgaria has been inhabited since the very early historical periods, and its history is rich and complex. The early historical and cultural development of education traces its roots to the time when the Thracians settled during the Bronze Age, and later, in the sixth century, when they were assimilated by the Slavs. In the second half of the seventh century, proto-Bulgarians settled in the territory of south-east Bulgaria, forming an alliance with the Slavs, and founded the state of Bulgaria in 681 C.E. At the end of the ninth century, Cyril and Methodius created and disseminated the Cyrillic alphabet, based on which a rich literary tradition and a sophisticated system of education were developed. From Bulgaria, Cyrillic writing spread across other Slavic countries such that in the ninth century Bulgaria could lay claim to be one of the first European countries to create its own church, school and literature. The Old Bulgarian language is recognized as the third literary language after the Old Greek and Latin languages.

In 1018, after extended wars, Byzantium conquered Bulgaria, though the response was that the Bulgarians immediately started the fight to recover their liberty and gained independence in 1186. A decade later, Bulgaria restored its previous power, and after years of cultural standstill, Bulgarian learning reached a new peak in the period of the Second Bulgarian Empire (1186–1396). The schools of literature and arts in Tarnovo, in the north of modern-day Bulgaria, developed the traditions of the Bulgarian culture.

In 1396, the Ottoman Empire conquered Bulgaria for a period of five centuries (1396–1878). During these years, the Bulgarian monasteries became educational and cultural centres that preserved the Bulgarian traditions, language and awareness. The monastery schools dominated the Bulgarian educational life until the late 1930s of the nineteenth century, when the 'teachers' in these schools were monks who could read and write. Monastic education was organized through small groups of young people who wanted basic informal education, and became a tradition in Bulgarian education, where the more educated people teach others as informal teachers.

The beginning of the eighteenth century saw the formation of the new Bulgarian nation and the development of a Bulgarian system of education. The pursuit of national independence progressed through the development of a national church, education and culture. In 1878, when the state of Bulgaria was once more restored after the Russian-Turkish war, Bulgaria preserved and developed further the traditions from the Bulgarian revival in education. A stable and democratic educational system was developed, accompanied by school legislation leading to different educational levels which were recognized as qualifying for some higher institutions on a regional basis. At that time, Bulgaria was recognized as having the highest literacy rate on the Balkan Peninsula, albeit there was still a lack of formal teacher preparation.

Bulgaria's participation in the First World War brought about a national catastrophe, leading to the country becoming unstable and the eruption of multiple civil wars. In the early 1940s, Bulgarian politics turned towards Germany, and as a result Bulgaria was occupied by Russian troops at the end of the Second Word War. In 1946, Bulgaria became a republic, and the Communist Party came into power. The Bulgarian school kept its national aspect and democratic character despite the ideological communist influence as well as the influence of the Soviet educational system. The beginning of the 1950s marked a period of great expansion for higher education, with overall developments that were in accordance with socialist ideas. At this time (about 1955), the formal system of teacher preparation began, based on the subject-orientated faculties at the universities (Bankov, 2007a), a model adopted from the former Soviet Union that still persists to this day.

The new democratic changes in Bulgaria started on 10 November 1989, and a new state constitution was developed and approved in 1991. In the area of education, new educational forms have been established, and some private schools have appeared. A series of recent legislative amendments and initiatives have created a process of educational reform designed to improve the quality of education. The reform is influenced by current trends towards internationalization and globalization; the need for greater freedom of choice; and the political, social, demographic, technological and economic changes that have occurred in Bulgaria over the last two and a half decades. The reform seeks a more flexible school organization that reflects the market economy and principles of autonomy; central education requirements for assessing student achievement and school accreditation; linking school financing to student enrolment and to educational quality; and more local influence on educational matters.

On 1 January 2007, Bulgaria became a member of the European Union, an important event in the modern Bulgarian educational development which now means that not only the legislation but also all educational entities have to be in line with the European requirements and norms. This gave a new direction to educational reforms and attracted appreciable European funds to support the needed changes and revisions of the normative documents and the implementation of their regulations.

Governance and normative documents

In Bulgaria, education is a state responsibility, with the Ministry of Education controlling virtually all aspects of the system. Regional educational inspectorates, made up of civil servants appointed by the Ministry of Education, are responsible for hiring school principals as well as for the administration and finances of local schools. The schools (their principals) are responsible for the hiring of teachers and support staff, whilst individual teachers make decisions on instructional methods and classroom process. Teaching methods are taught during teacher education courses.

Soon after the democratic changes established in 1989, the main educational law (Law of Public Education, 1991) was developed, passed in the Parliament and quickly came into force the same year. The structure of the new educational system is described following as well as the types of schools are that are legitimated by this law. For the last two and a half decades, social and cultural life in Bulgaria has continuously changed, circumstances which demand many revisions and amendments to the law, which have been made frequently during the past years when legislation has been constantly evolving.

Eight years later, a new curriculum law (Law of the Level of Education, General Educational Minimum, and Curriculum, 1999) was introduced in the country, and subsequently the national content standards and respective programmes of study were developed for the Bulgarian schools in all subjects and grades for general education. The main purpose was to improve the quality of basic education and to prepare citizens for successful life and work in a global world and economy. This requires the development of a new standards-based curriculum with an emphasis on skills and competencies components, especially lifelong learning skills as opposed to the widely spread traditional 'informational' approach which relied heavily on prescribed content and lecture-based pedagogy.

These ambitious goals were further elaborated by the National Program for Development of the School and the Pre-School Education and Training, 2006–15, published in 2006. This programme is based on the understanding that valuing the student's learning is the main component. All educational changes as well as the interests of the other parties in the educational process should be subordinated to the main goal, namely ensuring equal access to quality educational opportunities. The beginning of the programme (pp. 3–6) outlines the main problems of school education in 2006. Some of them are still topical to the present time, namely: (1) instructions that promote memorization and reproduction, not thinking, independence and developing skills; (2) an insufficient system for effectively evaluating the quality of education; (3) the large number of dropouts; (4) low social status and insufficient authority of the teacher; (5) old-fashioned management of the education system; and (6) a financing plan that does not stimulate development of the educational institution (i.e. schools). This programme also provides for the introduction of a national standardized assessment system and envisages reforms (e.g. a change of the structure of the educational system) for changes in other normative educational documents. Based on this, a proposal for a new law on preschool and school education was developed shortly after the publication of the above-mentioned programme. Although for the past few years the proposal has been discussed, corrected and debated in the Parliament many times, at the time of writing it has still to be agreed upon.

The Bulgarian educational system

According to the Law of Public Education (1991), there are three levels of education: preschool education (children aged from 3 to 6 or 7 years), school education (students aged from 6–7 to 18–20 years) and higher education (see Figure 1.1).[1,2] School education includes the two levels of basic education and secondary education (Schmidt et al., 2011).

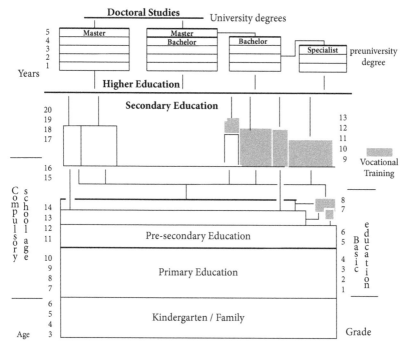

Figure 1.1 Structure of the educational system in Bulgaria.

Basic education (grades 1–8) comprises primary schools (grades 1–4) and pre-secondary schools (grades 5–8). Within the framework of the same educational level, additional vocational qualification could be obtained by running vocational-technical programmes upon completion of grades 7 or 8. After successful completion of grade 4, a Certificate of Primary Education is issued. A Certificate of Basic Education is issued after successful completion of grade 8.

Secondary education is divided into secondary general (comprehensive and profile oriented) and vocational. Secondary general education can be attained at secondary comprehensive schools (duration of studies, four years) or profile secondary schools (duration of studies, four or five years). Students can enter the profile secondary schools, beginning in grade 8 (rarely in grade 9), after passing entrance examinations on Bulgarian language and literature and/or mathematics, or on some other subjects according to the profile of the school. Most of these schools offer intensive foreign language instruction, and studies in the profile secondary schools are usually regarded as demanding, which is why they are considered 'the best places' for secondary education. Secondary vocational education can be attained at vocational training schools, beginning in grade 9 within a four-year training period, or beginning in grade 8 within a five-year training and intensive foreign language instruction. There are also vocational schools offering a three-year education. The professional qualification obtained gives access to the labour market. After successfully completing the last year of secondary school and passing the written examinations (*Matura*), a diploma of secondary education is issued. The qualification must obligatorily mention the chosen branch of specialization, where appropriate.

Education in Bulgaria is compulsory up to age 16 years. The school year in Bulgaria begins on 15 September at all levels and ends 30 May for primary schools, 15 June for pre-secondary schools and 30 June for secondary schools. The year ranges from 180 to 200 days and is divided into two terms: from September to the end of January, and from February to the year end. Schools are closed twice during the school year: for about fourteen days at the end of December and beginning of January, and for about ten days at the beginning of April. Figure 1.1 shows the overall structure of the education system and indicates the following types of schools in Bulgaria:

1. Junior: grades 1–4
2. Middle: grades 5–8
3. Primary: grades 1–8
4. Secondary: grades 9–12
5. Profile secondary: grades 8–12
6. Comprehensive: grades 1–12
7. Vocational training schools: from grade 8 or 9 through grade 12
8. Vocational schools: from grade 7 or 8, offering a three-year course; from grade 9, offering courses of up to four years; or after secondary education acquisition, a two-year course
9. Sport schools
10. Art schools
11. Special schools for children with special educational needs (SEN)
12. Culture schools

According to the National Statistical Institute (2012/3), there are 2,606 schools in Bulgaria. Most of them are funded by the state, whilst 128 private fee-charging schools are run by individuals or organizations and have been in existence since 1990.

The average class size in primary schools is about twenty-one students; in pre-secondary school, about twenty-two; and in secondary, about twenty-three students (National Statistical Institute, 2012/3). The dropout rate is between 2 per cent and 3 per cent. A weak point in the structure of the educational system is the transition to profile secondary schools. Even though the basic education formally finishes at the end of grade 8, the profile secondary schools start their education from the beginning in grade 8. This is a kind of inconsistency in the educational system, because the students entering the profile secondary schools do not formally finish their basic education. Also, the entrance examination for the profile secondary schools is considered a stressful event in the life of the candidates (about 45 per cent of the students finishing grade 7). This is not only because the exams are usually hard but also because students only have the chance to continue their education in a school that provides better training.

This could be proposed as one of the reasons for a change of the educational structure made by the National Program for Development of the School and the Pre-School Education and Training, 2006–15. The newly drafted law on preschool and school education takes this into account. According to the proposal, there are no profile secondary schools, and all students will complete their basic education after finishing grade 7. The secondary education will have two stages. The first stage, comprising grades 8, 9 and 10, offers a 'comprehensive education' where students may choose 'elective courses' according to their interests, by analogy with the profile subjects. The next stage of secondary education (grades 11 and 12) is planned to be real profile education, requiring students to choose fewer profile subjects but to study them in more detail. At the present time, this structure for secondary education is at the proposal stage only, with approval of the law yet to come into force.

Curriculum and programmes

The intended curriculum in all subjects for Bulgaria is centralized and determined by the Ministry of Education. There is a single curriculum for primary and pre-secondary education which is compulsory for all pupils. From grade 1 till the end of grade 8, there is only one curriculum in all school subjects. All students cover the same topics at the same level and have the same workload (study hours). From grade 9 until the end of secondary education, most subjects have two levels. Level 1 gives the basic knowledge and is intended for students who are not expected to go into a professional career involving this subject, whereas level 2 is more advanced. Both levels follow the same topics but at different depths, and some additional topics are covered for level 2. This is possible because there is a greater workload (study hours) for level 2. After grade 8, each student chooses one of the levels (for subjects that have two levels).

Students can move from one level to another on a particular subject, even if this does not happen often.

Profile secondary schools have additional lessons for the profiled subjects. In mathematics, for example, students in the comprehensive schools that do not have a mathematics profile study two academic hours (one academic hour is forty minutes) of mathematics per week. In contrast, students in mathematics profile secondary schools may study up to nine academic hours of mathematics per week. Mathematics profile curriculum offers few additional mathematics topics compared to the compulsory curriculum. But students in the mathematics profile secondary schools have much more time for practice exercises, experiments and problem solving.

In 2000, the Content Educational Standards for all subjects were approved by the Ministry of Education. These standards focus on what students are expected to know and be able to do at the end of each level of schooling (primary schools, pre-secondary schools and secondary schools). One year later, instructional programmes for each subject were developed for each grade. They describe the topics that students have to study in every subject at each grade level and the skills that they have to acquire. For the secondary education level, the standards cover both levels (for subjects that have two levels), as already described. These standards were developed on the basis of expertise but are not based on any preliminary assessment. It is expected that these standards will have to be assessed and revised.

In 2012, the European Social Fund sponsored the Bulgarian Ministry of Education to administer the project 'Improvement of the Quality of the General Education' (Project BG051PO001-3.1.04) whose slogan was 'For better education'. The aim of the project was to assist the implementation of the new law on preschool and school education that was expected to come into force very soon. A substantial part of the project was the revision of the Content Educational Standards and the instructional programmes for the basic education (grades 1–7). New Content Educational Standards and instructional programmes were developed for both stages (grades 8–10, and grades 11 and 12) of the secondary education. Special attention was paid to the profile education during the second stage (grades 11 and 12), because this is something new in the Bulgarian educational system both as a structure and as an educational philosophy. The project recognized that Bulgarian education is very much theoretically oriented, and students do not acquire practical skills. Therefore, the newly developed documentation recommends more 'real-life' orientation of instructions and advises teachers to implement this. For several reasons, however, the new law on preschool and school education has not come into force yet, so the results of the project (standards and programmes) are on paper only. These standards and programmes can be implemented in the future when the new law on preschool and school education comes into force.

Teacher education

In primary schools (grades 1–4), students usually have one teacher for all subjects, which reflects teachers' preparation and training. These teachers are prepared in university departments for primary education in the faculties of pedagogy. During their study, teachers have courses on different subjects in which the topics and the methods for teaching them are mostly considered on the primary school level.

The situation is very different for pre-secondary and secondary education. Starting from grade 5, classes have separate teachers for each subject. Every teacher is fully responsible for instruction on the corresponding subject for that class, or several classes. Usually, the same teacher teaches the same classes for the whole pre-secondary education (from grade 5 through grade 8). The same is applicable for the teachers in the secondary education (from grade 8 through grade 12). In some schools, especially in small towns and villages, the same teacher instructs the same classes for the whole period, starting from grade 5 until the end of grade 12.

This is why the philosophy of preparing teachers for pre-secondary and secondary education is different. It is expected that these teachers very well know the subject they teach. To attain proficiency, they have to study the subject matter in the appropriate faculty of their university. This is why typical institutions for the preparation of pre-secondary and secondary teachers are the education departments at universities. Usually, teachers are prepared to teach an additional subject that is more or less related to this main subject.

The preparation of pre-secondary and secondary mathematics teachers provides a good illustration. As already explained, they study at the faculties of mathematics in six universities in Bulgaria, and after successfully completion of their study, they receive a teacher certificate. Another route into mathematics teaching exists for people who have already received their bachelor degree (no teaching certificate) in mathematics, physics (or science) or engineering: the post-diploma qualification, which spans one year. Students study school mathematics–related courses as well as pedagogical and psychological courses.

Based on the studies of Shulman (1986, 1987), those who prepare mathematics teachers share the common understanding that during their preparation future mathematics teachers should learn three basic areas: mathematics, mathematics pedagogy and general pedagogy. What is specific for Bulgaria is that there is great emphasis on mathematics and very little on pedagogy. (The rough proportion of the workload (study time) spent for these three areas is 12:9:1.) It remains the case, however, that mathematics knowledge of the graduated future teachers is not good (Bankov, 2007b, 2008; Schmidt, 2011). Many reasons contribute to this, including the lack of interest among young people for the teaching profession. Bright students graduating from mathematics faculties can find much more attractive working places, usually in the software industry or banking. The main concerns in mathematics teacher preparation are that (1) future mathematics teachers do not have good problem solving skills; (2) after finishing the teacher preparation programme, future teachers have little knowledge of the school organization and the structure of the mathematics curriculum; and (3) there is not a teacher induction process.

The last of these concerns is common for all teachers in Bulgaria. New teachers are just put into the school 'jungle', hoping that they will survive. In most cases, this stressful start is a big problem for beginning teachers. This is only one of the reasons that make the teacher profession unattractive to young people who simply do not want to become teachers. The core of the problem is the low social status of the teachers, the low salaries and the fact that teachers are not respected by the public, which makes this difficult profession even more so. Some fifteen years ago, this problem was acknowledged as severe, and in 1998 an amendment to the Law of Public Education was enacted stating that 'Teachers (are) due honour and respect by the students, the administrative authorities and the public. Impairment of the dignity and authority of teachers is unacceptable' (Article 40, Paragraph 5). Nevertheless, teachers continue to command little respect and have a low social status within the Bulgarian population.

There are five levels of professional qualification for teachers in Bulgaria. These levels are conferred by the so-called Departments for In-service Training of Teachers. Three such departments in Bulgaria, attached to three different universities,[3] provide training for teachers and guide them in obtaining each level of professional qualification. The activities usually take place during vacations, holidays or weekends so that teachers continue their everyday teaching. Regulations provide requirements that should be met for each level of teacher professional qualification. For some levels, the requirements consist in passing exams; for others, a written exploration or thesis based on the teacher's practical experience is required. Each level is conferred only if a teacher meets the corresponding requirements. For the highest level, for example, teachers should defend a thesis that is very similar to the defence of a doctoral degree thesis.

Unfortunately, there are not many other opportunities for professional development of teachers after they enter the profession. Some universities or non-governmental organizations offer short-term courses (1–2 days each). Topics of the courses may vary: teaching methods, student assessment, subject-matter topics and so forth; to attend a long-term training course, teachers should temporarily leave the school (i.e. for one term), a reason why such training programmes rarely happen.

A problem discussed for many years has been the accountability of teachers in terms of evaluating the quality of their work. Fortunately, the first idea, to use pupils' achievement only, was rejected because of the value-added arguments. The last paragraph of the following section of the 'Assessment' describes the first attempt to use value-added models, at least on a school level. However, the problem with evaluating teachers' work still remains. Finding objective indicators and criteria is a requirement in the National Program for Development of the School and the Pre-School Education and Training (2006–15). They will be used in the implementation of differentiated payment for teachers, based on the quality of their work.

About 17 per cent of teachers are male, the rest being women, and a disquieting fact is that Bulgarian teachers are relatively old, a consequence of the fact that young people do not want to become teachers. According to the National Statistical Institute (2012/3), about 45 per cent of the teachers are age 50 years or older.

Developments in educational assessment

When the Law of Public Education (1991) came into force, the need for national assessment of the educational system became a priority. One of the Ministry's tasks was the development of national assessment standards. Few attempts have been made during the years, all of them with negligible success. As a result, whilst Bulgaria does not yet have assessment standards, the national assessment system has nevertheless been slowly developing.

During 1991 and 2001, several attempts for national assessment were made (i.e. of foreign language teaching, of general educational minimum on Bulgarian language and mathematics, implementation of the test assessment and examination at the end of grade 7, etc.), some of which were test based. In 2001, a centre for the evaluation of school education was created within the National Centre for Education. After some unsuccessful assessment attempts, it was reorganized into the Center for Control and Assessment of the Quality in School Education (CKOKUO) at the Ministry of Education. This way CKOKUO became and still is the official national testing agency. In 2010, the European Social Fund sponsored CKOKUO to administer the project 'Development of System for Evaluation of the Quality of the General Education' (Project BG051PO001/3.2-01). A part of this project was a development of strategy for internal and external assessment of the educational process, which also elaborated on guiding principles of assessment. This strategy cannot play the role of the assessment standards but is a suitable basis for the development of such standards.

External standardized tests were first piloted by CKOKUO in Bulgaria in 2007. Presently, national assessments are settled by the National Program for Development of the School and the Pre-School Education and Training, 2006–15. These assessments are census based (covering all students in the tested cohorts) and are administered annually at the end of primary (grade 4), pre-secondary (grade 7) and secondary (grade 12, *Matura*) levels. The new draft law on Pre-School and School Education envisions a new secondary education stage covering grades 8–10 and a national, census-based, annual assessment at the end of grade 10. The introduction of the test-based assessment and examinations in Bulgaria has been going through all the problems and difficulties typical for educational systems which have attempted this reform process.

Even though the assessment results are made known to the educational community (some of them are even published), they have not yet been put to a use that can significantly improve decision making, policy development and incentivizing school performance gains. Because there is no independent body controlling the administration of the tests, lingering concerns remain about the supervision of the test-taking process and the arrangement to counteract gaming in test taking.

In this sense, the returns to Ministry of Education investments in the assessment system are lower than their potential. In order to use assessment data for improvement and accountability purposes, the Bulgarian Ministry of Education needs to first address the above-mentioned concerns, ensuring that test results do reflect in an objective manner the knowledge of tested students. Further, the census-based assessment in Bulgaria needs to provide education stakeholders with information about the performance progress of individual schools and students and thus to facilitate the implementation of national policies for improving the quality of education.

Looking for a better way to improve the accountability of the schools, the Bulgarian Ministry of Education and CKOKUO, sponsored by the World Bank, administered in 2013 the project 'Pilot implementation of statistical models for estimation of the value-added of Bulgarian schools using national student assessment data'. The Project piloted several statistical value-added models (VAMs). The Bulgarian pilot implementation of the value-added models benefit from the availability of student-level data for the first cohort of students that took both the national assessment test in grade 4 (back in 2009) and the national assessment tests in grade 7 (2012). This has enabled the use of the tests scores from these two points in time in order to implement the value-added analysis. The subjects with a stable and common subject base across the education stages used for the pilot are Bulgarian language and literature and mathematics. Analysing the test results through value-added analysis is a new approach for the country. The findings from this pilot informed policy makers in Bulgaria about the advantages and limitations of VAMs in the context of the Bulgarian education system, its student assessment framework and the data collected and used by the education management information system. The project made recommendations not only about the appropriateness and future use of these models but also about the improvement of the quality of the testing instruments and the data needed for comprehensive analysis of the results. It was recommended that value-added modelling should be implemented with the next student cohort and that it eventually be used for future monitoring of school effectiveness.

The role of international studies

The first educational international study implemented in Bulgaria was the TIMSS study on trends of mathematics and science teaching, conducted by the International Association for the Evaluation of Educational Achievement (IEA) every fourth year, and started in 1995. The main TIMSS populations correspond to grade 4 and grade 8 in Bulgaria, and as a new member of IEA (since 1991), Bulgaria participated in grade 8 population in several TIMSS cycles, namely TIMSS 1995, TIMSS 1999, TIMSS 2003, and TIMSS 2007. Participation in the assessment process is optional, and Bulgaria missed TIMSS 2011, though it will participate for the grade 4 population in TIMSS 2015.

The history of the Bulgarian participation in TIMSS is a reflection of the policy makers' attitude towards international educational studies. In the early 1990s, it started with a kind of indifference and an expected satisfaction from relatively good results (in TIMSS 1995, Bulgaria scored among the top five countries in science and among the top ten countries in mathematics). After the decrease of the Bulgarian performance in TIMSS 1999 and especially in TIMSS 2003, when there was questioning of the appropriateness of the tests (Mullis. et al., 2004), there was a kind of distrust in the claim that 'assessment design and curriculum topics of TIMSS are not appropriate for Bulgarian education' (Mullis et al., 2004). After the next decrease in TIMSS 2007 (Mullis et al., 2008), it was decided that Bulgaria would not participate in TIMSS for the foreseeable future. But soon it became clear that for many reasons connected with influence and international educational contacts and collaborations, Bulgarian participation in TIMSS held international recognition and importance. Because it is expected that the grade 4 results could be better than these of the grade 8 students, it was decided to continue the TIMSS participation in the grade 4 population.

Bulgaria has participated in Progress in International Reading Literacy Study (PIRLS) (another IEA study) since its beginning in 2001. This is a reading literacy study focusing on grade 4 students. The performance of Bulgarian pupils in PIRLS has also been decreasing over the years (Mullis et al., 2012), but much more slowly than the decrease in TIMSS. This is probably because the quality of the basic education in Bulgaria has not changed a lot in contrast to the pre-secondary education (especially in grade 8), where the quality of education has been worsening from year to year.

The third important study in which Bulgaria has participated since 2001 is the OECD study Program for International Student Assessment (PISA). It assesses 15-year-old students on reading, mathematics and science, consecutively every three years. Bulgarian results on PISA are more or less stable from cycle to cycle (Challenges in School Education, 2013), even though not quite good—Bulgaria scores significantly below the international mean in all three areas. Because PISA assessment frameworks focus very much on practical applications of students' knowledge, these results show typical characteristics of Bulgarian education, namely, that it is very much theoretically oriented with little practical use and experience.

As a result of these studies, it became clear that mathematics education in Bulgaria is in deep crisis. According to the report Mathematics Education in Europe (2011), the average mathematics result in PISA 2009 for Bulgaria (as well as for Romania) is the lowest of all European countries (p. 16). The per cent of low-achieving students (p. 17) in mathematics is the highest for Bulgaria (and Romania). The same results are confirmed by TIMSS (p. 19). According to the same report, Bulgaria has the least number of hours for studying mathematics yearly (pp. 42–43). Some people argue that Bulgaria still has students with good achievement on the International Mathematics Olympiad (http://www.imo-official.org/). Although this is likely to be true, this fact shows only that there is an elite consisting of a few students who are very well prepared in mathematics, but hides the large-scale low mathematical literacy.

An important role of the international educational studies for Bulgaria is that they build experts in assessment, evaluation, educational research and testing. These are 'new professional fields' in the Bulgarian educational system, in which, thanks to Bulgarian participation in TIMSS, PIRLS, PISA and other studies, some people gained good experience and became valuable experts in these areas.

A look ahead

An important aim of the Ministry of Education is to move the new law on Pre-School and School Education and all concomitant documents and activities. Passing the law will be an important step towards the modernization of the Bulgarian educational system. Certainly, the law itself will not resolve problems but will give the normative basis for actions that could improve the educational system.

One of the important concomitant activities is the completion of the European project 'Improvement of the Quality of the General Education' (Project BG051PO001-3.1.04—'For better education') that was run especially to support the implementation of the law. This project developed the instructional programmes for the profile education in the second stage of the secondary school (grades 11 and 12), which will be created after the new law on Pre-School and School Education comes into force. These programmes are new features in Bulgarian educational system, and teachers need some training in order to implement them. The framework of the project foresees a short-term training of secondary teachers in this respect, which hopefully will happen soon.

The above-mentioned instructional programmes should reflect on the quality of pre-service teacher preparation. It is expected that not only pre-service, but also in-service teacher preparation will be the focus of future reforms of the Ministry of Education. Teachers, as an important part of the educational process, should have adequate training in order to be in line with the requirements of a modern and effective educational system.

Notes

1 Bulgaria occupies about 111,000 square kilometres of the Balkan Peninsula in south-eastern Europe. The population is about 7,360,000 people (2011 census). http://www.nsi.bg/census2011/indexen.php). According to World Bank data (http://ddp-ext.worldbank.org/ext/ddpreports/ViewSharedReport?&CF=1&REPORT_ID=9147&REQUEST_TYPE=VIEWADVANCED&HF=N&WSP=N) for 2012, GNI per capita is 6,870 US Dollars, and gross domestic product (GDP) growth is 0.8. The inflation for 2012 is 2.2 per cent. The social structure in Bulgaria is characterized by a high percentage of pensioners, approximately 40 per cent. (http://www.nsi.bg/otrasalen.php?otr=51&a1=2038&a2=2044&a3=2048#cont). The unemployment rate for 2014 in Bulgaria is 12.3 per cent (http://www.nsi.bg/otrasalen.php?otr=51&a1=2038&a2=2044&a3=2047#cont).
2 These subjects are Bulgarian language and literature, mathematics, physics, chemistry, biology, geography, history, philosophy, music and fine arts.
3 These universities are The University of Sofia, The Thracian University (in Stara Zagora) and The University of Shoumen.

References

Bankov, K. (2007a). 'The influence of the world educational changes on the teacher education system in Bulgaria', in M. T. Tatto (ed.), *Reforming Teaching Globally, Journal Oxford Studies in Education*, 75–95.

Bankov, K. (2007b). 'Is the preparation of mathematics teachers in Bulgaria effective?'. *Mathematics and Informatics*, 6, 3–12 (in Bulgarian).

Bankov, K. (2008). 'Comparative study of mathematics teacher preparation in six countries'. *Mathematics and Informatics*, 1, 6–13 (in Bulgarian).

Centre for Control and Assessment of the Quality of General Education (CKOKUO) (2010) Sofia. Development of the System for the Evaluation of the Quality of General Education (Project BG051P0001/3.2-01).

Challenges in School Education. Results from Bulgarian Participation in PISA 2012. (2013). CKOKUO, Sofia (in Bulgarian). http://www.ckoko.bg/upload/docs/2013-12/PISA_2012.pdf

Law of Public Education. (1991). State newspaper, 86, Sofia (in Bulgarian). http://www.mon.bg/opencms/export/sites/mon/left_menu/documents/law/zkn_prosveta.pdf

Law of the Level of Education, General Educational Minimum, and Curriculum. (1999). State newspaper, 67, Sofia (in Bulgarian). http://www.mon.bg/opencms/export/sites/mon/left_menu/documents/law/zkn_obr_minimun.pdf

Mathematics Education in Europe: Common Challenges and National Policies. (2011). Eurydice, Brussels. http://eacea.ec.europa.eu/education/eurydice/documents/thematic_reports/132en.pdf

Mullis, I.V.S., Martin, M.O., Gonzalez, E.J., and Chrostowski, S.J. (2004). *Findings from IEA's Trends in International Mathematics and Science Study at the Fourth and Eighth Grades.* Chestnut Hill, MA: TIMSS & PIRLS International Study Center, Boston College.

Mullis, I.V.S., Martin, M.O., and Foy, P. (with Olson, J.F., Preuschoff, C., Erberber, E., Arora, A., and Galia, J.). (2008). *TIMSS 2007 International Mathematics Report: Findings from IEA's Trends in International Mathematics and Science Study at the Fourth and Eighth Grades.* Chestnut Hill, MA: TIMSS & PIRLS International Study Center, Boston College.

Mullis, I.V.S., Martin, M.O., Foy, P., and Drucker, K.T. (2012). *The PIRLS 2011 International Results in Reading.* Chestnut Hill, MA: TIMSS & PIRLS International Study Center, Boston College.

National Program for Development of the School and the Pre-school Education and Training, 2006–2015. (2006) Ministry of Education (in Bulgarian) http://www.mon.bg/opencms/export/sites/mon/left_menu/documents/strategies/programa_obrazovanie.pdf

Republic of Bulgaria. National Statistical Institute. (2012/2013). http://www.nsi.bg/en/

Schmidt, W., Blomeke, S., and Tatto, M.T. (2011). *Teacher Education Matters. A study of Middle School Mathematics Teacher Preparation in Six Countries.* NY and London: Teachers College, Columbia University.

Shulman, L. (1986). 'Those who understand: Knowledge growth in teaching'.*Educational Researcher*, 15, 4–14.

Shulman, L. (1987). 'Knowledge and teaching: Foundations of the new reform'. *Harvard Educational Review*, 57(1), 1–22.

2

Croatia: An Overview of Educational Reforms, 1950–2014

Vlatka Domović and Vlasta Vizek Vidović

Introduction: Country context

As an independent state, Croatia has a relatively short history of less than twenty-five years and is one of the youngest members of the European Union; nonetheless, since ancient times its culture and history have been deeply embedded in the Central European and Mediterranean heritage. Until the nineteenth century, Croatia had been divided into two social and cultural circles. The northern part was predominantly linked with the Hungarian and later the Austrian Empire, whereas the Mediterranean (Adriatic) region was ruled or influenced by the Republic of Venice.

In the nineteenth century, similar to other national tendencies across Europe, Croatian nobility and intellectuals initiated political and cultural movements with the idea of preservation and enhancement of Croatian national culture and life, but at the same time new notions of entering into a political union with other South Slavs were also emerging. These ideas came into life after the First World War when the Austro-Hungarian Empire was abolished and Croatia become part of the Kingdom of Serbs, Croats and Slovenes, to be soon renamed into the Kingdom of Yugoslavia, which lasted until the beginning of the Second World War. After the war Croatia once again became a part of a new state—the Federal National Republic of Yugoslavia (FNRJ) with five other republics—Bosnia and Herzegovina, Macedonia, Montenegro, Serbia and Slovenia. During the 1950s, the harsh communist regime was replaced by a less rigid version in comparison to other Eastern European communist countries, leading to the change of the state name in 1963 to the Federal Socialist Republic of Yugoslavia (FSRJ). With the fall of the communist regimes in Eastern Europe in the last two decades of the twentieth century, the processes of dissolution of the Federal Socialist

Republic of Yugoslavia started in 1990. Unlike similar processes in some other communist countries, like Czechoslovakia or the Soviet Union, the dissolution of Yugoslavia was much more painful for Croatia, where the war for independence lasted for five years. Croatia achieved the status of an independent state in 1995. Establishment of the new state also brought changes to the political, economic and social systems, introducing democratic values and institutions and market economy (Godler and Domović, 1999).

Today, Croatia is one of the smaller European Union countries, with a territory of about 56,000 square kilometres and around 4,500,000 inhabitants. Three-quarters of them live in urban areas. Although some reside in smaller towns and cities, the majority live in larger cities. Among those, the capital city of Croatia, Zagreb, has the largest number of inhabitants. The rest tend to gravitate towards other larger cities, such as Split, Rijeka and Osijek.

Croatia has not been very successful in transitioning from a socialist system to a capitalist one and has been suffering a long economic crisis which started in 2008. The post-war transition period was hindered by material destruction of one-third of the territory combined with a negative demographic trend in general, a high rate of unemployment, a high number of people who got early retirements and a very unfavourable educational structure. The general unfavourable situation is worsened by psychological factors such as high expectations and hopes that changes of formal political and institution changes will result in economic welfare.

Political and socio-economic changes which took place during Croatian history have also influenced the developments of the educational system.

Historical perspective of changes in the Croatian education system

The beginnings of organized education in Croatia date from several centuries back. The first schools were run by various church orders within convents. The first secular school was opened in the fifteenth century in northern Croatia (Godler and Domović, 1999).

Year 1874 was a milestone in the reform of the public education in Croatia. In that year, the formalized system of four-year elementary education obligatory for all children was introduced by the first School Law passed on 14 October 1874. At the same time, only a few days later (on 19 October 1874), the first Croatian state university was founded, with three faculties—Law, Philosophy and Theology (Franković, 1958).

From that time until the breakup of the Austro-Hungarian Empire, the educational system in Croatia followed the patterns set up within the monarchy. In the period between the First and Second World Wars, the educational system in Croatia was developed within the political systems of the Kingdom of Serbs, Croats and Slovenes, and later of the Kingdom of Yugoslavia. Although the elementary education was compulsory, only about half of the school-age population attended schools (Franković, 1958), which means that illiteracy in the population was very high between the two World Wars.

After the Second World War, with the establishment of the Federal People's Republic of Yugoslavia, the school network was expanded, and in 1951 the duration of elementary schooling was extended to eight years. That model of an eight-year elementary school with two cycles (lower and upper) remains today.

In the years 1956 and 1957, legislative acts regulating secondary education were adopted (Franković, 1958). Students could choose to continue their education in the secondary general education schools (gymnasium, or in various types of three- or four-year vocational schools. The graduation from four-year secondary schools enabled pupils to continue their education at colleges or universities.

The first major educational reform in the former Socialist Federal Republic of Yugoslavia was introduced in the 1970s, dividing secondary education into two parts. For the first two years of all types of secondary schools, the uniform general curriculum was developed in order to offer quality general education for all children. In the subsequent one or two years of secondary education, diversification of curricula was introduced, with various professional programmes and certificates enabling students to more easily enter the labour market. However, these intentions were not realized because the uniform general curricula were too demanding for the large number of students, resulting in the increase of dropouts during the first two years. Also, the professional streaming of students in the second cycle of secondary education did not enhance the possibility of getting jobs.

In the period 1960–70, there was a significant move towards increasing accessibility to the higher education.

During the 1990s, the focus of policy makers was on creating the legislative basis for the Croatian educational system.[1] In reality, the changes in the education system were fragmented and reactive to social context. So Croatia's elementary educational system remained relatively intact until today, whereas the secondary schooling returned to the model preceding the 1970s, with general education schools (gymnasium) and three- and four-year vocational schools. The major reforms in higher education did not start before 2001, when Croatia joined the Bologna process.

Since 2000, there have been several initiatives for a serious rethinking of education policies in Croatia. In the year 2000, the White Paper on Croatian Education was created with the intention to serve as the basis for the comprehensive transformation of the Croatian educational system (Pastuović, 2001). According to the White Paper, the aim of the educational reform was the improvement of efficiency of the educational system through the following changes:

- Transition to a six-year elementary school
- Introduction of a nine-year compulsory education
- Modernization of the curriculum
- Education of teachers for a six-year elementary school
- Introduction of state examinations based on external evaluation
- Reform of the university system in accordance with the Bologna Declaration
- Decentralization of financing and management of the educational system

Subsequently, in 2001 the Center for Educational Research and Development was founded as a special research unit within the Institute for Social Research in Zagreb in order to support the implementation of the reform through policy projects focusing on the key problems identified in the White Paper.

Although the White Paper was positively accepted by various stakeholders, comprehensive reform was hindered by the lack of continuity in political structures responsible for the implementation of the proposed reform. Frequent changes of the key actors responsible for governing the educational sector led to short-term cosmetic changes rather than to broader, long-term reforms.[2]

The second attempt to introduce a holistic approach to educational changes was described in a new strategic document—the Education Sector Development Plan 2005–10 (2005). The developmental priorities stated in that document were as follows:

- Improving the quality and effectiveness of education
- Stimulating the continuing professional training of teachers and other education sector employees
- Developing strategies for improving the management and efficiency of the education system
- Promoting education for social cohesion and economic growth and development

The above strategic documents were again implemented partially, stimulating a remedial approach to the elementary school programmes and postponing the deeper structural and curriculum reform.

This attempt to modernize elementary school programme and teaching methods was introduced in a document entitled the Croatian National Educational Standard (CNES). The main goals were the reduction of the encyclopaedic knowledge contents and the introduction of student-centred teaching methods. In the experimental phase from 2005 to 2006, CNES was tried out in forty-nine elementary schools. In the school year 2006/7, based on CNES recommendations, the new Teaching Plan and Programme for elementary school was officially adopted (Pregled postignuća, 2007). This Teaching Plan and Programme is still in place. Its main critique addresses the fact that the CNES was not based on the implementation of the modern curricula theory, but was more or less focused on the reduction of the too detailed and redundant content. On the other hand, the planned continuous support to teachers in developing new skills related to student-centred teaching methods did not reach the level of sustainability. Although the planned validation of CNES implementation was never completed, a new measure for raising the quality of education was launched. In September 2006, the Council for the National Curriculum was appointed by the Minister of Science, Education and Sport with the task of designing the National Curriculum Framework (NCF) as a document for the preschool, elementary and secondary education. The first step in the development of NCF was the creation of the Strategy for the Construction and Development of the National Curriculum for Preschool Education, General Compulsory and Secondary School Education (2007), where the development and acquisition of key competences based on the European key competences framework for lifelong learning was emphasized as the main priority. In 2010, the Council accomplished its task by releasing the National Curriculum Framework for Preschool Education and General Compulsory and Secondary Education.

> The basic characteristic of the *National Curriculum Framework* is a transition to a system based on competence and student achievement (learning outcomes), unlike the previous (i.e. current) one, which focuses on content.... The *National Curriculum Framework* instructs teachers to overcome subject specialisation, and to take part more or less equally in developing students' core competences by applying the principle of shared responsibility—in particular by making explicit the values that are intertwined with cross-subject (cross-curricular) topics. (2010: 9)

The *National Curriculum Framework* is again an example of a huge undertaking which mobilized a lot of educational experts, academics and practitioners but was not elaborated further and consequently did not influence teaching practice.

Based on the Education Sector Development Plan 2005–10, at the level of the secondary education the most important objectives were introduction of 'a standardised external examination to evaluate students' knowledge and competencies at the end of grammar school and other four-year secondary schools', development of a new National curriculum for secondary schools and the restructuring of the too narrowly specialized vocational education programmes in accordance to the labour market needs (Education Sector Development Plan 2005–10: 30–31). The objective which has been more or less successfully implemented is the final state exams for all the four-year secondary school students, which are coordinated by the national Centre for External Evaluation of Education. Other objectives described in the Education Sector Development Plan 2005–10 were further elaborated in the separate strategic document *Development Strategy of Vocational Education System in the Republic of Croatia 2008*–13. The main objectives of the reform of the vocational education set out in this document were the development of curricula based on competencies and learning outcomes related to labour market needs, building of the mechanisms of comparability and recognition of Croatian vocational qualifications in Europe (European Qualifications Framework), creation of a system of vocational education and training that allows lifelong learning and mobility.

The Education Sector Development Plan 2005–10 acknowledged the importance of the implementation of the wide higher education reform which had begun with Croatia formally joining the Bologna Process at the Conference of Ministers in Prague in May 2001. The construction of the institutional basis for implementing the reform of higher education in Croatia was laid out in the Act on Scientific Activities and Higher Education, which was passed by the Croatian Parliament in 2003.

The Act indicated three strategically important priority objectives for the period from 2003 to 2005. The first was the building of the system of quality assurance of higher education, for which purpose the Agency for Science and Higher Education was to be established and entrusted with evaluating the quality of institutions of higher learning and their programmes. Along those lines, each institution of higher learning would be obliged to form its own unit for quality assurance. The second objective was the establishment of the necessary services connected to the application of the European Credit Transfer and Accumulation

System (ECTS) in Croatia, including those for monitoring and recognition of foreign diplomas, as well as establishing the European Network of Information Centres/National Academic Recognition Information Centre (ENIC/NARIC) national office. The third objective was the reorganization of a studies format based on the three-cyclic model also involving the major curricular reform aimed at the development of competence-based study programmes and a student-centred teaching approach. The Act of 2003 also stipulates the organizational integration of each university, because Croatian universities were previously loosely coupled clusters of more or less financially and legally independent constituencies. By 2005, all higher education institutions were required to make hasty preparations for about seven hundred new programmes, which were to be accredited and implemented in the academic year 2005/6, when the first generation of 'Bologna' students were enrolled. In spite of the resistance of the academia who were not used to such profound changes implemented in such a short time, the higher education reform moved on, and at the present moment the efforts are being invested into evaluating its results and planning future improvements. It should be noted that the transformation system had significant repercussions to initial teacher education, which will be further described later on.

Another important issue raised in the above-mentioned strategic documents was the accountability of the entire educational system and its outcomes. It has been recognized that accountability is closely linked to the functioning of external quality assurance mechanisms, which did not exist at the time. As building the necessary infrastructure in a relatively short period of time became a priority, several public institutions were established, each of them responsible for the development of a specific segment of the educational system. In 2004, the Agency for Science and Higher Education was founded, as well as the National Centre for External Evaluation of Education. In 2005, two institutions were founded: the Agency for Vocational Education and Training, and the National Centre for External Evaluation of Education. In 2006, the Education and Teacher Training Agency and the Agency for Adult Education were founded.[3] These institutions have primarily been oriented towards capacity building for the implementation of multiple approaches to quality management at different levels of the educational system, including monitoring of pupils'/students' achievements and supporting teachers' professional development as well as carrying out institutional accreditation in higher education.

As the role of international comparative research in education become more prominent across Europe in 2006, Croatia participated for the first time in the PISA project. Parallel to participation in international assessments, in 2006/7

Croatia piloted the first standardized national examinations for students in the first grade of secondary schools as the overall external assessment of students' achievements (Pregled postignuća, 2007, 55). Although those national examinations did not continue after the pilot phase, they served as a preparation for the introduction of state graduation examinations at the end of secondary education, locally referred to as the state *Matura*. The *Matura* exam was officially introduced at the end of the school year 2009/10 and is still being carried out on a regular basis. In the meantime, its function was broadened as it became a screening tool for entrance to higher education. The standardized assessment of students' achievements led to the project of self-evaluation by primary and secondary schools, which became a regular practice. The annual school self-evaluations serve as a basis for annual school development plans.

The implementation of Sector Development Plan 2005–10 was accompanied by extensive change in education legislation. In 2008/9, the following important legal acts were passed: the Act on Quality Assurance in Science and Higher Education, the Act on Education in Primary and Secondary Schools, and National Pedagogical Standards for the Elementary and Secondary System of Education, followed by the Act on Vocational Education.

An overview of historical changes and trends in the Croatian education system from early beginnings to present times has shown an increase of various initiatives, resulting in a large number of policy documents in the last two decades. But due to various factors such as a lack of human capital who could enforce changes; a general lack of coordination between various stakeholders in education; the inherited mindset from the previous political regime, which manifests in the lack of readiness to accept personal responsibility for implementation of policy decisions; and the prevalent belief among policy makers that an education system is an expenditure and not an investment in the future, as well as prolonged economic crisis, a serious apprehension emerges that most of the planned reforms will be remembered only as declarative intentions and easy-given promises that could not be fulfilled. On the other hand, this relative failure in the realization of the planned educational reforms should be perceived in a wider political and social perspective, where the 'young' state was too eager to harmonize its education system with the requirements of the European Union. In order to achieve fast results using shortcuts, the support from international institutions, experts and consultants was accepted without deeper contextualization of their suggestions and advice, resulting in the fragmented actions which were not embedded in a wider policy framework.

It can be assumed that such an interplay of internal and external factors was experienced as stressful, sometimes leading to learned helplessness among educational experts and policy makers.

Present context, main features and key challenges

In this section, the actual educational context and main features as well as key challenges in the specific educational subsystems will be presented. The result of the policy interventions into the educational system can be best described as a bricolage of 'something old, something new' without a coherent and comprehensive approach to educational reform. For example, in spite of the International Standard Classification of Education (2011) (dividing the basic system of education into pre-primary, primary, lower secondary and upper secondary), the Croatian pre-tertiary education sticks to the old scheme which remained unchanged for more than fifty years. The main difference in comparison with those in other countries is a shorter primary education. The overall educational system is divided into the following segments: preschool education, elementary school education, secondary school education, higher (including teacher) education (Figure 2.1). Each segment will be portrayed separately so that the specific features of each can be described and the specific problems discussed.

Preschool education

In Croatia, there is a long tradition of preschool education because women were encouraged to work outside of home in socialist times, and the state was supposed to help families by organizing public care for children. Generally, the families and other stakeholders are satisfied with the quality educational services delivered in preschool institutions. On the other hand, as the resources were always restricted, the shortage of institutions, especially in rural areas, is still noticeable. It should be noted that in the last twenty years, the ratio of preschool children who attend kindergartens has significantly increased, by approximately 20 per cent. Even though preschool education in Croatia is not compulsory, it represents the starting point of the educational system. The Preschool Education Law from 1997 stipulates that early childhood education can start when the child is six months old, but in the existing practice, children enter preschool institutions when they are one year old. Preschool education takes place in various types of

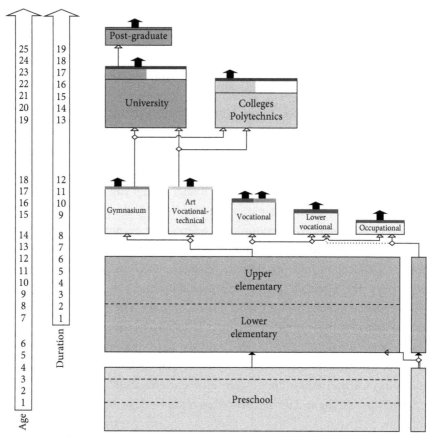

Figure 2.1 The contemporary system of education in Croatia.

institutions—nurseries, kindergartens, play groups, children's libraries, children's wards in hospitals, mobile kindergartens, orphanages, elementary schools—which can be founded by the local governing bodies, physical and legal persons, religious communities and citizens' associations.

Despite the variety of institutions, the prevailing organizational form of the preschool education is that of the kindergarten, in which children spend from five to ten hours per day. In addition to the so-called common regular programme, kindergartens also offer specialized programmes (foreign languages, sports, music, dramatic and visual arts expression). In 2009/10, 58 per cent children of preschool age attended preschool institutions on a regular basis. This situation cannot be considered satisfactory as there are always long waiting lists for places in nurseries and kindergartens, especially in bigger cities. Because of the shortage of public preschool institutions, the private initiatives have been welcome in this sector as compared to other educational subsystems. So at this moment, out of the total number of preschool institutions (N = 673), 35.40 per cent are private, with 19.60 per cent of attending preschoolers. To ensure equal educational opportunities, all the children enrolling in primary school are obliged to attend a preparatory programme, the so-called 'little school', prior to enrolment. These programmes are organized in kindergartens or schools for a duration of 150 hours, encompassing 99.60 per cent of preschoolers.[4]

Elementary education

Elementary school education is provided through the network of public elementary schools (851) and by a few private elementary schools (8).[5] In 2012/13, there were 851 elementary schools with 333,575 pupils, and 31,263 teachers.[6] In addition to teachers, elementary schools have on their staff a school principal, who directs and manages school affairs, and the professional support personnel such as psychologists, special education teachers, librarians and so on. The elementary school in duration of eight years is the compulsory part of education in the Republic of Croatia for children between the ages of 7 and 15, and corresponds to International Standard Classification of Education (ISCED) levels 1 and 2.

The structure of elementary education has been most resistant to changes in the last fifty years. Elementary school is divided into two levels: the first level comprises grades 1–4; and the second, grades 5–8. The curriculum is comprehensive and compulsory for all children. These two levels differ in the form in which a curriculum is delivered.

The curricula in grades 1–4 are organized into six teaching subjects, which are taught by a single teacher (the so-called class-teacher). The curricula in grades 5–8 are divided into thirteen subjects, each taught by a subject specialist. The transfer from the single class-teacher programme, which ends with grade 4, into a subject specialists' programme, which starts with grade 5, is considered to be one of the most critical transitions in the whole education system. For many pupils at the average age of 10, such abrupt change in their exposure to more subjects and to a larger number of teachers is too abrupt and too demanding, especially as it does not correspond to their cognitive and emotional level of development.

The rate of completion of the elementary school education is very high. Almost all enrolled pupils complete their elementary education (99.6 per cent)[7].

Secondary education

After the completion of the compulsory elementary school, more than 95 per cent of students continue their education in secondary schools (corresponding to the ISCED 3 level), although secondary education is not compulsory. In school year 2012/13, there were 687 secondary schools in Croatia, out of which forty-one were private, with 181,384 students and 24,702 teachers.[8]

The main characteristic of secondary education is streaming in three directions: academic (gymnasium), vocational schools and art schools. Whereas academic (gymnasium) and art schools are four-year secondary schools, there are two types of vocational schools, the four-year and the three-year vocational schools. Roughly 70 per cent of the secondary school population attends vocational schools, of whom about 44 per cent are in the four-year programmes, and the remaining 26 per cent are in the three-year programmes.[9]

In the 2010/11 school year, the state graduation examination (*Matura*) was introduced, serving as a requirement for enrolment into higher education. At the end of the four-year cycle, practically all gymnasium students and the majority of vocational four-year students take this final exam. Students who complete the three-year vocational programmes can only enter into employment. If they want to continue their education at the tertiary level, they must enter the fourth grade of the secondary school programme.

Art schools allow students to pursue specific programmes of study and training in the fields of ballet, music and visual arts. Some art schools have programmes which cover the complete secondary school curriculum, and students who complete them can apply for the *Matura* exam. Some other art schools (such as, e.g. secondary music schools) have only those programmes which cover a particular art subject. Students enrolled in such schools must therefore at the same time attend some other four-year secondary school in order to apply for the *Matura* exam.

Although three-quarters of secondary school students attend vocational schools, the experts who analyse vocational school programmes (Lowther, 2004) claim that Croatian vocational education has not adjusted quickly enough to changes in the economy, the needs of the labour market and technological developments. In general, the curriculum is assessed as too fragmented and focused on development of narrow subject-specific skills, instead of providing broad theoretical and practical basis for flexible, adaptable employment. The latest Development Strategy of the Vocational Education System in the

Republic of Croatia 2008–13 identified these problems and formulated the following goals:

- Development of qualifications based on competences and learning outcomes
- Continual adjustment curricula with labour market needs
- Development of vocational education which fosters lifelong learning and mobility
- Strengthening teacher competences which support student-centred teaching
- Establishment of quality assurance system in vocational education

Efforts in implementation of the above-mentioned strategy resulted in a significant decrease in the number of overspecialized programmes from more than four hundred specializations to around two hundred programmes with relatively clearly defined learning outcomes.[10]

Higher education

Higher education in Croatia is based on the binary system, and it can be acquired at the university and professional higher education institutions. Most of the total number of students (ca 195,000[11]) study at the public higher education institutions (87 per cent). In Croatia, there are seven public universities which are situated in larger cities, offering 1,086 programmes at all three levels.[12] The other public institutions of higher education are professional polytechnics (13) and colleges (3)[13], offering eighty-eight programmes.[14] The private higher education institutions (three universities, two polytechnics, twenty-four professional higher education schools) offer seventy programmes.[15]

Higher professional schools and polytechnics offering higher education are not a part of the university system. They offer specialist professional programmes and relevant diplomas but do not provide programmes leading directly to a PhD.

Educational analysts often point out that the numbers of enrolled students in different academic sectors is not well balanced with labour market trends and needs. For example, in 2011/12, more than 50 per cent of students were enrolled in master's programmes in social sciences, and only about 3 per cent in life sciences and 10 per cent in engineering.[16] Also, it should be noted that Croatia falls behind the attainment level of tertiary education in the European Union, which in 2012 reached 35.7 per cent among thirty- to thirty-four-year-olds, whereas Croatia achieved attainment level of only 23.7 per cent.[17]

The major reform of higher education started formally in 2001 when Croatia joined the Bologna process. In July 2003, the Croatian Parliament passed the Act on Scientific Activities and Higher Education, which paved the way for the incorporation of the basic principles of the Bologna process. Although there was substantial accumulated evidence that the Croatian higher education system was not very efficient prior to the Bologna process (Godler and Domović, 2008), with large numbers of dropouts and so-called 'eternal' students, discipline-oriented curricula and low mobility, these reasons would have not by themselves led to change without external influence imposed by the Bologna principles.

Bologna reform was perceived as an externally imposed political decision, and it provoked considerable resistance and mistrust among the academic community. From the present perspective, the feeling of high pressure was the result of too many simultaneous changes in too short a time. What the implementation of Bologna process meant for Croatian higher education was a multilevel reform encompassing a new approach to governance and management in higher education, leading to integrated universities and the introduction of a new structure (three-cycle model) together with ECTS credits and development of competence-based curriculum, combined with a demand for new approaches to teaching and learning, as well as the implementation of comprehensive system of quality assurance.

Full implementation of a new three-cycle model started in academic year 2005/6 after accreditation. The reform has been supported by several rounds of European Union projects (Tempus, CARDS) focusing on curricula development and implementation of quality assurance mechanisms.

The first experience with new programmes revealed that most institutions did not have adequate infrastructure and necessary human resources. The reform was mainly focused on formal aspects of programme restructuring such as shorter one-semester courses, smaller groups of students, adjusting demands to sixty ECTS per year, the introduction of diploma supplements and student evaluation of teachers. That changes were not followed by achieving deeper understanding of concepts such as competence-based curriculum, constructive alignment of learning goals and outcomes, student's workload and student-centred approach to teaching and the role of institutional self-evaluation as a tool for improvement. The Bologna process also encouraged universities to broaden their traditional missions of research and teaching by strengthening the so-called third mission, that is, cooperation with community and business.

The important impulse for rethinking these concepts and their implications for teaching practice in higher education was given by the re-accreditation process of higher education institutions, which started in 2010. The re-accreditation process is steered by the provisions in the Act on Quality Assurance in Science and Higher Education (2009) and an independent public institution, the Agency for Science and Higher Education (ASHE), is responsible for implementation of external quality assurance mechanisms such as re-accreditation of all higher education institutions, accreditation of non-university study programmes, audit, and thematic evaluations.[18]

Based on the recommendations of the re-accreditation reviewers the higher education institutions started the process of deeper transformation in their curricula, teaching staff development and establishment of student support services.

Teacher education

Across the world in the last decade, the accumulated research evidence strongly indicates that the teacher quality is significantly and positively related to the student's attainment. It has triggered the major shift in the perception of the role of teachers in achieving high-quality education outcomes. The latest Education and Training Monitor 2013 (EC) emphasizes that 'teaching staff are arguably the most important in-school factor affecting the learning outcomes of students. They have an indispensable role to play in any intervention measure tackling early school leaving, whether related to school climate, supportive and individualized learning environments, early warning systems, or cooperation with parents' (p.33).

In line with these arguments, the special attention in this chapter will be devoted to the issue of teacher initial education and professional development in Croatian context.

In Croatia, there are different categories of teachers, depending on the educational level at which they teach: preschool teachers, teachers in grades 1–4 of elementary school (class-teachers), subject teachers in grades 5–8 of elementary school, subject teachers in secondary academic schools (gymnasium), teachers of general education subjects in secondary vocational schools and teachers of vocational subjects in secondary vocational schools.

The implementation of the Bologna process in 2005 had significant consequences for the initial teacher education system in Croatia. In the past, the education of preschool teachers and classroom teachers was conducted by teacher colleges which organized professional study programmes, whereas subject teachers were educated at universities. The major change introduced by the reform of higher education has been universitization of all initial teacher education programmes. In that way, the long-lasting dualism in the education of class and subject teachers was finally overcome. Since the beginning of the academic year 2005/6, the duration of studies for class and subject teachers has become five years, at the end of which a master's degree is awarded. Although a master's degree is compulsory for all categories of schoolteachers to enter the profession, the compulsory requirement for preschool teachers is a bachelor's degree, although the option of continuing their studies at the master level is available.

The exception of these are teachers of vocational subjects who do not study at teacher education faculties but get their master's degree in other professional fields. They are required to take an extra year of study in order to obtain teacher qualification, usually during their induction period in schools.

The programme for pre-primary schoolteachers is organized according to the simultaneous model at the faculties of teacher education. At the BA level, all programmes for pre-primary schoolteachers have a ratio of about 40 per cent academic content to 60 per cent educational studies and practice in kindergartens. The admission requirement for prospective pre-primary teachers is a graduation certificate from a four-year secondary school. Because the number of applicants always exceeds the number of open places at teacher education institutions, students have to take entrance exams.

Initial education for prospective teachers in lower elementary school (grades 1–4) is carried out at teacher education faculties. The curriculum has been designed according to the integrated model of undergraduate and graduate level (five years, ten semesters) leading to the award of a master's degree in education (three hundred ECTS credits). This model has been chosen based on the assumption that teacher education lasting continuously for five years would be best suited for the acquisition of competencies necessary for teaching all curriculum in grades 1–4. After graduation from the teacher education faculties, teachers are qualified to teach six subjects in the lower grades of elementary schools: mother tongue, science and society, mathematics, visual arts, music arts and physical education. On average, the ratio between the theoretical and practical parts of the curriculum is fifty/fifty. The school-based teaching practice has been incorporated into the regular programmes, but the number of hours for school practice has not been unified across teacher education faculties, ranging from forty to sixty days (Domović and Vizek Vidović, 2011).

In upper elementary and secondary schools in Croatia, the teaching is organized by subjects taught by specialized subject teachers. Study programmes for subject teachers are organized in two cycles—BA level (180 ECTS credits) and MA level (120 ECTS credits) at the faculties which deliver programmes for specific academic disciplines (such as Faculty of Science or Faculty of Art and Humanities). Subject teachers are educated according to the concurrent model. At the BA level, students mostly take two disciplines (academic subjects), whereas educational studies, teaching methodologies and teaching practice are studied at the master's level. These courses cover sixty ECTS credits, which are distributed across two years. After graduation, students receive the professional title of Master of Education in specific disciplines and are usually qualified to teach two subjects (Domović and Vizek Vidović, 2011). Special cases are teachers in secondary vocational schools who teach theoretical parts of vocational subjects, and professional instructors in school workshops or in companies.

Teachers of theoretical parts of vocational training are, as a rule, graduated professionals (such as engineers, economists, medical doctors), whereas instructors of practical work and exercises most often complete higher or secondary school in their relevant vocational branches (Domović and Matijević, 2002). The education of vocational schoolteachers is not carried out at special institutions, but is organized at teacher education faculties as a type of lifelong learning programme with a sixty-ECTS workload. These teachers are obliged to complete the special programme of pedagogical training during their first year of service, which enables them to obtain teacher qualifications.

All novice teachers spend one year of induction period in schools supervised by their mentors. Mentors are experienced teachers appointed by the Ministry of Science, Education and Sports. Their role and tasks are regulated by a special act on induction, and they are paid extra for this task. Mentors are not offered any specialized training in mentoring. After the completion of the induction period, a mentor writes a report on the development and achievements of his or her mentee. A positive report allows the novice teacher to take the state exam, which allows them to get full responsibility as professional teachers.

The Act on Education in Primary and Secondary Schools (2008) defines continuous professional development as the right and obligation of all school staff. Recognizing the importance of lifelong learning of teachers, the Teacher Education and Training Agency has developed the INSET (In-Service Education and Training) Strategy for Professional Development of Teaching and Non-Teaching Staff (2014–20)[19] with the overall objective of improving the quality and effectiveness of the institutions responsible for the provision of education and training.

Continuous professional development is organized and coordinated by the appointed institutions, such as the Agency for Vocational Education and Training and the Education and Teacher Training Agency. The areas of professional development are divided into four categories: education in various academic disciplines (subjects), in educational sciences and teaching methodologies, information communication technology (ICT) and educational policy and management. Participation in approved programmes is verified by a certificate of attendance. Teachers are expected to attend several programmes per year, but the exact number of hours has not been specified.

However, although significant changes have occurred in teacher education in the last decade, quite a few problems and challenges still remain. Some relevant strategic documents and procedures are still missing, such as national qualification standards for the teaching profession or a model of teacher licensing, although some projects have recently been started with support from EU funds.[20]

Another challenge is the issue of universitization, which in some degree weakened the link between academic courses and school-based practice, especially regarding insufficient support to school-based mentors.

It has been observed that upgrading teacher initial education programmes puts more pressure on teacher educators for reaching higher research attainments, which shifted the focus from their teacher educator competences.

The general comment regarding teacher continuous professional development is that new strategy has not yet been fully implemented. Also, the offered programmes do not fully take into account the results of the studies on teacher educational needs.

Besides, it is possible to identify some other problems in this subsystem of teacher education, such as the absence of quality assurance measures, the lack of development of connections among higher education institutions conducting teacher initial education and institutions providing continuing professional development of teachers, a vague connection between continuing professional development and teacher advancement, and the absence of the system of (re) licensing in the teaching profession (Domović and Vizek Vidović, 2011).

Recent challenges and developments in Croatian education system

The main challenges for the Croatian education system are the lack of continuity in strategic approach, the coordination gap between document developments (policy level) and implementation (practice level), lack of consensus among policy makers and other stakeholders about the education as a public good and the best investment in the future, and unwillingness to base strategic measures on accumulated evidence about educational achievements and needs of students and society.

Regarding the continuity, it is evident that during the last twenty years there was an impressive production of different strategic documents which sometimes overlap, and sometimes there were periods without clear goals or priorities for education. For example, there is a four-year gap between the last Sector Development Plan (2005–10) and new comprehensive draft of the Strategy of Education, Science and Technology (2014)[21] which is now waiting for approval by the Parliament. This long-awaited strategy is perceived with mixed feelings by the educational community. Generally, it has been positively received in public debate because of its comprehensiveness, underlying expertise, and operationalization of concrete measures, but the open question is whether there will be resources for its implementation in a planned time frame.

The coordination gap between document developments (policy level) and implementation (practice level) manifests in various ways. In many occasions, the planned strategic measures are poorly communicated from policy level to schools, universities and teachers and students. For example, in direct communications with different representatives of educational community, it has been perceived that teachers are mostly not aware of guidelines introduced by the National Curriculum Framework. Sometimes, measures are introduced as pilot projects without proper follow-up steps and evaluation of their outcomes, and then are simply abandoned, being replaced by new ones offered by the next generation of policy makers. One distinctive example is higher education, where some key concepts brought forth by the Bologna process, such as learning outcomes, student-centred teaching or ECTS credits, are still not fully understood among teachers or students.

The lack of consensus among policy makers and other stakeholders about education has been especially emphasized during the prolonged economic crises, since 2008. The comparative data show that although there were some cuts in budgets for education in all EU countries, Croatia belongs to the group of countries with the lowest percentage of expenditure for education and with a continued and significant decrease. For example, in the period from 2008 to 2010, annual expenditure per student in € PPS (per person sharing) has decreased in pre-tertiary education by 4 per cent, with the most dramatic drop in tertiary education a decrease of 28.4 per cent.[22]

It should be also noted that while at the EU level about 77 per cent of expenditure in education is devoted to personnel expenditure, in Croatia the percentage for personnel expenditure amounts to more than 90 per cent.

Although in the last decade a significant amount of data on different aspects of the Croatian education system and its effectiveness have been collected in various national and international studies, the accumulated evidence was usually ignored by policy makers. For example, since 2006 Croatia has been participating in three PISA cycles achieving continually below average results in all three measured literacies. These data did not attract great attention either from policy makers and educational professionals or from the general public and media. The question may be raised, what is the purpose of such expenditure if the results are not used in rethinking improvements in education? It should also be noted that other national surveys reveal that students as well as their teachers and parents express dissatisfaction with the curricula, which they perceive as outdated, overloaded with factual details, with too many fragmented compulsory subjects, not supporting the acquisition of lifelong learning skills and generally not preparing students for 'real' life.

The consequence of all these inconsistencies and deficiencies is an educational practice with unused innovative potential, sometimes anxious about unclear top-down expectations, keeping to old, safe modes of functioning with prevalent teacher-centred and discipline-focused practice at all educational levels. Reflecting on all these developments, educational practitioners put forward the question: What really prompts educational changes, and how will they be supported in implementing those changes? Apparently, they perceive the focus to be less on real internal social needs and more on acceptance of external trends without deeper analysis and adaptation to a local context.

Notes

1   For example: the Elementary School Act in 1990; the Secondary School Act in 1992; and the Higher Education Act and the Law On Scientific Research Activities in 1993; Preschool Education Act in 1997.

2   In the last twenty-five years, the Ministers of Education on average completed only about half of their mandate, resulting also in a significant fluctuation and shortage of trained staff in the Ministry departments.

3   In 2010, two agencies—the Agency for Vocational Education and Training and the Agency for Adult Education—merged into the Agency for Vocational Education and Training and Adult Education.

4   Source: Ministry of science, education and sports: http://public.mzos.hr/Default.aspx?sec=2195 (retrieved 25 September 2014).

5   CBS data basis, Croatian Bureau of Statistics: http://www.dzs.hr/default_e.htm (retrieved 25 September 2014).

6   CBS data basis, Croatian Bureau of Statistics: http://www.dzs.hr/default_e.htm (retrieved 25 September 2014).

7   CBS data basis, Croatian Bureau of Statistics: http://www.dzs.hr/default_e.htm (retrieved 25 September 2014).

8   CBS data basis, Croatian Bureau of Statistics: http://www.dzs.hr/default_e.htm (retrieved 25 September 2014).

9   Strategija razvoja sustava strukovnog obrazovanja u Republici Hrvatskoj 2008–13. (2008) Zagreb: Ministarstvo znanosti, obrazovanja i sporta. p.8.

10 Source: Agency for Vocational Education and Training and Adult Education: http://www.asoo.hr/default.aspx?id=1345 and Strategija razvoja sustava strukovnog obrazovanja u Republici Hrvatskoj 2008–13. (2008). Zagreb: Ministarstvo znanosti, obrazovanja i sporta (retrieved 21 September 2014).

11 Source: Agency for science and higher education: https://www.azvo.hr/index.php/hr/statistike (retrieved 22 September 2014).

12 Source. Agency for science and higher education. https://www.azvo.hr/index.php/hr/statistike/broj-studijskih-programa-po-vrstama-visokih-ucilista (retrieved 22 September 2014).

13 Source: Ministry of science, education and sports. http://public.mzos.hr/Default.aspx?sec=2254 (retrieved 22 September 2014).

14 Source: Agency for science and higher education. https://www.azvo.hr/index.php/hr/statistike/broj-studijskih-programa-po-vrstama-visokih-ucilista (retrieved 22 September 2014).

15 Source: Agency for science and higher education. https://www.azvo.hr/index.php/hr/statistike/broj-studijskih-programa-po-vrstama-visokih-ucilista (retrieved 22 September 2014).

16 Source: Croatian Bureau of Statistics: http://www.dzs.hr/Hrv_Eng/ljetopis/2013/sljh2013.pdf (retrieved 29 September 2014).

17 Source: EC—Education and Training Monitor (2013), p. 41 http://ec.europa.eu/education/library/publications/monitor13_en.pdf (retrieved 4 October 2014).

18 The extensive overview of the Croatian higher education can be found on ASHE website: https://www.azvo.hr/index.php/en/o-nama/propisi

19 See http://www.azoo.hr/images/pkssuor/Strategija_HR2-Final.pdf (retrieved 2 October 2014).

20 For example: IPA project: Development of the national qualification standard for teachers as a basis for the implementation of a teacher licensing system. See http://www.nskzaucitelje.hr/eng/project (retrieved 2 October 2014).

21   Source: Strategija obrazovanja, znanosti i tehnologije—Radni materijal (Strategy of education, science and technology). (2014). http://www.universitas.hr/wp-content/uploads/2013/10/Strategija-OZT.pdf (retrieved 4 October 2014).
22   Source: EC—Education and Training Monitor (2013), p. 14 http://ec.europa.eu/education/library/publications/monitor13_en.pdf (retrieved 4 October 2014).

References

Act on Elementary and Secondary Schools. (2008). *Zakon o odgoju i obrazovanju u osnovnoj i srednjoj školi.* Zagreb: Narodne novine 87/08.

Act on Quality Assurance in Higher Education. (2009). *Zakon o osiguravanju kvalitete u znanosti i visokom obrazovanju.* Zagreb: Narodne novine 45/09.

Act on Vocational Education. (2009). *Zakon o strukovnom obrazovanju.* Zagreb: Narodne novine 30/09.

Croatian National Educational Standard. (2005). *Hrvatski nacionalni obrazovni standard, HNOS.* Zagreb: Ministry of Science, Education and Sport.

Development Strategy of the Vocational Education System in the Republic of Croatia 2008–2013. (2008). Zagreb: Ministry of Science Education and Sports.

Domović, V. and Matijević, M. (2002). 'For a "new school"—Different teachers: Towards a reconstruction of teacher education system in Croatia'. *Metodika*, 5(3): 33–49; Zagreb: Učiteljska akademija.

EC. (2013). Education and Training Monitor. http://ec.europa.eu/education/library/publications/monitor13_en.pdf

Education Sector Development Plan 2005–2010. (2005). Zagreb: Ministry of Science, Education and Sports.

Franković, D. (1958). *Povijest školstva i pedagogije u Hrvatskoj.* Zagreb: Pedagoško-književni zbor.

Godler, Z. and Domović, V. (2008). 'Croatian higher education and the implementation of the bologna process', in D. Palomba (ed.). *Changing Universities in Europe and the 'Bologna Process', A Seven Country Study.* Roma: ARACNE, 101–24.

Godler, Z. and Domović, V. (1999). 'Clear Needs, Uncertain Responses: Change in the Croatian Education System', in K. Mazurek, M.A. Winzer and Cz. Majorek (eds), *Education in a Global Society: A Comparative Perspective.* Needham Heights, MA: Allyn and Bacon, 271–84.

International Standard classification of Education. (2011). Paris: UNESCO.

Lowther, J. (2004). 'The quality of Croatia's formal education system', in P. Bejaković and J. Lowther (eds), *Croatian Human Resource Competitiveness Study.* Zagreb: Institut za javne financije, 14–27.

National Curriculum Framework for Pre-school Education and General Compulsory and Secondary Education. (2010). Zagreb: Ministry of Science, Education and Sports.

Pastuović, N. (ed.) (2001). White Paper on Croatian Education. Zagreb: The
   Government of the Republic of Croatia.
Pregled postignuća 2004–2007 *(Overview of Achievements 2004–2007)*. (2007). Zagreb:
   Ministry of Science, Education and Sport.
Preschool Education Law. (1997). *Zakon o predškolskom odgoju i naobrazbi.* Zagreb:
   Narodne novine 010/97.
Strategy for the Construction and Development of the National Curriculum for
   Preschool Education, General Compulsory and Secondary School Education.
   (2007). Zagreb: Ministry of Science, Education and Sport.
Strategy of Education, Science and Technology—Proposal *(Strategija obrazovanja,
   znanosti i tehnologije—nacrt)* http://www.mzos.hr/datoteke/Strategija-2014.pdf

3

Cyprus: Exploring Educational Reform 2004–2014

Eleftherios Klerides and Stavroula Philippou

Introduction

Within the *problématique* of the book, this chapter focuses on recent education developments in the Republic of Cyprus. The education system in the Republic is examined as a case undergoing reform for the last ten years, and is thus explored as being in a state of transition rather than a description of what 'is' in a fixated present. We specifically focus on the period starting in the year 2004, when a comprehensive reform programme, the so-called 'Education Reform', was launched against the background of accession to the European Union (EU). Relations between the Republic of Cyprus and European Communities were initiated in 1961 when the Republic became the sixteenth member state of the Council of Europe; approximately forty years later, in May 2004, it entered the EU as the applicant and only recognized state on the island, a fact which has exerted further pressure to resolve the 'Cyprus Problem'. Hence, the year 2004 can be considered as a landmark year also because of the rejection of the UN Secretary General's Cofi Annan's Plan for the reunification of the island on the basis of a bi-communal and bizonal federal state. Cyprus has been divided since the inter-ethnic hostilities of 1963–67 and the withdrawal of the Turkish-Cypriots from the Republic of Cyprus, the partnership state between Greek-Cypriots and Turkish-Cypriots, which was established in 1960 after decades of British colonial rule (1878–1959). This state did not, however, satisfy the aspirations of either community, as both were engaged in multifaceted conflict to respectively claim either *Enosis* (Union with Greece) or *Taksim* (partition of Cyprus between Greece and Turkey). The Greek-led coup and the Turkish invasion in 1974 consolidated separation, dividing the island into two ethnically distinctive areas (Greek-Cypriots in the south and Turkish-Cypriots in the north). In 1983, a 'Turkish Republic of Northern Cyprus' was founded in the Turkish-occupied north, but not recognized by the international community.

Focusing on 2004 as the year of initiating reform is not to say that education issues discussed in this chapter were not present also before 2004. In fact, we suggest that the origins of the Education Reform are traced a long way back, but more recently in the 1997 UNESCO Report on Cyprus education, which we briefly discuss as a milestone in the first part of the chapter. More generally, the aim of this first part of the chapter is to provide a brief sketch of the beginnings, development and nature of education in Cyprus, as well as the main challenges that education faces in an era of Europeanization and globalization, arguing that politico-ideological and sociocultural specificities of education and its historical trajectory are conditions that made the emergence of the Education Reform possible. In the second part of the chapter, a brief account of the Reform is described before we closely explore curriculum and higher education reforms in the third and fourth parts of the chapter, respectively. School curriculum and university education, we argue, are the two sub-sectors of education that attracted more attention in political rhetoric and have been transformed within the context of reform, and their transformation reflects and is guided by *global* and *European* 'policyscapes' (Carney, 2009) and 'travelling reforms' (Coulby et al., 2006), by Greek *national* culture and identity, and by *local*, postcolonial anxieties or priorities, ideologies and histories. The last part of the chapter, the conclusion, opens up new lines of scholarship on 'Cyprus education', suggesting that we need to engage in a more systematic way with the interplay between intersecting global, European, national and local forces.

Mapping Conditions of Reform Initiation

The education system of Cyprus is a segregated system of education consisting of the Greek-Cypriot system and the Turkish-Cypriot system. These two different sub-systems are the product of complex processes of the borrowing and transfer of education forms and patterns from England, Greece and Turkey, and subsequently, local adaptation, indigenization and the dialectical evolution of education imports (Kizilyürek, 1999; Klerides, 2009, 2011; Persianis, 2006, 2010). The focus of this chapter is on the Greek-Cypriot system of education, which has been controlled and administered by the Republic of Cyprus since the mid-1960s, following the withdrawal of the Turkish-Cypriots from the partnership state and the establishment of an Education Ministry.

In particular, the origins of the Greek-Cypriot system are located in the late nineteenth and earlier twentieth century against the background of the spreading of Greek national ideals and values on the island, as well as the advent of British colonialism and the British plan to modernize the island on the basis of European standards and institutions (Charalambous, 1997, 2001; Klerides, 2009, 2011; Philippou and Klerides, 2010). Within the context of the 'external dimension' of the nation-building project of the Greek state (Kitromilides, 1989) and as part of the British imperial space, ideals and ideologies, policies and practices of modern European schooling found their way to the island and determined the beginnings of this system. The ideological and philosophical orientation of this system, its objectives and content, its institutional framework of governance, and its structure as well as its teacher policies and training were to a large extent a product of borrowings from Greece and England, which, however, were translated and transformed in the course of interaction with locality, giving Greek-Cypriot education its unique character.

Despite the recent reading of the Greek-Cypriot system as a *mélange* (Gregoriou, 2004; Philippou and Klerides, 2010; Klerides, 2011, 2013), this system is often considered to have been offering 'Greek education' to the youth because it has been framed by a mobile ideology of hellenocentricism and its locally adapted and evolved parallel version of hellenocypriocentrism. Drawing legitimacy from the idiom of Cyprus as an inseparable part of the 'imagined community' of Hellenism, the Greek nation, these ideological tokens have promoted the full identification of education in Cyprus with the education of Greece, even after the creation of a Cypriot state in 1960 (Persianis, 1978, 2006, 2010; Charalambous, 1997; 2001). In this politico-ideological *zeitgeist*, Greek-Cypriots followed and implemented the education policy of Greece, at least in secondary education; Greek-Cypriot curricula were modelled on those of Greece; textbooks and other teaching material used in Greek-Cypriot schools were imported from Greece; and Greece offered places for university education to Greek-Cypriot students. Most importantly, Hellenocentrism and hellenocypriocentrism have ruled out any other alternative ideology to inhabit the system, negating alterity as a danger of de-Hellenization.

These two ideologies in education were historically challenged by colonial education policy and the education agendas of the communist movement on the island in the 1920s–1940s (Charalambous, 2001; Persianis, 2006). In recent times, they have been criticized on the grounds that they prioritized the making

of educational subjectivities loyal to the cause of *Enosis* and Greece, and by
disseminating and solidifying irredentist Greekness, they played a key role in
the alienation of Greek-Cypriots and Turkish-Cypriots and the legitimization
of their confrontation and eventual segregation (Bryant, 2004; Makriyianni
and Psaltis, 2007). These ideologies are held to sustain and perpetuate division,
thus preventing reconciliation and the reunification of the island (Psaltis, 2008;
Philippou, 2009). Opponents of these ideologies, who are simultaneously
advocates of Cypriotism, the ideology which brings to the fore the Cypriot
dimension of the identity of Greek-Cypriots and Turkish-Cypriots and sets
them apart from the Greeks and the Turks as citizens of Greece and Turkey,
respectively, believe that if Cyprus is going to be re-united in the future,
education must be reformed and transformed at present in order to contribute
to Greek-Cypriot and Turkish-Cypriot rapprochement. In this line of argument,
the subjects of history and history textbooks often attract overdue attention
(Philippou, 2012a; Klerides, 2014a).

Independence from the education policies of Greece, at least in part, was
sought during the 1976–80 reforms carried out by Chrysostomos Sofianos,
then Education Minister. A curriculum development unit was established; the
teaching of the history of Cyprus, citizenship education and Greek-Cypriot
literature were introduced in schools, as well as many other measures aiming
at the strengthening of Cypriot statehood (Sofianos, 1986). The first university,
the University of Cyprus, was established in 1989, following fierce debates over
de-Hellenization, as this was perceived as a step away from the entrenched
tradition of Greek-Cypriots studying in Greek universities (Theophilides,
2012). It was also after 1974 that a new Greek-Cypriot education policy, often
qualified as 'independent' to connote difference from the education policy of
Greece (Koutselini-Ioannidou, 1997), was initiated and emerged in parallel
with hellenocentric and hellenocypriocentric policies. This 'independent
policy' is arguably a 'borrow-and-mix' approach to policy making (Klerides,
2014b) confirming and perpetuating, albeit in a different form, the character of
education as a *mélange*.

Despite disagreement about the politico-ideological orientation of policy
and education, less contested issues have been often recognized as major
problems and are also derived from policy borrowing and hybridization,
complex indigenization and the evolution of Cyprus education. First, there is
a gap or discontinuity between primary and secondary education (Psaltis, I.,
2008). During the British colonial period, primary education was administered
and controlled by the Colonial Government of Cyprus, whereas secondary

education was under the responsibility of the Orthodox Church of Cyprus and local communities (Persianis, 1978). State and Church produced different administrative structures, different attitudes and perceptions, and made use of different curricula, resulting in discontinuity between the two sub-sectors. Second, there is a disparity in status between schools offering general education and technical schools at the upper secondary level. Often, attendance at technical schools has been regarded as a sign of academic failure rather than a choice to pursue a career in technology, trades or administration (Persianis, 2010). This tendency reflects the historical growth of education in Europe and particularly in Greece, especially the tendency to see any deviation from an academically oriented curriculum as 'non-education' (Pyrgiotakis, 2001). The nine-year course of compulsory education (six years of primary education and three years of lower secondary education) was introduced in 1994 to bridge the gap between primary and secondary education, and the Comprehensive Lyceum in the mid-to-late 1990s to address the disparity between general and technical education. But according to the Education Reform Committee (ERC, 2004), commissioned to examine the education system and submit proposals for reform, both initiatives failed to bring about the desired results.

The historical-cultural context within which the Greek-Cypriot system is embedded also accounts for other challenges. Greek-Cypriots are often said to set a high value on education, with extremely high motivation among parents, especially for academic qualifications. This strong motivation is often explained by historians such as Persianis (2010) as a response to the trauma of the Turkish invasion, which provoked a sense of insecurity in which education came to be regarded as the one possession that could not be taken away. Yet, this motivation is translated as intense competition to gain entrance to universities in Cyprus and abroad, which prompts parents to supplement schooling with private tuition, to the extent that it creates an informal complementary education system, 'the shadow educational system' (Bray et al., 2013). Also important is the problem of the focus of education on the transmission and acquisition of information, originating in the Greek (or French) tradition of encyclopaedism (Persianis, 2010). Teachers focus on covering a large amount of material (*yli*), and there is a rush through the curriculum: 'Everything has to be done in such a hurry' is their frequent complaint. In this regard, learning becomes more coaching than education, and the joy of learning disappears (Koutselini, 2010).

Obviously there are many more challenges one could comment on and analyse; however, our focus in the preceding paragraphs aims to highlight the long, cultural-historical and political-ideological roots and conditions of reform initiation in the period under study. Before we proceed to the analyses of the cases of school curriculum and university education in the last decade, we need to account for one of the more recent drives of the reform, the UNESCO Report (1997).

Fuelling the Reform: the UNESCO Report

The origins of the current education reform are traced to the mid-1990s (Klerides, 2014b), when the Government of the Republic of Cyprus submitted a request via UNESCO to undertake an appraisal of education in co-operation with the International Institute for Educational Planning (IIEP), with the aim of reforming and aligning the country's system to European and international policies and practices. Following consultations with stakeholders, UNESCO published in 1997 a report on Greek-Cypriot education with the title *Appraisal Study on the Cyprus Education System*, focusing on pedagogical issues, on issues of education research and evaluation and on teaching personnel management. This report was a very first attempt to introduce ideals and ideologies of 'post-bureaucratic regulation' (Maroy, 2009) or 'governing through data' (Grek and Ozga, 2010) to the Greek-Cypriot system. Post-bureaucratic governance revolves around rhetorics of quality, autonomy and transparency, and focuses on outcomes, benchmarking, efficiency, accountability and performativity.

In their report, the consultants of the IIEP pointed to some of the long-standing challenges of the system and made concomitant proposals for upgrading education. They highlighted the gap between primary and secondary education, and between general and technical education at the secondary level, proposing the merging of the Department of Primary Education, the Department of Secondary Education and the Department of Technical Education in the Ministry of Education and Culture (MoEC) into a single department as a way to address these gaps. The IIEP suggested that although they are in accord with the aims of education of states within the European Community and with the countries having membership of OECD, the aims of education should be broken into key issues, and a set of indicators and performance targets should develop out of these issues, which would allow the measurement of progress towards the achievement of the aims of education. The IIEP also recommended the creation of a specialized policy-making body, which the education system was (and is still) lacking, as well as the establishment of a national research and evaluation unit, which would be in charge of data collection for purposes of quality improvement, strategic planning and evidence-based policy.

In the area of teacher management, the IIEP determined that waiting lists for appointment in schools, date of application for placement in waiting lists and age as modalities of recruitment 'are detrimental to the quality of education', and suggested that this system 'requires urgent and radical review' (UNESCO, 1997: 4). Also requiring review, according to IIEP, is the teacher promotion system, which is (also) based on years in service and age, and which fails to recognize excellence and to utilize the services of the most able teachers in an effective manner; the dual role of the inspectors as inspectors and advisors; and the system of evaluation of teachers and schooling by the Inspectors, with a necessity to shift from processes to outcomes. The consultants recommended the devolution of powers at district and school levels and the strengthening of the role of school principals in the management and development of schools. An upgrading of in-service teacher training was also suggested, including the limitation, or abolishment if possible, of the secondment scheme in the staffing of the MoEC.

Education Reform (2004–13)

Given that none of these policy proposals were put into practice (Klerides, 2014b) and with Cyprus being just one step before accession to the European Union, the need for an immediate qualitative upgrading and modernization of all levels of education was proclaimed by President Tassos Papadopoulos as a main goal of his administration (2003–8). To achieve this goal, the Council of Ministers appointed an Education Reform Committee (ERC) in the fall of 2003, comprised of seven academics affiliated with American, Cypriot and Greek universities and higher education institutions, with the mandate to examine education and submit proposals for a comprehensive reform. In August 2004, the Committee submitted to the MoEC a report, entitled *Democratic and Human/Humane Education in a Euro-Cypriot Polity: Prospects for Reconstruction and Modernization*, which put forward policy proposals for 'the reformation of the structural-institutional framework of education governance, the restructuring of school system from Nursery to University, the renewal of the content of education and pedagogy-didactics, and equally important, the reconceptualization of the ideology and the philosophical foundations of the system' (ERC, 2004: 17).

The report was favourably accepted by many stakeholders, including political parties, teacher unions, parent associations, student associations and academics. Nevertheless, the Church of Cyprus, along with the right-wing party of Democratic Rally (DISY) (the party of Opposition), former education ministers, educators and journalists, disagreed with some proposals. The issue that caused controversy and intense conflict was the ERC's position that 'the ideological-political framework of Cyprus education remains Helleno-Cypriocentric, narrowly ethnocentric and culturally monolithic' and the subsequent proposal for 'the ideological re-orientation and redefinition of the aims and objectives of Cyprus education' and 'the elimination of the narrow ethnocentric, monocultural and, by extension, ethno-dualistic elements of the system' (Hellenocentric and Turkocentric) (p. 95). Both these proposals and reactions are not unfamiliar and indeed allude to two specific periods in the history of education in Cyprus: the 1930s and the conflict between the British colonialists and the Cypriots Hellenists, and the 1976–80 and the Sofianos reform programme (see e.g. Persianis, 2006; Kazamias, 2010).

A few months after the publication of the Report, on the occasion of commemorating the '(Greek) Letters Day' on 30 January 2005, the President of the Republic announced the intention of the Government to embark upon 'radical revolutionary reform', based on the proposals of the ERC. Since that date, the term 'Education Reform' had become a hegemonic concept in the education politics of the Republic of Cyprus penetrating all levels and aspects of education. For Persianis (2010), a leading historian of education in Cyprus, this initiative was the first real major education reform since the founding of the Republic, and its aim was declared to be the creation of 'a democratic and human/humane school'. The initiator of this term, Professor Andreas Kazamias, the President of the ERC, and one of its subsequent users, Professor Giorgios Tsiakalos, the President of the Curriculum Review Committee (CRC) and also a member of the ERC, invested this polysemous term with rather different meanings. While Kazamias used this term to denote a school which would promote neo-humanism and would cultivate to pupils all the necessary virtues for active, democratic and critical citizens as per the model of Ancient Greece envisioned by Socrates and Aristotle (ERC, 2004), Tsiakalos described this school as one which would be inclusive of all students irrespective of social, racial or ethnic background, gender, or physical or mental ability (CRC, 2008). Despite this essential difference, both academics employed the idiom of 'a democratic and human/humane school' to denote opposition to international trends aiming at transforming schools on the basis of the needs of the market economy and particularly to neo-liberal, techno-economistic and market-driven, education agendas of the EU (see Philippou, 2012b; Theodorou and Philippou, 2013).

The proposals of the ERC were structured under six areas or 'critical zones', the third of which was the school curriculum under the title 'Content of Education: Curriculum, School knowledge, and Pedagogic-didactic process', and, the fourth of which was 'Higher and University Public and Private Education' (ERC, 2004, 5). It is to these two areas of reform that we now turn in the third and fourth parts of the chapter, as they attracted most attention in the decade that followed the launch of the Reform. They are also the two sub-sectors of the system in which education change materialized, albeit not necessarily in the suggested direction and pace, and, this change is guided by an interplay of intersecting global, European, national and by local forces.

School Curricula Review

The ERC proposed the revision and upgrading of school knowledge and the modernization of school pedagogy-didactics. Conceptualizing the official curriculum as a political-ideological text, the Committee envisioned school curricula that would include not only skills and performance-based indicators in crucial areas for the 'knowledge society', such as mathematics, sciences, reading, foreign languages and technology. Equally important, the setting up of indicators and competences was urged in areas which go 'beyond the Knowledge Society' and are related to a democratic and anthropocentric school—such as community, character, prudence, democratic ethos, friendship, solidarity and critical thinking. This envisioned democratization of education structures and contents also included educators, as the Report suggested the provision of space for teacher participation in decision-making procedures and their recognition as 'autonomous professional pedagogues', which was manifested particularly with its call for a departure from the single textbook policy (ERC, 2004). The Report highlighted the European context as one of the most important reasons why reform was necessary; it named the state as 'euro-cypriot' in its title and invited for a conscious shift towards 'Europe' and the EU as a discursive source for a re-definition of Cypriot citizenship which would enable students to participate in the *'cosmopolis'* of the EU as *'homo Europaei'*, as active and democratic citizens (ERC, 2004: 40). Though at some points rigidly and directly opposing neo-liberal economic agendas over education, and proposing humanistic education as a counter-ideal, the former discourses continued to surface especially when issues of evaluation were at stake, thus rendering 'Europe' both a model of democracy and humanistic/liberal ideals and a source of policies of standardization, competitiveness and economic rationalism in education (ERC, 2004; see Philippou, 2012b).

In 2007, the MoEC prepared a new reform report with the title *Strategic Planning for Education: A Comprehensive Review of our Education System*. This report, as noted in the foreword, 'will serve as a roadmap for the implementation of the education reform and its objectives, as these were articulated and expressed in the Report of ERC ... therefore, the strategic planning does not represent another reform, but it is an attempt to systematize and operationalize it' (MoEC, 2007: 1). However, and despite declaring that it attempts to implement the Education Reform as envisioned by the ERC, the Strategic Planning for Education distanced itself from controversy surrounding the Committee's proposal for 'the ideological re-orientation and redefinition of the aims and objectives of Cyprus education', confirming instead the Greek orientation of the country's system. It stated that 'the provision of education to children and young people is based on our Greek tradition ... [and] an integral part of an education with a democratic and humane content, is to inspire love towards the motherland ... [and] to preserve the memory of our occupied territories' (MoEC, 2007: 1–2). The introduction of new curricula and timetables is suggested as a means of achieving this ideal pupil, portrayed as a person achieving a common foundation of knowledge, skills and attitudes during their compulsory education around eight tenets: use of the mother-tongue; satisfactory use of two foreign languages; acquisition of math skills and scientific, technological culture; acquisition of competencies in the use of information and communication technologies; development of humanistic and environmental culture, acquisition of social and political competencies; development of autonomy and initiative; development of metacognitive competencies (MoEC, 2007). As far as the portrayal of teachers is concerned, kernels of neo-liberal discourse begun to infiltrate this text, as professional autonomy was now linked to teacher efficiency (Theodorou, Philippou and Kontovourki, under review).

The Government of Demetris Christofias of AKEL, which succeeded the Papadopoulos Government in 2008, also ranked education very high in its priorities. According to press reports, at a Meeting of the Education Council on 29 July 2008, President Christofias noted that 'the Government adopts the principles of the ERC's Report on the Education Reform, sharing the ERC's vision for a democratic school serving the needs of the people/the agora of the demos, a democratic school for the citizen and not a school serving the market economy' (cited in Klerides, 2014b: 33). Immediately after he became Education Minister, Andreas Demetriou announced that the year 2008/9 would be the 'Year of the Education Reform'. To speed up the implementation of the Reform, several committees or councils were appointed by the Council of Ministers, the most important of which was the Curriculum Review Committee (CRC) in July 2008 with the mandate to develop a new curriculum for a ten-year course of public compulsory education.

The CRC presented in December 2008 a document entitled *Curriculum for the Public Schools of the Republic of Cyprus*, which was framed as a key document for the transition from policy to school curriculum reform by serving as guidance for those later involved in the development of new curricula texts. This document stressed the significance of school curricula for the broader education reform, drawing on Europe as an exemplary model: '[…] in the early 1970s, a decade of intense pedagogical debates and fundamental education reforms in Europe, the relevant efforts were 'sealed' by the phrase education reform is the reform of curricula' (CRC, 2008: 11). Indeed for the second half of the decade in focus in this chapter, education reform was mainly materialized through a process of curriculum review outlined in this document as progressive in allowing democratic participation, recognizing the pedagogical autonomy of teachers and addressing all dimensions of education. The 'Principles of Curriculum Structure and Implementation' presented in this document again included 'a unified and coherent curriculum from preprimary education to the lyceum' as well as differentiation, cooperative, multisensory and experiential learning, the reconceptualization of homework and others; these elements were construed as a break away from an oppressive agenda of subject-centred curriculum to be replaced by a child-centred curriculum. In this document, the international, and more particularly 'Europe', was in complex interplay with the 'local': the Committee argued that it did not draw the new curriculum's aims from economy experts (citing DELPHI technique as an example) or from EU documents, but that it rather opened it up to public discussion (for rendering the curriculum review process a 'public endeavor'), so that local needs and priorities were addressed. It named 'Greek culture/civilization' as the framework of education and of a 'democratic and human/humane school', 'wherein the children of the Greek-Cypriot community are supported in autonomously and confidently forming their identity (national, religious, cultural), whilst at the same time learning to respect the characteristics of the children of the other communities of the Republic of Cyprus as well as those of their peers with origins from other countries. For children with different origin there has been care so that they can holistically develop their own distinct identity' (CRC, 2008: 3–4; cf. Philippou, 2012b).

The publication of this document aimed at providing the theoretical foundation and guidance by means of three broad categories of aims and objectives for the work of twenty-one Subject Area Committees which were subsequently formed to develop new curricula texts. Most of these committees developed texts for both primary and secondary education in an integrative way (addressing both ERC and UNESCO recommendations on this matter; however the recommendation to address the disparity of status between general and technical secondary education was not tackled), whereas a small number focused only on secondary education; a separate committee was formed for preprimary education, but it was also expected that preprimary education would be considered by all committees. These committees were comprised of fifty-three appointed academics from Cyprus and Greece, Ministry officials/ technocrats and teachers who had responded to an open call for volunteer teachers in February–March 2009. According to the MoEC, about 320 primary and secondary educators (approximately 3 per cent of the practicing teacher population) applied and all were accepted to participate in these committees (as a manifestation of the reform as a 'public endeavour' and of the recognition of teacher importance), though evidently not always as equals to the other members (cf. Kontovourki, Theodorou and Philippou, 2014). The committees produced a draft syllabus per subject area published in March 2010 for a period of public debate, at the end of which the curricula were edited and finalized as a unified text in printed form in two volumes and disseminated to schools in September 2010. The 'Office for the Review of the New Curricula' was replaced by an 'Office for the Promotion of the New Curricula' and the next steps in the introduction and implementation of the new curricula involved seminars for inspectors and school principals in fall 2010; compulsory mass professional development seminars in December 2010 and January 2011 for all primary schoolteachers and various other seminars for secondary schoolteachers (especially for lower secondary); a piloting of the curriculum and related teaching materials with teachers who had participated in the committees or other volunteer teachers; the production of related teaching materials by seconded teachers; the publication of guides and guidelines for teachers and parents regarding the reform; school-based professional development; the development of an online teaching material depository for the uploading of new material.

That the new curriculum texts appear as a compilation of syllabi with the subject area serving as the main axis of organization of the committees, the development of the official texts and later of professional development and production of teaching material, points towards a strengthening of special didactics and their construction of knowledge in each subject area, a point also made by Philippou and Karageorgi (under review) who compared the previous with the new primary curriculum texts. The new curricula in many subject-areas also signal an attempt to shift from content-based teaching to outcome-based learning, aligning Greek-Cypriot education with international practices. Since no other measures were implemented in this regard, such as changes in regimes of inspection or of teacher evaluation, recruitment and promotion, it could be suggested with reference to Bernstein's (1996) conception of pedagogic practice that the education system focuses on 'processes' rather than 'outcomes' as a mode of control and governance. 'It is well known', as Persianis (2012) notes, 'that in Cyprus there are no established national levels and indicators so as to assess the academic results of pupils, especially of our school graduates in a valid and reliable way' (p. 23; see Campbell and Kyriakides, 2000). The need or demand for an emphasis on standards, benchmarking, performativity and effectiveness has gained much prominence in recent times due to the country's poor results in international achievement tests such as TIMMS and PISA, and, is legitimized on the basis of the country's relatively high public expenditure on education—before the economic crisis Cyprus was proportionally the first country in the EU in terms of public expenditure on education, at 7.8 per cent of gross domestic product (GDP) compared to the average 5.2 per cent in the European Union.

However, not all academics, educators, teachers and politicians on the island subscribe to the principles of benchmarking, performativity, and effectiveness. Echoing debates from curriculum theory and the sociology of curriculum in the Anglo-Saxon world since the 1970s, the ERC (2004), for example, doubted whether the clear-cut articulation of all aims and objectives of schooling is feasible, let alone desirable to measure their success, and, challenges the 'validity' of setting up standards posing the question 'who, what criteria are used and what processes are applied to define these standards' (pp. 278–85). The ERC also pointed out that these policies or practices reduced curricula to what is 'measurable', degrading the humanities and social sciences, assuming that everyone has the same abilities for learning and failing to take into account the specificities of learners, an argument put forth also in their analysis of the new curricula from the perspective of inclusive education by Symeonidou and Mavrou (2013). A discussion of the uncomfortable balance between neoliberal and social justice discourses is also conducted by Theodorou and Philippou

(2013) in their analysis of European and intercultural education discourses in policy and curriculum documents of this last decade.

Teachers responded in diverse ways to these activities and while they were positive to the change and its necessity, they were largely against the removal of the single textbook policy. The MoEC gradually adopted a more mediocre approach that existing school textbooks would continue to be used, while new material would be created to supplement or replace the textbooks when the new curriculum goals or subject area syllabus objectives were not met. Thus, much of the discussion and guidelines provided to teachers centred on their increased flexibility in taking initiatives and developing instructional interventions to achieve quality and effective teaching, a rhetoric which was actually a deterioration from the 'autonomous professional pedagogue' envisioned in the ERC 2004 Report (Theodorou, Philippou and Kontovourki, under review), suggesting a move to more restricted or governable forms of teacher professionalism (see e.g. Beck, 2008; Hargreaves, 2010). Before we conclude this part of the chapter, we need to note that during the current academic year and after a change in government in March 2013, the new curricula are being evaluated so that decisions are made for the nature and direction of the reform.

Higher and University Education Reforms

The sub-sector of higher and university education was another key critical area of concern for the ERC. In their Report, the ERC (2004) proposed the expansion of public higher education with a substantial increase in the number of university places. In part, this proposal was legitimized on the grounds of increasing local demand for university education and academic qualifications. The ERC's call for more university places was also justified as being essential to reduce the phenomena of private tuition after school and 'student emigration' to Greece and other countries. The long-standing dependency of the ERC on the ideal of university education in Greece itself was proving to be a barrier to re-thinking innovative reform of Cypriot higher education. From the perspective of the Report's Cypriotist ideology, stressing among other things the independence of Cyprus from Greece (and Turkey), it was specifically said that this practice undermines the Republic's capacity to formulate its own higher education policy as an autonomous state and member of the European Union, and thereby to shape its own course of economic, technological and cultural development according to the needs of local society.

Furthermore, the Report of the ERC drew upon elements from EU higher education discourse as reflected in the 2000 Lisbon Strategy for growth and employment. Recognizing universities as 'key partners' in research and growth, the ERC (2004) suggested that the Republic ought to develop a strategy for the promotion of university education and research and not just for local economic ends. More importantly, it recommended that the country's higher education sector must be aligned with EU policies, starting with a commitment to the EU 2002 Barcelona goal of raising public expenditure on research to 3 per cent of GDP by 2010. The Report of the ERC also echoed the Bologna Declaration, which Cyprus signed in 2001. Urging both the state and the (soon-to-be-created) universities to actively participate in the making of the European Higher Education Area, the ERC maintained that universities should be integrated into the European Union's various mobility and cooperation networks, while the MoEC should upgrade existing or establish new quality assurance and accreditation systems in order to facilitate comparability and harmonization of educational outcomes. Above all, the ERC subscribed to EU notions of 'autonomy' and 'transparency' in governance, as well as to the socially inclusive rationale of widening participation in higher education, which all fit perfectly with the democratizing spirit of the Report.

At the same time, however, the ERC (2004) argued against the Bologna Process, warning that it poses several dangers, including the commercialization and transnationalization of higher education, the adaptation of universities to the needs of the labour market with the parallel marginalization of the humanities and liberal arts, and the cultivation of techno-economistic and instrumental identities and subjectivities characterized by a lack of humanistic ideals and values. These arguments allude to wider criticism in Europe and beyond, articulated against Bologna and the ideology of neo-liberalism in higher education (see e.g. Moutsios, 2013), and are partly derived from the Report's neo-humanistic philosophy.

Indeed, within a short period of time after the publication of the Report (2004) and the launching of the Education Reform (2005), the landscape of higher education in the Republic of Cyprus has fundamentally changed, with the establishment of new public and private universities (Klerides, 2014b). In addition to the University of Cyprus (UCY), two new public universities were founded with a view of diversifying higher education provision. These are the Open University of Cyprus (OUC), which was legally established in 2002 and admitted its first students in September 2006, and the Cyprus University of Technology (CUT), which was founded in 2003 and admitted its first students in September 2007. The OUC was created to provide distance and continuing education and lifelong learning, which are often treated in the Bologna Declaration as the foundation for the enactment of 'knowledge societies' (see e.g. Keeling, 2006). In the Report of the Preparatory Committee for the Establishment of the OUC, it was stressed, echoing now the social dimension of the Bologna Declaration, that this institution 'will provide opportunities to non-privileged sects of society to gain access to higher education and to upgrade their knowledge and qualifications' (quoted in Theophilides, 2012: 607–8). According to official rhetoric surrounding the establishment of the CUT (Persianis, 2010; Theophilides, 2012), the University was created with a focus on conducting applied research and to offer programmes of study in undergraduate and postgraduate levels in the areas of applied sciences and applied arts, which were not offered by the UCY.

There are several different reasons behind the creation of two new public universities (see Klerides, 2014b), including, as mentioned above, local pressures of sociopolitical ilk; pressures to open up university education to the masses of the Cypriot society; and to reduce phenomena of private tuition and student emigration to Greece. Other local factors include pressures from political and business circles from Limassol, the second largest city on the island, demanding the creation of a second university based in their city; and from the teaching personnel and students of the Higher Technological Institute, which saw the possibility of a second university as an opportunity to upgrade their status and degrees. In fact, the creation of the CUT put into practice in part the Government's strategy to upgrade a number of public institutions of tertiary education, such as the Higher Technological Institute, the Nursing School and the Forestry College. These institutions have been operating as state departments at least since the 1960s and satisfying the needs of the state and economy by providing professional training leading to two- or three-year diplomas. Finally, there were pressures deriving from the European level, especially EU accession talks with the European Commission. In the late 1990s, against the background of the Government's anxiety to convince the Commission that it was making all necessary preparations to align the country's education system with European standards, particularly to link economic growth with higher education, and thus to become a full member state of the European Union, then-Minister of Education and Culture Ouranios Ioannides prepared and sent a note to the Commission expressing the Government's commitment not simply to create two new public universities (Persianis, 2010). In the same document, always according to Persianis, the Government also promised to allow the establishment and operation of private universities in the Republic, a commitment translated into legislation in 2005.

Within a context of local and European pressures to establish a differentiated system of higher education and an educational market characterized at least in theory by competition between institutions, five private universities were also founded or upgraded from the status of college and recognized as 'universities' in following external evaluation of their programmes. These are the European University Cyprus (EUC), the University of Nicosia (UoN), Frederick University (FU), the Neapolis University Paphos (NUP) and University of Central Lancashire–Cyprus. The EUC, the UoN and FU admitted their first students in September 2007, the NUP in September 2010 and UClan-Cyprus in September 2012. The EUC is a member institution of the Laureate International Universities network and the UCLan–Cyprus is a franchised English university operating on the island, whereas FU is the only non-for-profit institution. Although the first three of these universities, the EUC, the UoN and FU, were formally established as universities in 2007, they all have a long history in tertiary education offering vocational training and education (two-year diplomas, four-year bachelors and two-year masters), often in collaboration with Anglo-American universities, and satisfying the needs of the local economy. The EUC was founded in 1961 as a business school with the name of Cyprus College, and the University of Nicosia in 1980 as Intercollege. Frederick University was initially established as Nicosia Technical and Economics School and was renamed in 1975 as Frederick Institute of Technology.

In addition to the pressures sketched above, the recognition of private universities drew much of its legitimacy from a local vision to make the Republic a regional hub of excellence in higher education (Persianis, 2010). Since at least the mid-1990s, political elites and business leaders in Cyprus have envisioned making the Republic a destination for higher education studies, especially for students from neighbouring countries in the Middle East and from countries of the former communist block, including Russia and China. However, a 2009 report on higher education, entitled *Strategy for the Development of University Education and Research in Cyprus* and commissioned by the MoEC following a relevant recommendation of the ERC, noted that Cyprus does not have the infrastructure to become a regional hub of higher education, nor does it fulfil some of the basic criteria to attract foreign students. To mention just one example, although private universities offer programmes of study in English, their status is rather low; on the other hand, public universities have the status to attract foreign students, but they are unable to do so because Greek is their language of instruction. Instead, the report, which was carried out by the Education Minister himself, Andreas Demetriou, in co-operation with a group of academics from public and private universities, recommended that university education ought to grow first in order to cover local demand, taking simultaneously small and careful steps towards internationalization.

In the same report, several policy proposals are put forward which are in sharp contrast with the logic of a higher education market. The report stresses that planning and coordination mechanisms in private university education should be created, not least to avoid the excessive growth of graduates in some disciplines—for example, the numbers of teachers and nurses outstrips available jobs; and a strategy of allocating programmes of studies in public universities should be formulated and implemented—for example, the Medical School to be established at the UCY and the School of Nursing at the CUT. Moreover, the report suggests that the so-called 'student grant', a grant given by the state to all students studying either in Cyprus or abroad, should be provided on the basis of socio-economic criteria. In light of this grant, it seems that the state provides indirect funding for private universities, making the emerging system of private university education a locally specific form of public private partnership (see e.g. Robertson, 2009).

The Report of the ERC set up the framework for at least another key development in higher education. Against the background of the ERC's proposal for the unification of the legislative and institutional framework of the governance of public and private institutions of higher education, a Committee of Experts was appointed in 2008 by the MoEC. The Committee was given the mandate to produce a framework for the modernization and unification of the legislation on universities and other institutions of tertiary education. In 2009, the Committee submitted its recommendations to the Ministry in a Report entitled *Law-Framework for Higher Education in Cyprus*, which is yet to be put in practice. Drawing heavily on EU higher education discourses, the Law-Framework encourages the internationalization of universities and embraces European models of governance and research, reiterating the importance of university autonomy and accountability as the basis of the new social contract between higher education sector and society. It also alludes to Anglo-Saxon practices of governance confirming that the University Council, consisting of a mixture of academics and non-academics (politicians, business leaders, etc.), is the highest authority within universities. The Law-Framework proposes the creation of a pan-Cypriot council that would be responsible for the making of higher education and research policy, and recommends the modernization of the higher and tertiary education structures of the MoEC, with the reorganization of the Department of Higher Education to include an emphasis on research.

The absence of policy making and research structures in the Republic's education system reflects the local history of education, especially a lack of research culture and tradition. Despite the recent expansion of university education, research and innovation remain at the margins of the system, and this manifests itself in the Republic's public expenditure for research, which was before the economic crisis well below the EU average (1.8 per cent), at 0.45 per cent. Thus, it seems that the system of university education in the Republic has been developing more in line with the objectives of the European Higher Education Area than with the aims of the EU's Research Area.

Indeed, as a result of the proliferation of private and public universities, the 'massification' of higher education has now become the norm in the Republic of Cyprus, like in many other places in Europe (and the world). Under the banner of Bologna, university degree structures in Cyprus have EU's three discrete cycles of study—bachelors (*ptychio*), which is four academic years of full-time study; masters, with duration of eighteen months to two-year full-time study; and doctorate, where the minimum length of full-time study is three academic years. Also, all public and private universities have introduced the European Credit Transfer System, with the EUC already being awarded the ECTS Label. Student and staff mobility, both outward and inward, is also part of the system, as is the Diploma Supplement, with the UCY, the UoN and FU acquiring the Diploma Supplement Label. Also in line with EU harmonization, the Republic has invented quality assurance and accreditation bodies: the Council for the Recognition of Higher Education Qualifications of Cyprus, which was legally established in 1996 and began its operations in 2000; the Council of Educational Evaluation—Accreditation, which is a member of the European Network of Quality Assurance; and the Evaluation Committee of Private Universities, which was established in 2005. Based on the recommendation of the ERC, the Ministry of Education and Culture created in 2007 a new national body of quality assurance and accreditation, the Cyprus Agency of Quality Assurance and Accreditation in Education, which will eventually replace all these three bodies. Finally, for Cypriot universities, 'synergies' with other European universities and the EU's targeted financial support for research under its 'Framework Programmes' or through the European Research Council and the Marie Curie scheme, are very significant.

Conclusion: Blending the local, national, European and global

In this chapter we argue that the Education Reform of the Greek-Cypriot education system has been discursively identified in political rhetoric and largely materialized through the development, introduction and implementation of new official school curricula texts. We also suggest that the Reform has been further materialized through the expansion of higher education and the proliferation of universities. It becomes clear from the analysis of both these cases above that recent developments in education reflect and are guided by European and global 'policyscapes' and 'travelling reforms', by Greek national culture and identity, and by local, postcolonial priorities or anxieties, ideologies and histories. As a result, we suggest in this final part of the chapter, the Greek-Cypriot system of education appears to veer between the global, the European, the national and the local.

Indeed the analysis presented in this chapter is part of a broader study exploring 'Cyprus education' as being in a state of tension and contradiction, and veering between different discourses produced in local, national, international and global spaces. As we have previously studied, this veering between discourses of national and local identity between 1960 and 2010 (Philippou and Klerides, 2010), in this chapter we have broadened the scope of the analysis to also account for the global and the European, as it is in constant interplay with the national and the local through the example of the Education Reform in general and the school curricula and university reforms in particular during the last decade. Though a common phenomenon, as we have briefly argued in the first part of the chapter, such veering, oscillation or hybridization is amplified, becomes especially clear or more visible in times of transition and produces new gaps, antinomies, paradoxes and inconsistencies which invite further research and constitute a challenging, yet necessary, agenda of future study into their emergence, formation and nature in the case of Cyprus education and its sub-systems.

References

Beck, J. (2008). 'Governmental professionalism: Professionalising or deprofessionalising teachers in England?'. *British Journal of Educational Studies*, 56(2), 119–43.

Bernstein, B. (1996). *Pedagogy, Symbolic Control and Identity: Theory, Research, Critique*. London: Taylor & Francis.

Bray, M., Mazawi, A. and Sultana, R. (eds) (2013). *Private Tutoring Across the Mediterranean: Power Dynamics and Implications for Learning and Equity.* Rotterdam: Sense Publishers.

Bryant, R. (2004). *Imagining the Modern: The Cultures of Nationalism in Cyprus.* London: Tauris.

Campbell, R. and Kyriakides, L. (2000). 'The national curriculum and standards in primary schools: A comparative perspective'. *Comparative Education,* 36(4), 383–95.

Carney, S. (2009). 'Negotiating policy in an age of globalization: Exploring educational "policyscapes" in Denmark, Nepal, and China'. *Comparative Education Review,* 53(1), 63–88.

Charalambous, D. (1997). *The Founding of the First Public Gymnasium in Cyprus.* Nicosia: Pancyprian Gymnasium. (in Greek)

Charalambous, D. (2001). *History of Teachers' Unionism in Cyprus.* Athens: Greek Letters. (in Greek)

Coulby, D., Ozga, J., Popkewitz, T. and Seddon, T. (eds) (2006). *World Yearbook in Education 2006: Education Research and Policy.* London: Routledge.

Curriculum Review Committee (2008). *Curriculum for the Public Schools of the Republic of Cyprus.* Nicosia: Ministry of Education and Culture. (in Greek)

Education Reform Committee (2004). *Democratic and Human/Humane Education in a Euro-Cypriot State: Prospects for Reconstruction and Modernization.* Nicosia: Ministry of Education and Culture. (in Greek)

Gregoriou, Z. (2004). 'De-scribing hybridity in "unspoiled Cyprus": Postcolonial tasks for the theory of education'. *Comparative Education,* 40(2), 241–66.

Grek, S. and Ozga, J. (2010). 'Governing education through data: Scotland, England and the European Education Policy Space'. *British Education Research Journal,* 36(6), 937–52.

Hargreaves, A. (2010). 'Four ages of professionalism and professional learning'. *Teachers and Teaching: Theory and Practice,* 6(2), 151–82.

Kazamias, A. (2010). 'Modernisation and conservatism in Cyprus education: The Sisyphean course of education reform, 2004–2009'. *Comparative and International Education Review,* 14, 46–79. (in Greek)

Keeling, R. (2006). 'The Bologna Process and the Lisbon Research Agenda: The European Commission's expanding role in higher education discourse'. *European Journal of Education,* 41(2), 203–23.

Kitromilides, P. (1989). '"Imagined communities" and the origins of national question in the Balkans'. *European History Quarterly,* 19, 149–94.

Kizilyürek, N. (1999). *Cyprus: The Impasse of Nationalisms.* Athens: Black List.

Klerides, E. (2009). 'National identities on the move: Examples from the historical worlds of Greater Britain and Hellenism'. *Comparative Education,* 45(3), 435–52.

Klerides, E. (2011). 'Cypriots first: Identity, education and conflict regulation on a divided island', in T. Hanf (ed.), *The Political Function of Education in Deeply Divided Countries.* Baden-Baden: Nomos, 37–60.

Klerides, E. (2013). 'Comparative research in education in an era of globalisation: Possibilities, puzzles, priorities', in Ch. Theofilides and I. Pirgiotakis (eds), *Education Research: Theoretical Puzzles and Praxis*. Nicosia: University of Nicosia Press. (in Greek)

Klerides, E. (2014a), 'Cyprus history debates, 2002–2010', in S. Lässig, M. Repoussi and L. Cajani (eds), *History Education Under Fire. Textbooks and Curricula in International Perspective*. London: Routledge.

Klerides, E. (2014b). *Education Reform in Cyprus (2003–2013)*. World Bank Working Document. Washington, DC: World Bank.

Kontovourki, S., Theodorou, E. and Philippou, S. (2014). *Caught between worlds of expertise: Primary teachers amidst official curriculum development processes in Cyprus*. Paper accepted for presentation at the 2014 Annual Meeting of the American Educational Research Association, Philadelphia, PA, United States.

Koutselini, M. (2010). 'Education reform and the curriculum: A critical approach'. *Comparative and International Education Review*, 14, 95–112. (in Greek)

Koutselini-Ioannidou, M. (1997). 'Curriculum as political text: The case of Cyprus (1935–90)'. *History of Education*, 26(4), 395–407.

Makriyianni, Ch. and Psaltis, Ch. (2007). 'The teaching of history and reconciliation'. *The Cyprus Review*, 19(1), 43–69.

Maroy, C. (2009), 'Convergences and hybridization of educational policies around "post-bureaucratic" models of regulation'. *Compare*, 39(1), 71–84.

Ministry of Education and Culture (2007). *Strategic Planning for Education: A Comprehensive Review of Our Education System*. Nicosia: MoEC. (in Greek)

Moutsios, S. (2013). 'The de-Europeanization of the university under the Bologna Process'. *Thesis Eleven*, 119, 22–46.

Persianis, P. (1978). *Church and State in Cyprus Education*. Nicosia: Violaris Press.

Persianis, P. (2006). *Comparative History of Education in Cyprus*. Athens: Gutenberg. (in Greek)

Persianis, P. (2010). *The Politics of Education*. Nicosia: University of Nicosia Press. (in Greek)

Persianis, P. (2012). 'A brief historical review of the Greek education of Cyprus during the first fifty years of its independence (1960–2010)', in *Education in Cyprus from 1960 to 2010: Proceedings of the Scientific Conference*. Nicosia: MoEC.

Philippou, S. (2009). 'What makes Cyprus European? Curricular responses of Greek Cypriot Civic education to Europe'. *Journal of Curriculum Studies*, 41(2), 199–223.

Philippou, S. (2012a). 'Beyond the history textbook debate: Official histories in Greek-Cypriot geography and civics curricula', in R. Bryant and Y. Papadakis (eds), *One Island, Many Histories: Rethinking the Politics of the Past in Cyprus*. London: I.B. Tauris, 51–70.

Philippou, S. (2012b). 'Europe as an alibi: An overview of 20 years of policy, curricula and textbooks in the Republic of Cyprus—And their review'. *European Educational Research Journal*, 11(3), 428–45.

Philippou, S. and Karayiorges, Y. (under review). 'Philosophical orientations of primary education curricula in Cyprus (1996 and 2010): Issues of continuity and change'. (in Greek)

Philippou, S. and Klerides, E. (2010). 'On continuity and change in national identity construction: An initial note on Greek-Cypriot education, 1960–2010'. *The Cyprus Review*, 22(2), 119–32.

Psaltis, C. (2008). 'Mapping the field of intercommunal relations: A socio-psychological analysis'. *International and European Politics*, 11, 133–43. (in Greek)

Psaltis, I. (2008), *The Transition From the Primary School to the Gymnasium*. Nicosia: Parga Publishers. (in Greek)

Pyrgiotakis, I. (2001). *Education and Society in Greece*. Athens: Greek Letters. (in Greek)

Robertson, S. (2009). 'Europe, competitiveness and higher education: An evolving project', in R. Dale and S. Robertson (eds), *Globalisation and Europeanisation in Education*. Oxford: Symposium.

Sofianos, Ch. (1986). 'The education reform in Cyprus, 1976–1980: Attempts—dependencies—reactions', in A. Kazamias and M. Kassotakis (eds), *The Educational Reform in Greece: Attempts, Deadlocks, Perspectives*. Rethymno: University of Crete Publications. (in Greek)

Symeonidou, S. and Mavrou, K. (2013). 'Deconstructing the Greek-Cypriot new national curriculum: to what extent are disabled children considered in the 'humane and democratic school' of Cyprus?', *Disability & Society*. DOI: 10.1080/09687599.2013.796879

Theodorou, E. and Philippou, S. (2013). 'When/if European and intercultural education meet: a discourse analysis of educational policy and curriculum texts in Cyprus', in P. Aggelides and Ch. Hadjisoteriou (eds), *Intercultural Dialogue in Education: Theoretical Approaches, Political Convictions and Pedagogical Practices*. Athens: Ekdoseis Diadrasis, 133–75. (in Greek)

Theodorou, E., Philippou, S. and Kontovourki, S. (under review), 'Between autonomy and autonomies: teacher professionalism amidst curriculum reform in Cyprus'.

Theophilides, Ch. (2012), 'University education in Cyprus: mapping the field', in S. Bouzakis (ed.), Comparative Education. Athens: Gutenberg. (in Greek)

4

The Czech Republic: 25 Years of Educational Transformation and Growing Inequalities 1989–2014

David Greger

Introduction

This chapter offers a brief and analytic overview of educational policy development since the demise of the communist regime in November 1989 in the Czech Republic. It argues that developments, especially those taking place in the early phase of the transformation process, have led to many structural changes and the introduction of early selection in the school system; new educational policy granted relatively high autonomy to schools and encouraged a decentralization of public policy and education system. All these changes have resulted in growing inequalities and differentiation of the education system.

This chapter is therefore structured into two main parts. The first part describes the process of transformation in the last twenty-five years, structured into four phases, whilst the second part documents the level of educational inequalities in the Czech education system.

The Transformation of the Czech Education System from 1989

In 1989, the Czech Republic underwent a transition from a totalitarian political system and centrally planned, state-owned economy to a democratic governance respecting human rights, the restoration of private ownership and a market economy. These changes also affected the education sector which, until then, was under the exclusive control of the central power. The transition thus started the large education transformation process that can be schematically divided into four phases.

The first, earliest phase of the educational transformation lasted only a few months just after the political turnover in 1989, and within our theoretical framework it is called *deconstruction*. This early period is well recognized and documented in all societies in transition—Birzea (1996) labelled this early period *de-structuring* and Čerych et al. (2000) termed it *a period of annulation or correction*.

The main aim of this period was to redress immediately the most visible shortcomings in education caused by the totalitarian regime. *De-ideologization* of the legal documents, including curricula programmes, and *de-monopolization* of state education, facilitating the setting up of private and denominational schools, and stipulating that parents and students should be free in their choice of an educational route and school, were among the most important tasks of this first stage of transformation. Rigid political and ideological control of the system was replaced by the broad level of school autonomy that Čerych (1997) characterized as 'unusually large and unparalleled in many western European countries.' School autonomy concerns a wide range of competencies, from curriculum determination to admission requirements and the content of examinations. Čerych (1997) argues that such school autonomy represented a complete departure from the old system and was the key factor in the bottom-up nature of the reform process in the first phases of educational transformation in the Czech Republic. Among other forms of direct action negating some features of the old education system that were built into the previous regime, we could mention abolition of the mandatory centrally prescribed number of pupils admitted to different types of schools, or facilitating other foreign languages than Russian to be taught, Russian often being the only foreign language that had been taught.

However, as pointed out by Kotásek, Greger and Procházková (2004), some measures within the first wave of reforms had destructive effects (e.g. abolition of the institutional system for in-service teacher training, destruction of the infrastructure of vocational centres and reducing the level of public preschool education).

Other measures prompted the *restoration* of the traditional *gymnázia* (secondary grammar schools, called *multi-year gymnázia*) operating on the basis of early selection and segregation of children with high cultural capital (at the age of 11), but failed, among other things, to restore the status of teachers as state (public) employees with appropriate remuneration. In the first stage of transformation, and even later, there was no doubt that most of the measures were necessary and fruitful. The trend of '*negating the past and restoring the* "*status quo ante*'" was pursued—particularly in political and academic circles—with a lack of profound knowledge of West European and global developments in education policies and without a constructive view of the long-term prospects of the development of democratic schooling.

The second phase (1991–2000) of educational transformation in the Czech Republic was labelled by Kotásek, Greger and Procházková (2004) *partial stabilization*. After the first, most urgent and quickly made changes in education during the deconstruction phase, the partial stabilization period was characterized by gradual, partial legislative, organizational and pedagogical measures. The trend of retaining the 'status quo' with a deliberate partial adaptation to new conditions was promoted, above all, by representatives of the school administration and conservative teachers. This period was still mainly one of bottom-up reform, where the main changes and innovations were promoted by individual, institutional and local activities. Reforms were mainly spontaneous, arising from the pedagogical terrain and later based on operational, '*ad hoc*' *measures*. Partial stabilization is reflected at the legislative level by several amendments to the Education Act dating from the communist period. Among the key players in policy making at that time, the role of non-profit associations like NEMES, PAU and IDEA have to be mentioned. These agencies and other expert teams were preparing their proposals for the reform of Czech education where the state did not yet play the leading role in middle- and long-term educational policy development. These proposals prompted discussion on the future of Czech education and the first programme for the reform of education entitled 'Quality and Accountability' was prepared by the Ministry of Education, Youth and Sports (MoEYS) in 1994. Even though this report had no direct influence on education, it was the first attempt to formulate a comprehensive policy with a long-term perspective. Thus the second half of the 1990s could be perceived as a turning point in policy formulation, where the state, represented by MoEYS, started to play a steering role in the process.

Public opinion polls analysing the demand for schooling from different stakeholders were conducted from 1995 until 1999 (for more, see Kotásek, Greger and Procházková, 2004; Walterová and Černý, 2006). Knowledge of international and global trends in education was fostered by the active involvement of the Czech Republic in international large-scale studies of student achievement (e.g. The Programme for International Assessment (PISA), Trends in International Mathematics and Science Study (TIMMS) and Progress in International Mathematics and Science Study (PIRLS)—for summary of results, see Straková, 2003) and participation in other OECD projects, especially reviews of national policies for education (in the Czech Republic, 1996, 1999). The other driving force of internationalization was the negotiations and preparations for EU accession at that time. This led to the preparation of the extensive strategic document *Czech Education and Europe* (1999).

Thus the second half of the 1990s was not only characterized by the partial adaptation and implementation of the changes required by the overall social transformation, but it was mainly the preparatory period for the next (third) phase of transformation—*reconstruction*. Here it is obvious that the placing of the phases of transformation on a time-line is a difficult endeavour, as there are no static lines and borders. Thus the other possibility is to consider the phase of partial stabilization only for the first half of 1990s and to consider the second half of the decade as already being the start of the reconstruction phase. The blurring of the borders between the different phases and their overlapping nature is even more obvious if we take into account the different dimensions of educational transformation (e.g. curriculum, monitoring and evaluation, structure of education system, as discussed below), where different developments did not reach the same stage at the same time. The discussions about the future of national education were, according to Kotásek (2005a, b), started in the second phase of transformation and they came to a head in the next reconstruction phase, when the White Book (MoEYS, 2001), the Long-Term Plan for the Development of Education and the Education System in the Czech Republic, was prepared and approved by the government and later followed in 2004 by the new Educational Acts (Educational Act—The collection of Laws on Pre-School, Basic, Secondary, Tertiary Professional and Other Education No. 561/2004, and Collection of Laws on Pedagogical Staff No. 563/2004). According to Kotásek (ibid.) the last phase of transformation lasts from 2005 onwards and is the period of *implementation* of the systemic reform prepared in the previous reconstruction phase. This leads to the conclusion that *systemic reform has not yet been achieved, and thus the transformation process is still seen as an open-ended process.*

Analyses of the process of transformation have so far been rather static and sketchy. To clarify it more effectively, some important obstacles to this schematic understanding and the lively process of change that started from spontaneous initiatives will be pointed out. Changes are still happening at the micro-, or intermediate, level, even though the macro level seems to be now in its final phase, ready for implementation. What is more, the implementation process is not easy, especially for the top-down reforms, where it presents special difficulties. Critics of the reforms (most often articulating their concerns in the domain of curriculum and evaluation) argue that the reforms are not well prepared and, in particular, have not been explained and communicated to the wider public (parents and other stakeholders) and that teachers are not ready to accept these reforms. Thus the process of implementation is long term, and there is a need for well-developed support structures.

A detailed explanation of the educational transformation has also not been sufficiently elaborated within the context of national politics. The preparation of systemic reform was made during the long period when the Social Democrats held power (even though the government was a coalition with other parties), lasting from 1998 until 2006. However, from 2006 up until today, there have been nine ministers of education installed in office, meaning that the average time in office was shorter than one year. The frequent change of ministers of education, with different political backgrounds and priorities, has not surprisingly led to policy reformulations or even negations. Thus we might be observing the '*reforms of reform*', or what Birzea (1996) calls a *counter-reform*. The most visible 'counter-reform' is in the field of evaluation, where many measures prepared by the previous government and codified in law have been postponed or are being gradually wound up. To understand the process of educational transformation in the Czech Republic, we shall thus analyse the *tension between continuity and discontinuity*, which is considered to be the main feature of transition (e.g. Birzea, Mitter). The current stage of development of education we could see either with Kotásek (2005a) as an implementation phase that requires a lot of effort and time or as a process of redefinition and reformulation of systemic reform. For both alternatives, there are several obstacles to policy formulation or implementation, for example finances and management, but especially human resources. The risk of reforming the reforms over and over again is thus the biggest obstacle to any change. It might lead to disconnection of the macro from the micro level and thus prevent change from taking place as it has been designed to do.

Diversification, tracking/streaming and early selection in the Czech education system

The reforms affecting the structure of the education systems represent the most visible changes. They could be undertaken as comprehensive and holistic reforms of the whole educational structure, or they might be represented by rather moderate changes (prolonging the length of compulsory education or at some particular level of education, e.g. prolonging primary education from four to five years and extending the length of basic school from eight to nine years, as happened in the Czech Republic). These reforms are most visible in the

Structure of the education system in the Czech Republic

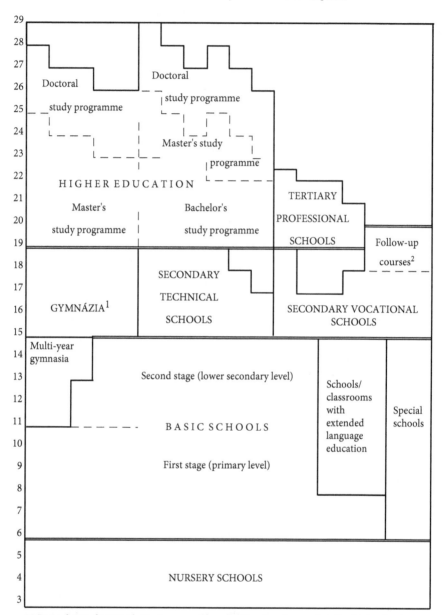

1/ Compulsory education lasts nine years. The majority of pupils complete it at basic schools.
Pupils who study at a multi-year gymnázium accomplish it in the relevant years of gymnasium.
2/ A follow-up study is designed for graduates at three year courses of secondary vocational
schools' students. It gives them the opportunity to improve their qualifications and pass
Maturitní zkouška, which opens up access to tertiary education study.

case of the creation and development of new types of educational institutions. In the development of the Czech Republic, this is the case especially for *multi-year gymnázia*.

The *multi-year gymnázia* (these are multi-year general secondary schools with an academic orientation, lasting eight or nine years in most cases, combining both lower and upper secondary education), which had operated in Czechoslovakia until 1948, were re-established by a 1990 amendment to the Education Act. Restoration of the multi-year *gymnázia* is the most striking example of the trend of *negating the past and restoring the 'status quo ante'* that was widely used during the deconstruction phase. During the communist period, only four-year *gymnázia* existed (upper secondary general education) and all children aged 6 to 14 were educated in the comprehensive (common or single-structure) school (*jednotná základní škola*) comprising primary and lower secondary education. The basic single-structure school was established in 1948, after the communists came into power, and replaced the existing school structure which had parallel and separate branches of study for pupils aged 11 to 14 years. The pre-communist system of early selection had already been widely criticized by researchers since the 1920s from the perspective of social justice and equality of educational opportunity.

Nevertheless, the main characteristic of socialist education in the basic school was a unified curriculum and progress through it at the same pace for all pupils, the emphasis being on sameness and mediocrity. After experiencing the single-structure school during forty years of 'real socialism' in Czechoslovakia, highly educated parents and representatives of elites did not believe in the ability of this common single-structure school to respect individual students' different learning styles, interests, personal traits and other individual differences.

As a result of that disappointment with the single-structure (common) school, they required the restoration of segregation at an early age, even though this was not in line with global educational perspectives and developments in Western countries as they had developed from the 1950s with the quest for comprehensive schooling. The aim in establishing the multi-year *gymnázia* was to provide a more demanding education, facilitating further academic studies, for students as young as 11 who showed a higher level of cognitive capacity. The establishing of the multi-year *gymnázia* is thus the result of social pressure and the strongly articulated demand of more educated parents. (For more detailed discussion of the development of comprehensive schooling and the restoration of multi-year *gymnázia*, see Greger, 2005).

Admission to six- and eight-year *gymnázia* programmes is based on selection consisting of various types of written and oral examinations designed by *gymnázia* teachers (normally in the mother tongue and mathematics) and sometimes intelligence or student aptitude tests provided by private companies. The decision concerning admission, on the basis of examination results as the main criterion, is taken by the *gymnázia* principal who is also a civil servant. The intake numbers are determined by the school administration (approximately 12 per cent of the relevant age group) and range from 6 to 14 per cent depending on the region. The number of applicants for six- and eight-year *gymnázia* programmes is approximately double the intake number.

The restoration of early selection during compulsory education was widely criticized by researchers, as well as pointed out by OECD experts. The government-promoted White Paper of 2001 reiterated that the two streams (selective *gymnázia* and the second stage of basic school) of education should be gradually merged and that internal differentiation should take place within the basic school. The inclusion of this recommendation in the new education bill, in the form of the gradual abolition of the lower years of six- and eight-year *gymnázia*, prompted public debate, on the part of parents with higher levels of education and socio-economic status, which was dominated by the requirement that a more demanding level of education be retained for their children.

The pressure exerted by the parents, *gymnázia* directors and teachers and academics in the media, not to mention their political influence, prevented the proposed reform and was one of the reasons the bill was rejected by the Parliament as a whole in 2001. The new Education Act from 2004 introduced only one national curricular document for the two parallel types of lower secondary education—the Framework Educational Programme for Basic Education— which is the foundation for the development of school educational programmes at both basic schools and at six- and eight-year *gymnázia*. Moreover, the number of teaching periods at basic school gradually increased so as to be equal to those in *gymnázias* in quantitative terms, and the salary levels of teachers at both types of school have been made identical. However, the *numerus clausus* is preserved (~12 per cent of 11-year-olds) as well as the selective admission proceedings for six- and eight-year *gymnázia*, which discriminates against children with lower cultural capital. Analysis of PISA 2003 data has revealed (Matějů and Straková, 2005) that children coming from the two lowest quintiles (bottom 40 per cent) of the socio-economic and cultural status make up only 15 per cent of the students at multi-year *gymnázia*, while the children coming from the two highest quintiles (top 40 per cent) represent 70 per cent of the student body at these schools. And using recent data from the Czech Longitudinal Study in Education, we have shown that both aspirations as well as success at admissions to multi-year *gymnázia* are highly influenced directly and indirectly by parents and their level of education (Straková and Greger, 2013).

Multi-year *gymnázia* are the most visible structural example of differentiation of the Czech education system post-1989. However, to draw the full picture of diversification of the Czech education system, we must mention several other types of selective schools and characteristics of the system. Another type of early selection in the Czech Republic is *schools and classes with a specific focus* which provide extended teaching in some subjects: foreign languages, physical education and sports, mathematics and natural sciences, music, visual arts and information technologies. The specialized curriculum is employed from the first, third or sixth grade. The proportion of pupils attending these schools in the overall population of basic school pupils is around 12 per cent. These schools thus already select students at the age of 6 for entry to primary schools, based mostly on the oral examination organized by individual schools. Parents show great interest in extended teaching in selected subjects—particularly languages and sports (demand is twice as high as the number of places available), hoping for their children to achieve better results as compared to those in other basic schools.

Admission to this type of basic school is also up to school directors, who decide on the basis of entry examinations designed by the school and taken by children at the age of 6, 8 or 11. Again, pupils from families with higher cultural capital are in a more favourable situation. Secondary analysis of fourth-graders' data from PIRLS and TIMSS 2011 (Greger and Soukup, 2014) have shown that, similarly to multi-year *gymnázia*, schools or classes with a specific focus on foreign languages are also attended by children from families with higher cultural capital. And analysis of eighth-graders' TIMSS 2007 data (Greger and Voňková, 2013) has shown that all the schools with a specific focus are attended by students with more privileged home backgrounds compared to schools with no specific focus. Schools with a specific focus are often second-choice schools for those fifth-graders who did not make it to a multi-year *gymnázium*.

Both multi-year *gymnázia* and schools or classes with a specific focus are examples of tracking or streaming and early selection of students with high cultural capital based on declared or measured cognitive abilities. However, other types of school also attract parents with high cultural capitals. There are also public primary schools which offer parents supplementary classes or services for a fee (e.g. parents are paying for teaching/conversation in a foreign language with a native speaker or for Montessori classes with teaching assistants). Parents from higher social strata thus have a wide range of choices within the Czech education system. Even though private schools have been

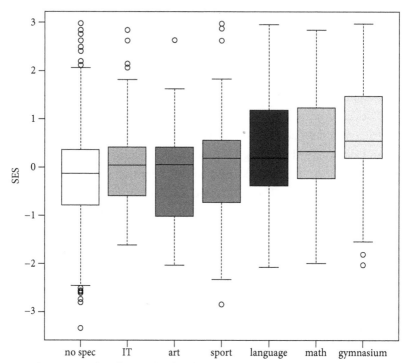

Graph 4.1 Box plots for standardized socio-economic status of students in different tracks.

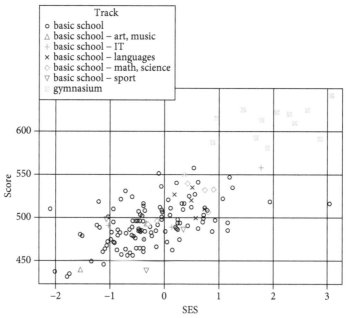

Graph 4.2 Average school SES and the math score, comparing different tracks.

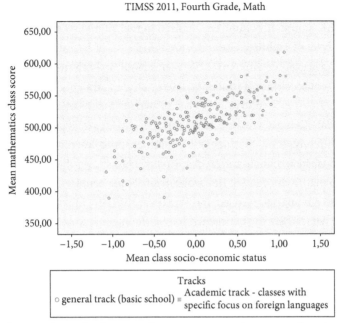

TIMSS 2011, Fourth Grade, Math

Graph 4.3 Relationship between class socio-economic status and math score.

allowed and launched in the post-socialist period, the percentage of students in these schools, compared to other education systems, is relatively low (2 per cent in primary school and 3 per cent in lower secondary, compared to OECD average 10 per cent and 11 per cent, respectively—OECD, 2014). However, educated parents have a wide range of choices within the public sector and often demand a selective type of institution. This is supported by the high autonomy granted to individual schools and their principals, who are reflecting demands from parents for more selective school settings or schools with a specific focus. The focused schools or classes are thus rising in numbers: however, because the Ministry of Education does not collect data on school enrolment practices, official statistics do not exist.

The highly differentiated education system in the Czech Republic, with early selection and differentiation of education pathways as described above, is also documented by research data. The analyses of the PISA data show that the Czech Republic belongs among countries where the impact of family background on student performance is very high and also where the differences between schools are above the OECD average (the differences in results between schools are 1.5 times larger than the OECD average). What is more, the schools largely differ in their socio-economic background. The school's socio-economic background explains 37 per cent of the variance in the students' test results. This is the seventh highest value among the countries involved in the 2003 PISA study.

An analysis of eighth-graders in the TIMSS study has also shown similar results—above average differences between schools in both measured outcomes as well as composition of students. These studies also highlighted growing inequalities in time. Straková (2010) has shown in analysis of TIMSS 1995, 1999 and 2007 data that growing use of tracking in the Czech Republic leads to the growing differentiation of student achievement and learning experiences of students in various schools and tracks. Straková has shown that between-school variance in math achievement has grown from 21 per cent in 1995 to 32 per cent in 2007, and our analysis (Greger and Voňková, 2013) documents the same trend for science data, where the between-school differences accounted for 12 per cent of variance in science results in 1995 and 19 per cent in 1999; and from 1995 to 2007, it has almost doubled to 23 per cent of variance attributable to differences between schools. Both analyses further showed that the information on which type of track or school a student attends and his or her family background explain most of the differences in average achievements of individual schools.

Furthermore data of fourth-graders has been analysed from TIMSS 2011 to see whether the relatively high dependency of students' results on family background also apply to primary education. Comparing all EU countries which participated in the TIMSS 2011 study, Greger and Soukup, 2014) have found that out of twenty EU countries, the Czech Republic exhibits the third highest dependency of school average results on school socio-economic status (after Malta and Hungary) in primary education (see Graph 4.4 below).

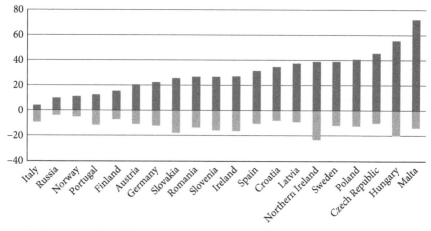

■ % of variance explained by pupils SES   ■ % of variance explained by school SES

Graph 4.4 TIMSS 2011, fourth grade, mathematics (Greger and Soukup, 2014).

Conclusions: Bringing equity back to an education policy agenda

The educational post-Socialist transformation since 1989 was described in part 1, and it was shown that the main drivers of change in society were a move from centralism to decentralization and local school autonomy, and from a supply driven to a more demand-sensitive school system. However, in the case of equity it could be seen that parents' demands (as well as demands of other stakeholders) might be hindering equity. Educated parents' demands for the restoration of early selection could have been one of the drivers of growing inequalities and differentiation of the education system.

After the political changes of 1989, the social dimension of education was not at the forefront of public debates and was not seen as urgent in comparison to the other areas and problems of education, for example, de-monopolization of state education and creating space for freedom in school choice (resulting in the foundation of private schools and the restoration of early selection in multi-year *gymnázia*); de-ideologization and de-indoctrination of the content of education; and loosening of governance and control from the centre, accompanied by the introduction of a broad level of school autonomy. Thus, in the early 1990s, people were stressing the importance of reshaping and refocusing education from a communist past to capitalism and a modern future. Because previously the socialist education system emphasized equality in education (strongly in ideology and rhetoric and also supported by some policy measures), the new establishment did not tackle these issues.

To understand the extent of the change that has been achieved in this dimension, we have to briefly go back to the socialist era and characterize it further. Between 1948 and 1989, educational policy was constructed in line with the official ideology of communist political elites that aimed to eliminate the mechanisms of social reproduction in education and that emphasized the possibility of upward mobility, especially for those coming from the lower social strata, enabling them to achieve higher levels of education. The goal was equality of educational opportunity, and this was widely understood to be in line with the concept of equality of results. The understanding of equity at that time has been characterized by many authors as 'statistical justice' (see, e.g. Štech, 2008), meaning that the main aim was to achieve the representation of different social classes at upper secondary and tertiary education at a ratio equivalent to their representation in society overall—that is, a statistically equal representation of all classes.

For that purpose, many other characteristics than just students' ability were monitored in the process of admission to upper secondary and tertiary education (so called *kádrová kritéria*)—for example, class origin and socio-economic status of the family, the political affiliation of the parents, rural/urban origin and gender. The equality of educational opportunity was to be reached especially by proper selection and control of student intake at higher levels of education according to preset criteria (quota system). According to this practice of selection of students, the educational system was perceived by communist officials as being by definition equal and just. Thus there was no need for research into educational inequalities. Even though the quota system has led to some positive results (e.g. equalizing the opportunity for achieving higher levels of education between women and men), Shavit and Blossfeld (1993), based on international data analysis, came to the conclusion that the impact of social origin on student attainment at higher levels of education was generally the same in former socialist countries and in capitalist countries. Many other researchers also support the notion that 'Communist positive discrimination', applied through the quota systems, did not lead to significant results in reducing socio-economic inequalities in access to education (see e.g. Matějů, 1993; Hanley, 2001). Kreidl (2005) challenges this conclusion on a methodological as well as theoretical basis. Kreidl also shows by data analysis that during periods of the most orthodox Communist egalitarianism in Czechoslovakia (1949–53 and 1970–73), socio-economic inequality in access to secondary and tertiary education did indeed decline. The quota system was thus the main instrument for achieving equality of educational opportunity in the 'real socialism era', even though there is disagreement on the effects of this policy.

In the views and experiences of many of the general public, however, the quota system was often seen as largely politically biased, and many efforts for equality were perceived as a way to mediocrity in achievement and collectivism. So the fight against inequalities was not on the political agenda and was not present in discussions on how to shape and reform the education system for a new democratic society. Neither the general public nor policy makers were interested in equity-related issues.

In the early years of the transformation process, the goal of achieving equal educational opportunities was thus mainly advocated by non-government organizations (NGOs) and active individuals. Both often supported and later accompanied by international organizations and supranational agencies, it was the NGOs who have brought an agenda of equal educational opportunity to the forefront since the early 1990s and who started the actions (e.g. Roma teachers' assistants) that were later implemented and supported by the state. The NGOs thus replaced the role of the state in the early years of transformation, and they remain the engine of further progress. In the case of education for Roma children, it is thus NGOs who run many of the progressive programmes (e.g. mentoring) as well as influencing policy formulation. The leading role of NGOs is also apparent in the case of programmes targeted towards equal opportunity between women and men and in programmes for gifted students. This 'third sector' is an important actor in transformation and in the policy formulation process.

The other important actor to be mentioned here in the promotion of equality of educational opportunity is represented by international and supranational organizations. In the Czech case, two organizations should be particularly stressed—the European Union and the OECD. The major impact of the European Union is seen especially in legislative improvements in post-communist countries. The Czech Republic, among other countries, had to prepare new legislative documents, especially with respect to disadvantaged groups (including national minorities, women and the disabled) and combating discrimination. This was one of the criteria to be fulfilled for entering the European Union on 1 May 2004 and led, according to many authors (e.g. Davidová et al., 2005) and organizations, to the high quality of the legislation in the 'new member states' in the case of respect for minorities and disadvantaged groups, which is in many respects better than the legislation of 'old member states'. Nevertheless, the quality of legislation is not always translated into reality and practice in this area. Presently, the European Union also plays a very important role in fostering equity through the financial resources that come into the new member states through European Social Funds. The programmes for disadvantaged groups and for combating educational inequalities are largely financed from these sources.

Another important actor to be mentioned here is the OECD, whose activities have contributed to educational change, especially through the analysis of the status of the education system. In the second half of the 1990s, two country reviews of national policies for education (OECD, 1996, and follow-up review) were developed. The presence of the OECD experts and their suggestions for the development of Czech education were very useful in this period of the search for an appropriate long-term plan and policy formulation. These reviews pointed out (among many other things) the selective nature of education and recommended abolition of the newly reconstructed selective multi-year *gymnázia*. More generally, throughout its review the OECD stresses the importance of the equity perspective for policy analysis. Also, many analyses of educational inequalities in the Czech Republic, including some of those mentioned in part 2 of this chapter, are based on data from the OECD and IEA. This is important because the Czech Ministry of Education has no other data on schools' social composition and student achievement. Without large-scale international studies like PISA and TIMSS, the identification of high and growing inequalities would not be possible.

The selective nature of the Czech education system and the existence of multi-year *gymnázia* is widely criticized by researchers, whilst quite recently all political parties in the Czech Republic have also recognized it as a problem, the identification of which was made possible by the data evidence. Nevertheless, there is a lack of political will to change the selective nature of education because, as the political parties repeatedly explain it, the 'general public wants to retain these selective schools'. Thus twenty-five years after the demise of Communism, we have recognized that educational inequalities and high differentiation of the Czech education system is a problem and that there is a need to bring it back to the political agenda. However, from recognizing the problem to combating educational inequalities, there is a long way further to go.

Acknowledgement

This chapter is the output of research grant 'Unequal schools—unequal chances' No. P407/11/1/1556, supported by the Czech Science Foundation (GACR).

References

Birzea, C. (1996). 'Educational reform and power struggles in Romania'. *European Journal of Education*, 31(1), 7–107.

Čerych, L. (1997). 'Educational reforms in Central and Eastern Europe: Processes and outcomes'. *European Journal of Education* 32(1), 75–96.

Čerych, L., Kotásek, J., Kovařovic, J. and Švecová, J. (2000). 'The education reform process in the Czech Republic', in *Strategies for Educational Reform: From Concept to Realisation*. Strasbourg: Council of Europe Publishing.

Czech Education and Europe. Preaccession Strategy of Human Resource Development. (1999). Prague: Tauris.

Davidová, E., Lhotka, P. and Vojtová, P. (2005). Právní postavení Romů v zemích Evropské unie. [The legal status of Roma in the European Union countries]. Praha, Triton.

Greger, D. (2005). *The development and debating of the comprehensive school model in the Czech Republic and other Central and Eastern European Countries (CEECs).* Paris: AECSE. Available at http://www.aecse.net/cgi-bin/prog/gateway.cgi?langue=fr&pass word=&email=&dir=myfile_colloque&type=jhg54gfd98gfd4fgd4gfdg&id=564&tele charge_now=1&file=greger.vo.pdf.

Greger, D. and Soukup, P. (2014). *Sekundární analýzy výsledků šetření PIRLS 2011 a TIMSS 2011.* [Secondary data analysis of TIMSS 2011 and PIRLS 2011]. Prague: Czech School Inspectorate. Available at http://www.csicr.cz/getattachment/1686a360-d008-478d-ab0c-b92c623be997.

Greger, D. and Voňková, (2013). *Tracking Effects on Mathematics Achievement in the Czech Republic.* Paper presented at IRC 2013 conference in Singapore.

Hanley, E. (2001). Centrally administered mobility reconsidered: The political dimension of educational stratification in state-socialist Czechoslovakia'. *Sociology of Education* 74, 25–43.

Kotásek, J. (2005a). 'Vzdělávací politika a rozvoj školství v České republice po roce 1989—1. Časť. [Education politic and the education system development in Czech Republic after 1989—1st part] *Technológia vzdelávania*, 3, 7–11.

Kotásek, J. (2005b). 'Vzdělávací politika a rozvoj školství v České republice po roce 1989—Pokračovanie'. [Education politics and education system development in Czech Republic after 1989—Continuation] *Technológia vzdelávania*, 3, 7–11.

Kotásek, J., Greger, D. and Procházková, I. (2004). *Demand for Schooling in the Czech Republic (Country Report for OECD).* Paris: OECD. Available at http://www.oecd.org/dataoecd/38/37/33707802.pdf.

Kreidl, M. (2005). *Socialist Egalitarian Policies and Inequality in Access to Secondary and Post-Secondary Education: New Evidence Using Information on Detailed Educational Careers and Their Timing* [On-line]. California Center for Population Research. Available at http://repositories.cdlib.org/ccpr/olwp/CCPR-058-05/.

Matějů, P. (1993). 'Who won and who lost in a socialist redistribution in Czechoslovakia?', in *Persistent Inequality. Changing Educational Attainment in Thirteen Countries.* Boulder: Westview Press, 251–71.

Matějů, P. and Straková, J. (2005). 'The role of the family and the school in the reproduction of educational inequalities in the post-Communist Czech Republic'. *British Journal of Sociology of Education*, 26(1), 15–38.

Ministry of Education, Youth and Sports (MoEYS). (1994). *Quality and Accountability. The Programme of Development of the Education System in the Czech Republic.* Prague: MoEYS.

Ministry of Education, Youth and Sports (MoEYS). (2001). *National Programme for the Development of Education in the Czech Republic.* White Paper. Prague: Tauris.

OECD. (1996). *Reviews of National Policies for Education: Czech Republic.*
    Paris: OECD.

OECD. (2014). *Education at a Glance 2014. OECD Indicators.* Paris: OECD.

Shavit, Y. and Blossfeld, H. P. (1993). *Persistent Inequality. Changing Educational
    Attainment in Thirteen Countries.* Boulder–San Francisco–Oxford: Westview Press.

Štech, S. (2008). 'A "Post-egalitarian" society—From statistical towards liberal justice'.
    Orbis Scholae, 2(2), 7–17.

Straková, J. (2003). 'International large-scale studies of educational achievement—The
    involvement of the Czech Republic'. *Czech Sociological Review*, 39(3): 411–24.

Strakova, J. (2010). *Trends in differentiation of student achievement and learning
    conditions in the Czech compulsory education. Findings from TIMSS.* Paper presented
    at IRC 2010 conference in Gothenburg.

Straková, J., and Greger, D. (2013). 'Faktory ovlivňující přechod žáků 5. ročníků na
    osmileté gymnáziu'. [Transition of fifth-graders to multi-year grammar school] *Orbis
    Scholae*, 7(3): 73–85.

ÚIV. (1999). *Priority pro českou vzdělávací politiku.* [Priorities for the Czech Educational
    Policy.] Praha: Tauris.

Walterová, E. and Černý, K. (2006). 'Vzdělávací potřeby pro 21. Století'. [Educational
    Demands for the 21st Century] *Orbis Scholae*, 1(1), 60–76.

5

Estonia: An Overview, 1970–2014

Doyle Stevick

Introduction

Estonia has quietly emerged from its half-century of Soviet domination to become one of Europe's—and the world's—leading educational performers. According to the 2012 PISA results, Estonia surpassed the 'Finnish miracle' in mathematics and approaches its northern neighbour's levels in reading and science, despite having a much smaller economy, a large and largely segregated Russian-speaking minority population and a 20 per cent national poverty rate. When compared only to other free democratic countries, rather than select Asian cities or city-states under authoritarian regimes, Estonia's performance is all the more remarkable. Rather than capitalizing on decades of freedom, stability and prosperity like Finland, Estonia has had to navigate unrelenting change and reform with limited resources while serving multiple goals, from consolidating democratic institutions and a market economy to purging the ideological heritage of Soviet schooling. On the shifting sands of perpetual reform, Estonia has managed to build up a *Learning Tower of PISA*; the strength of its structure derives in no small part from its ability to maintain stability amidst constant change.

Estonia's journey, emerging from authoritarian foreign rule to become an educational leader in Europe, involved not simply overturning all things Soviet, though the rhetoric may have suggested as much. Indeed, it is critical to distinguish between policies and practices from the Soviet era and specifically Soviet practices and policies. During the Soviet period, despite its marginal position and tiny size, Estonia managed to capitalize on its status as a full republic within the Soviet system to have English-language immersion schools and music schools in all major cities since the 1960s, plus specialized boarding schools for talented pupils in physics, math and sports; its own national Ministry of Education; and even a separate institute for teachers' ongoing professional development and the preparation of study aids, and all the other perquisites of republic status.

The period from Perestroika through early independence was a mixture of vocal denunciation of the most visible and ideological Soviet legacies, together with more silent continuities and more modest adjustments (Krull and Trasberg, 2006). Paradoxically, independence did not signify a simple shift from top-down to bottom-up efforts in education. The new openness beginning with Perestroika saw a proliferation of grass-roots efforts and change and innovation at the ground level. Upon independence, new policies issued by the state began to standardize many practices with more top-down approaches, a dynamic only accelerated when Estonia was compelled—however willingly—to adopt a broad package of European regulations to earn admission into the European Union. Estonia formally adopted the policies and regulations that it had to in order to secure membership in Western multinational organizations like NATO, the European Union, and many others—even a deeply unpopular Holocaust commemoration day for schools (Stevick, 2010)—but it had learned during the Soviet period how to pay lip service when necessary and to deviate selectively from foreign prescriptions in order to maintain greater national autonomy in the implementation of education policy and practice.

Estonia's small size and population provides it with a manageable scale and yet limits its ability to have the degree of specialization and adaptability possible in societies with much greater resources. Its successes, in turn, cannot be attributed to some secret ingredient that can be singled out and transplanted to other contexts, but are rather the product of continuous tweaking and adjusting of most aspects of an entire system with deep contextual roots. Estonia was especially notable for its equity in education, showing small variance in scores among students while both increasing its high performers and reducing its low performers in science, according to PISA (PISA Results in Focus, 2012). The country is nevertheless generally cognizant of its challenges, limitations and problems; its majority population, however, may be insufficiently attentive to the country's failure to gain the support of its Russian-speaking minority for education reforms related to language policy in particular. The country's apparent lack of happiness was reflected in students' scores on those measures, which were among the world's lowest, and top politicians in the government have begun to speak about making schools into happier places. It remains to be seen whether Estonian society will continue to regard academic achievement as an end unto itself or as a means to other ends.

Estonian education in its historical context

Estonia's recent and rapid transition from the Soviet Union to the European Union reflects its long history as a borderland between different powers. Situated just below its Finno-Ugric cousin, Finland, and bordering Russia and Latvia, Estonia has a long shoreline on the Baltic Sea that has long fostered its links to Scandinavia and the medieval cities that constituted the former Hanseatic League. Generally dominated by foreign powers, Estonia was subject to competition between local Baltic German lords and the Russian empire before a brief period of independence was ended and the country overrun alternately by the Soviets, Nazis and then Soviets again. By contrast, its prior period of Swedish domination is seen as a golden age, notable for the establishment of Tartu University in 1632. The complex reality of the institution includes significant discontinuities as well as complex language politics in its duelling German and Russian languages of instruction; it would be centuries before Estonian would become the *lingua franca* of Estonia's leading institution of higher education, which today is shifting further away from its former colonial languages to more use of English. The simplification and selective rendering of this complex past is perhaps inevitable and reflective of broader trends in both Estonia's and Estonian education's contemporary relationship to its Soviet past and desire to establish—or at least represent—continuities with its brief period of independence.

A primary function of Estonian education has been to create a national consciousness and elite cultural class on the model of the Germans, who could create the basis for an independent society from its peasant roots. In the late stages and aftermath of the First World War, when the new Soviet Union was still reeling from the turmoil of the Russian revolution and Germany's forces were considerably weakened, Estonia was able to establish its first independent state with liberal ethnic policies and mother tongue education guaranteed by the constitution. These policies were perhaps a reaction to forced Russification policies in the nineteenth and early twentieth centuries, but they had broader support in the 90 per cent ethnically homogeneous Estonia of the 1920s than the roughly 60 per cent ethnic Estonia of the early 1990s.[1]

During the Soviet period, Estonians had a number of educational accomplishments despite the loss of political independence in their territory. Estonians received eleven years of schooling, compared to ten for Russians, in part so they could master the hegemonic tongue, but this extra year in effect was the success of maintaining education in the national language. There were also elite schools for highly promising Estonians as well as textbooks produced by Estonians in the Estonian language rather than simply translations of Russian textbooks. The ministers of education Eisen and, to a lesser degree, Gretskina were particularly noted for their engagement with students, teachers and education professionals while maintaining a surprising degree of independence within a totalitarian state. The geopolitical realities surrounding Estonians prepared them well for managing foreign pressures and expectations on their educational practices, sometimes openly, often less so.

Out of the Soviet Union

The first main period in the development of Estonian education away from Soviet control dates to the Teachers' Conference of April that called for the authorities in Moscow to decentralize the compulsory curricula of general education by dividing their contents into central and national components (Kärner et al., 2013). This call and conference were notable not just for their dramatic character but because they were the products of forces that had already been in motion for some time by early 1987. The renewed curriculum was supposed to pave the way for replacing subject-centred instruction, dominant during the whole Soviet period, by a more learner-centred instruction. Even today, this shift is only partially successful. The culmination of these trends was the passage of the Law of the Republic of Estonia on Education (1992), which established the general principles of organization, governance and financing of the system of education. Its stated goals were broad: promoting the development of the individual, the family and the Estonian nation, as well as national minorities; preserving Estonian economic, political and cultural life and nature in the global economic and cultural context; cultivating loyal citizens; and establishing the basis for continuing education for all. Still, the law was more a reflection and institutionalization of the changes that had occurred than a new set of prescriptions for how things should change. In a period of transition when no laws exist, writings laws is a fundamental stage in establishing independence and takes precedence over using the law as a tool to promote reform and change.

Through this initial phase, the purge of Soviet materials was paramount. The mandated photographs of Gorbachev began to disappear from the walls, and students began to display both the banned colours of the national flag and, on certain occasions, the traditional regional folk costumes that, although not banned under Soviet policy, still played an important role in public expressions of traditional national and Estonian identity. The 'red' subjects were eliminated, and the ideological textbooks removed. Social sciences rooted in Marxism were pushed aside, together with aspects of history that justified the question for empire by Russia or with Russia at the centre. The Russian language was no longer required. Middle school students no longer had to learn how to assemble and disassemble an AK-47 or how to replace parts with materials from the forest. Such universal military and paramilitary training was eliminated, returning only in very limited form in recent years. The monopoly of the state over educational provision was ended, making it possible for parents, religious organizations, non-profits or profits to enter schooling, from preschool through tertiary education. Required education, extended in 1986 by the Soviets to twelve years starting at age 6, was soon reduced to nine required grades, beginning when children are 7. The policy of allocating an extra year of study to the minority population for language mastery—something that Estonians experienced as a minority during the Soviet times to improve their Russian—was not extended to the Russian-speaking minorities in newly independent Estonia, who received the same number of years as ethnic Estonians.

Looking to the West: International influences in newly independent Estonia

In the wake of the 'Singing Revolution', a period of great national solidarity and displays of national identity, Estonians proclaimed the Republic of Estonia, a second independence day, on 20 August 1991, just ten days before the traditional start of the new school year. Many classrooms lacked new materials to replace what had been purged, and for older students, it was often an exciting time as teachers and students attempted to sort out, side by side, what was happening. Russia remained an existential threat in the mind of many Estonians, and the push for integration with the West was strong. Educators often looked to the West for alternative educational approaches, driven by a sense of restoring what would have been the natural progression of the country; many believed that Estonia's level of development and prosperity would have paralleled Finland's and sought to reassert its connections to its Nordic and Scandinavian peers.

Western countries were happy to oblige, seeking to influence the direction of Estonian education. Europe took a comprehensive approach, through the OSCE and the European Union in particular, and to a lesser degree, the Council of Europe. The United States could concentrate its aid on more 'ideological' subjects, particularly in areas like civic education and economics. Though both Europe and the United States promoted democratic governance and market economies, they had considerably different emphases in the philosophy of law (e.g. eternal principles, as in the American Constitution, or an ever-changing policy tool informed by a commitment to universal human rights, as in more European approaches). European institutions worked in all sectors, including vocational education, special education and higher education, to name a few.

Few foreigners were proficient in the languages of the region, and particularly not the most difficult Finno-Ugric languages, such as Estonian and Hungarian, which provided these countries with greater latitude to reflect international hopes back to foreign powers and donors while maintaining autonomy in practice. But the new internationalism of education reform shifted the languages of importance from Russian to regional languages such as Finnish and Swedish, and also German, but especially English. Educators in different fields, whether they were leaders domestically or not, were artificially privileged by their fluency in Western languages, and for those who were functional in English at the time of independence, great opportunities awaited. One by-product of this dynamic was the further exclusion of native Russian speakers, and national representatives in such partnerships, often working through established networks of trust rather than a merit system, did little to reach out to Russian-speaking communities or participants except when they offered the prospect of additional foreign funding. Independent actors such as the George Soros's Open Society Foundations played a powerful role as well and focused whenever possible not on delivering foreign expertise but on building local capacity and facilitating cooperation within the region; meetings of educators from the Baltic states, for example, would often revert to Russian to communicate effectively.

Subtle continuities: Maintaining Soviet-era practices

Estonia's purge of Soviet influence in education did not, as the expression goes, 'throw out the baby with the bathwater'. Rather, the drama of the splash may have largely obscured the baby: Estonian education had a number of continuities from the Soviet period that are less frequently addressed. But even then, not all practices from the Soviet era were necessarily Soviet: some represented practices that had survived Soviet times. Among these continuities, Estonia maintained a network of heavily subsidized kindergartens; public schools made sure kids had free or highly subsidized lunches in grades 1–9, and in cases of need school lunches were provided free even in secondary school. Vocational education and special day and boarding schools for special needs students received ongoing public and state support. Special needs services were maintained in regular schools and kindergartens, and six public universities offer tertiary instruction in the Estonian language, no small achievement in a country of 1.3 million people. Other deeply encultured practices, like the relatively authoritarian style of school leadership, would persist for significant periods.

Levels of trust were not high, and much of the teaching force remained in place. Society was split over whether anyone with Communist party membership was fully discredited and should be removed from his or her position. More nuanced discussions involved the extent to which some Estonians and some of Estonia's Russians operated within the system to humanize it, promote independence, maintain cultural autonomy or were marginal. Although the Soviets wanted teachers to develop their students into Soviet citizens, the same teachers were then expected to become effective promoters of democratic citizenship and workers who could flourish in a market economy. In theory at least, the idea of citizenship as an ethnic privilege operated in practice. The extent to which teachers had once been true believers in the Soviet project, Marxist-Leninist philosophy or ideology is impossible to establish, though the prevalence of a detached 'neutral' teaching style often reflected teachers' non-committal relationship to the subject material. 'Red' subjects were often taught as material students simply had to learn for the examinations because it was required. This detached, 'neutral' teaching style frequently remained the standard practice after independence, yet it is seldom engaging or compelling for teaching participation and engaged democratic citizenship. Enduring low salaries and feeling politically marginalized, teachers had little positive experience with the political participation to promote the types of cooperation and behaviour that sustain a democratic society.

The Soviet era's lack of freedom and opportunity channelled many able and intellectually oriented people into the teaching force. With the end of the Soviet era, many new opportunities, combined with new economic pressures, both lured and impelled many such teachers out of the teaching force; many students who would have entered teaching opted instead for other professions domestically and other opportunities abroad. During the rough economic transition, particularly in the first years, salaries were an insufficient incentive to lure new teachers, and particularly to get Estonian teachers to bring their native-language fluency to teach in predominantly Russian communities. In these early years, many Estonians opted to work in Finland; northern Estonians frequently understood Finnish because Finland's television broadcasts reached the northern part of the country during the Soviet period, and others adjusted quickly because the languages are closely related. At this time, teachers of pension age often remained in the teaching force for extra income and security, and the teaching force greyed, which contributed to a more conservative teaching pool and a greater reluctance to embrace innovation and change. From about 2004, another wave of Estonians went to work in Ireland and other parts of Europe, driving many younger families as parents, often men, to work abroad, which added stress on children and, by extension, on teachers and schools as well.

Together with the teaching force, several areas of education have been debated in the public sphere but remain relatively consistent with their precedents in the Soviet era. Public education remains fully secular, for example. The schools for Russian speakers remain separate, though with the same curriculum. There has not been meaningful effort to create shared facilities for native Estonian and Russian speakers so that both populations could benefit from opportunities to speak each language among large groups of fluent peers. If one-third of the new countries of the post-Soviet period experienced armed conflict or ethnic conflict, Estonia avoided some of the potential for conflict through residential separation (beyond the capital city, Russian-speakers were largely concentrated in the north-east) and by separating schools into single language-dominant school instruction (Silova and Eklof, 2013).

Russian speakers; from (relatively) privileged majority to marginalized minority

The most notable continuity from the Soviet period that impacted on education was the demographic changes of the Soviet period. Estonia's one-time liberal minority policies were established when 90 per cent of the country's residents were Estonian. The people who settled (or were settled) in the country after the Second World War (mostly Russophone Eastern Slavs) were not recognized as Estonian citizens and are overrepresented among the 'persons with undetermined citizenship'. This group of de facto stateless individuals made up one-third of the entire Estonian population in 1992.[2] They were permitted to 'legalize' their presence and to apply for Estonian citizenship provided they had proficiency in Estonian. Most importantly, non-citizens had almost no political influence when crucial political decisions were taken. In 1989, Russophones made up about 40 per cent of the population but failed to elect a single Russophone representative to the first post-independence Parliament (1992–95). This Parliament adopted several important laws, including the Basic Schools and Upper Secondary Schools Act (1993), which envisaged transition to Estonian-language training in Russian upper secondary schools (the last three school years) to begin in 2000 (however, the deadline was postponed several times).

Inflexible ethnic policies of the early 1990s, especially in the field of education, migration and public use of languages, basically functioned to achieve two goals: promoting 'repatriation' of Russians (and other Slavs) to their 'historical motherlands' and facilitating acculturation (assimilation) of those who stayed.[3] Due in part to the purposeful activities of responsible Estonian academia and the influence of the European Union in the pre-accession period, Estonian ethnic policies were liberalized by late 1990s with the introduction of official integration programmes.[4] The minority school system was targeted for reform: in ordinary schools the transition was postponed to 2011, and it was permitted to keep 40 per cent of educational work in 'other' languages (de facto, Russian). In the 2013/14 academic year, every fifth student in Estonia still had Russian as the language of instruction in ordinary basic schools.[5]

The primary stated goal for minority-school reform was improving the competitiveness of minority youth on the labour market, their access to higher education and their integration into Estonian society. But these government rationales were not responsive to concerns in the Russian-speaking communities, which remain unsupportive of policies embraced by large Estonian majorities.[6] Many Russophones still lack adequate proficiency in the only official language, though there are significant generational differences.[7] Demanding professional linguistic requirements were established for both the public and private spheres, effectively excluding many ethnic Russians.[8] In addition, by promoting language reform from the top down, that is, from the university and college level, many Russians hit a dead end. These challenges have contributed to the evident drop-off in educational levels of the Russophone population; in the PISA results, they trail students of Estonian language schools, though the gap has narrowed; even so, the 1989 census revealed that for every 10,000 ethnic Estonians, 99 had higher education, compared to 119 for ethnic Russians and 130 for Ukrainians (though these figures may reflect age differences in the populations as well) (Eesti Rahvastik, 1995: 247). The Estonian school still lacks the facilities to accommodate efficiently the educational needs of non-Estonian speakers.[9] Many Russians are now studying in Estonian schools, but most minority youth are expected to attend Russophone upper secondary schools where Russophone teachers teach their Russophone co-ethnics through, most often, poor Estonian. In practice, educational interaction between ethnic communities can only be observed at the level of colleges and universities.

Language policy and education

With only 1.1 million speakers worldwide, Estonian exists in a context where it is vulnerable to the homogenizing forces of English, the regional dominance of Russian and a declining population of native speakers. Although non-Estonian language instruction is permitted to varying degrees, and foreign-language instruction is mandatory at three points within the public education system (i.e. at the latest in third, sixth, and ninth grades, with English being the most popular foreign language overall), legal guarantees and policies prioritize the position of the Estonian language in both Estonian and Russian-medium public education. In post-Soviet Estonia, schools play a crucial role in both the integration and cultural preservation of the country's Russian-speaking, minority-language community. Estonia funds a dual-track education system with schools offering Russian and Estonian as the primary medium of instruction from preschool through ninth grade. This bifurcated system, which has roots in the first period of independence but solidified during the Soviet occupation, enjoys the support of the government and the public. According to the Estonian Education Information System (EHIS), in the 2013/14 school year about one-fifth of all public school students at the basic school level (grades 1–9) study in Russian-medium schools (i.e. 22,269).

The public school system also functions as a way to integrate the Russian-speaking community through Estonian-language learning and exposure to a shared curriculum with the Estonian-medium schools. Russian speakers in Estonia have the choice of enrolling (1) in an Estonian-immersion programme (approximately 5,355 students from grades 1–12 are enrolled in this type of a programme), (2) in a Russian- or (3) an Estonian-medium school. The vast majority of Russian speakers opt to attend Russian-medium schools. In these institutions, the Ministry of Education has instituted a common curriculum with their Estonian-medium counterparts and has emphasized the need to improve Estonian-language instruction, which was not uniformly available or of high quality during the Soviet era. To this end, the 2013/14 academic year marks a landmark point in the integration efforts targeting students attending Russian-track upper secondary schools (*gümnaasium*). By the spring of 2014, all Russian high schools (grades 10–12) in Estonia must offer 60 per cent of the curriculum in Estonian. For schools in the heavily Russian areas of Estonia, such as Narva, which are over 95 per cent Russian speaking and only began to offer Estonian in 1991, this transition has been particularly challenging (Kiilo and Kutsar, 2013: 479–80). For Russian schools in more Estonian-dominant areas of the country, especially in Tartu (the major university city), the small cities and rural towns, this curricular transition has proceeded without much difficulty. Additional changes include the following: the first foreign language taught in Russian-medium general schools (first through ninth grades) must be Estonian; and Russian-medium kindergartens (starting from age 3) must offer Estonian-language instruction.

Language policy and schooling in Estonia also concerns other minority groups like the Võro, an autochthonous, regional-language community, akin to the Breton community in France. The Võro identify themselves as ethnic Estonians and are fully integrated into Estonian cultural, political and social life. This minority group speaks, to varying degrees of proficiency, Võro, an endangered local language. By the most recent estimates, about 74,400 people speak Võro (Koreinik, 2013: 2), or approximately 5 per cent of the ethnic Estonian population. In the newly independent Estonia, the state has accommodated and endorsed, on the basis of voluntary choice, regional-language instruction in south-eastern Estonian schools. Since 1995, a new phase in state-supported Võro-language education has begun, with a voluntary language programme offered in about half the schools where Võro has historically been spoken. In these schools, instruction in the state language is preserved and regional-language education is offered as an optional or after-school (*huviring*) course. The roots of this state support for regional-language education are many; it is a response to the organized initiative of Estonian regional-language activists, a growing awareness of general 'European' (i.e. the Council of Europe and the European Union) endorsement of regional and minority languages, and the government's continued appreciation of the regional languages as an enriching source of Estonian language and identity. In addition to regional-language education at the basic-school level (grades 1–9), a network of Võro-language preschools, or 'nests', have developed since 2011. A 'nest' offers regional-language instruction one day a week in the public kindergarten (for children aged 3–6) with the remaining days maintaining Estonian-language instruction.

The nest idea emerged as a result of new, post-Soviet networks of Finno-Ugric educators and language activists especially among the Võro, Karelians and Sámi. In 2013/14, fifteen kindergartens participated in the nest network.

Children with special needs and education

Special education has followed inclusion since the 1988 Teachers' Congress. The inclusive approach is reflected by the dual-option in education law since 1991 and was thoroughly elaborated in the Basic Schools and Upper Secondary Schools Act from 2010: everyone has a right to study at the local (regular) school, but there must be different (segregated) options as well, in case the local community is unable to provide proper circumstances. In practice, parents are empowered to insist upon education in the local regular school, while leaving the educational administration space to resist and manoeuvre. Special education is therefore a network of regular school-based services, self-contained classrooms and special schools (two-tier system).

At the initiative of parents, a new set of small and medium-sized private and municipal special schools were established in the 1990s to provide for children with moderate and severe intellectual and multiple disabilities. Some of those schools were rooted in Waldorfian principles. Day-care as well as extended vocational and semi-vocational educational options have expanded recently; residential arrangements for semi-independent adult life also exist. Parents with severely disabled children still struggle with the limited help provided. A number of educated people with disabilities are unable to find accommodation suitable for adults or to live outside parental care.

The range of semi-rural state residential schools that care for approximately 3–4 per cent of the school population has gradually diminished from twenty to approximately ten. A similar number of new and mostly urban schools were set up between 1987 and 1997. Following the depopulation of rural areas, a new wave of restructuring of residential schools is expected to begin in 2014. The heritage of regular school-based services has survived with some changes in appearance. Kindergarten and school-based services are increasingly concentrated in the cities. The traditional Soviet-style euphemism of calling most special needs services 'speech therapy', which accounts for 14–17 per cent of the school population, was superseded by the 2010 act, which set up special needs coordinators. Unfortunately, the 2011 regulation earmarking 11 per cent from the state-provided teacher salary funds for special needs was reduced in

2013 in order to raise the regular teachers' salary. Special education services have extended into tertiary education institutions since the new millennium.

Higher education in Estonia

The main challenge for Estonian higher education is maintaining quality while managing efforts to dramatically expand access and participation to higher education. Estonia's efforts to integrate instructional technology and the Tiger Leap policy have helped to boost IT, to bridge the digital divide and to bolster the country's reputation as 'E-stonia', with its global reputation for paperless government, electronic voting and broadly available internet, and the development of Skype.

Estonia's success in developing targeted, high-level research in niche fields such as genetics has helped it to avoid some of the pitfalls of the liberal market approach to tertiary education while preserving Estonian as the main language of instruction and offering the full spectrum of tertiary education. Developments within the higher education sector fall into their own periodicity. The years 1988–95 witnessed the diversification of higher education providers, the merger of research institutions with universities, and an escape from Russian/Soviet regulations and management schemes. As in the K–12 system, Marxist social sciences and the imperial approach to history disappeared, as did universal military training. Broad initial regulations were established by 1995–96 when higher education received substantial autonomy. Research witnessed the turn to Western paradigms and English-language high-impact journals and publishers in the social sciences. Former funding for military research and development was lost, and a number of experienced researchers were employed abroad. Foreign resources played an important role in this period, headlined by EU TEMPUS, George Soros's Foundation, the Nordic countries, the UK and the United States.

The years 1996–99 were the period of 'Intermediate' degree reform. Regular international evaluations were established for study programmes and accreditation of research teams. The universal graduation exams for secondary schools were established as the major qualifier for access to higher education. Public universities began to admit fee-paying students, which made possible the expansion of enrolment. The student enrolment in 2005 was 250 per cent of the 1995 numbers, and international donors continue to play a major role in this period. The years 2000–4 witnessed the rapid adoption of the Bologna framework; graduate schools, centres of excellence and competence, and curriculum development programmes were established, and with them a second wave of accreditation and evaluation. Facilities were upgraded, in particular, the first effort to bring improvements to student housing. With the Bologna process and EU accession, EU programmes providing access gain importance, and the overall role of donors decreases as a result.

Since 2005, investments in research and study facilities continued: buildings, dormitories and equipment as well as curriculum development, graduate schools and research centres of excellence are enabled largely through EU structural funds. Support expanded for innovation, English-language master programmes, Estonian-language terminology and textbooks, which since 2013 have electronic versions only. Only high-cost, non-profit programmes for training medical doctors, veterinarians, traditional engineers (metal, mining, construction), agronomists and foresters remained as the single, original core duties within their original institutions. Beginning in 2013, fees for the public universities were abolished (after seventeen years) unless students fail to collect enough credits per term.

Overall, the status and production of research has grown exponentially and embraces a wider range of topics with broader research methodologies. Newly studied topics include student harassment, special needs, student motivation, fair access and efficiency. With less than 1 million native speakers, more than thirty higher educational institutions enrolling around seventy thousand students is impressive, but the expenditure per student remains quite low, and this discrepancy causes a value conflict in the academy (Jaakson et al., 2013). Unfortunately, the challenging transitions have created some negative outcomes; the under-representation of some generations of the academy, and the shift to the West has marginalized the social scientists who never succeeded in learning English so that they could publish in the refereed English-language media.

Estonia's high educational performance

Given the challenges Estonia faces, it is not self-evident why Estonia has performed so well on the PISA tests. Some of it is attributable to a culture of hard work and professional competence, to maintaining the strengths of the previous period and to continuous modest adjustments and reforms that added up to substantive improvements. However, there are two particular efforts in Estonia that do not seem to be present in other countries, or not to the same degree at least, that may help to account in part for Estonia's relatively success in education. The first was the 1996 'Tiger's Leap' programme, which included schools but extended far beyond them. Because Estonia had been largely excluded from information technology developments for decades, it was able to leapfrog to the newest technology. Its coordinated effort to invest in free public internet access, paperless government, internet voting, and other markers of high-tech proficiency have received considerable media attention around the world, labelling the country 'E-stonia'. This effort was led in part by Education Minister Jaak Aaviksoo and included a strong component for schools. Computer labs, upgraded equipment and internet access were provided to most schools. Estonia's international reputation and profile was greatly enhanced by Estonians' participation in creating Skype and with the establishment of the NATO Cooperative Cyber Defence Center of Excellence in Tallinn after the country experienced cyberattacks in 2007.

The second unique feature is the *klassijuhataja* system, in which each class has a dedicated teacher who has responsibility for coordinating the activities of the class's teachers (up to twenty-four in basic school or thirty-six in secondary). Some schools even dedicate a pair of teachers to this function, while others make it a full-time position with no regular teaching responsibilities. This individual can monitor individuals and group relations, making sure no one falls through the cracks. This individual is attentive to the difference between the Estonian languages' multiple concepts for education; *haridus* is more formal and cognitive, whereas *kasvatus* is broader, including social development.

Ongoing challenges

Estonia faces a number of ongoing challenges to its education system. Rural municipalities have struggled with declining student numbers. After a birth rate of more than twenty thousand annually, the difficult economy of transition plunged the birth rate down by 40 per cent to roughly twelve thousand babies each year; it has since rebounded to about fifteen thousand, but the contractions and expansions are particularly difficult for planning enrolments and school closures. Indeed, Estonia has been closing twenty to thirty schools on a yearly basis, which constitutes a substantial percentage for a country with a 2013 total of 558 comprehensive schools. In some rural communities, children are bussed great distances to school, and while some savings are achieved within the educational budgeting process, new costs are imposed for bussing, drivers' salaries and other necessary services.

With these economic challenges, school leaders struggle to procure the resources their schools need. During the Soviet period, leaders who were linked to powerful people had greater success. In this respect, the situation is often quite the same. In Soviet times, school leaders were party members. Today, leaders must still navigate society's allocation processes, though today they reflect democratic party politics in governance and a market economy. A number of school leaders have undertaken entrepreneurial efforts to raise funds for their schools. Others feel obliged to take up membership in the locally predominant political party in order to gain necessary support or in fact need that membership and its connections to be appointed to the position in the first place. Leaders are not ostensibly neutral politically. These trends are complicated by a new effort to nationalize schools. The national government is opening a series of state secondary schools. These are often new or renovated schools, and the resources are offered to communities who could not fund them independently in exchange for the school gaining independence from the local community and becoming a national school. Because this process is new, its impact has not yet been studied, but this recentralization after decentralization process merits further attention.

There are also challenges within schools. Rather than maintaining its system of outside inspections of schools, legislation passed in 2006 requires schools to conduct their own self-evaluations. Such policies require a great deal of capacity building, when essential functions are outsourced from centralized, independent specialists to every site. Furthermore, the ability to take a fair, clear look at one's own work is quite different from hearing from others who are not invested in the local context and who have a comparative perspective from conducting inspections across scores of schools.

The state of the profession could be upgraded as well. Teachers have not established a politically influential union nor developed strong professional identities or group affiliation. If incentives were low to enter teaching, at least there had been clarity about compensation. Beginning in 2013, schools have the ability to allocate 20 per cent of the school salary budget as performance bonuses. It is unclear what effect this will have on teacher collegiality and morale, but it also destabilizes teachers' pay, making it more difficult to predict regular income. What criteria and process that, for example, small schools will use to compare an art teacher with a physical education teacher fairly and accurately are also unclear.

The teaching force must grapple with ever changing curricula. Initial efforts to define a national curriculum were launched in 1994, and beginning in 1997 the new curriculum was phased in to grades 1, 4, 7 and 9, extending to the next grades each year. The new curriculum entailed the development and implementation of new textbooks. Over time, the outcomes were elaborated and specified. With the renewed national curriculum of 2011, the legally binding National Curriculum for Basic Schools and National Curriculum for upper secondary schools were formally adopted by the Estonian government. These documents attest to a broad vision, including supporting the mental, physical, moral, social and emotional development of students. They support a science-based worldview, and pursue the attitudes and value judgements that are the basis for personal happiness and cooperation in society. These values are rooted in the Universal Declaration of Human Rights. In an effort to shift from knowledge to competencies, the subject content and number of outcomes have been reduced, while the learning environment is more precisely described (Kärner et al., 2013).

School leaders face a particularly difficult situation. Their work is dominated by financial concerns and general administrative matters. However, in policy and in public perception, they are situated as powerful leaders who have a vision of excellence and a strategy for pushing the school forward to meet that vision. The tension between expectations and reality is ever-present, but nowhere stronger than in the question of instructional leadership. Although this area dominates much thinking about school leadership internationally, it plays a small part of the actual job functions of Estonian school leaders and is often left to subordinates.

Acknowledgement

This chapter was assisted by contributions from Jaan Kõrgesaar, Juri Ginter, Karmen Trasberg and Hasso Kukemelk, University of Tartu; Vadim Poleshchuk, Legal Information Center for Human Rights; and Kara Brown, University of Carolina, United States.

Notes

1   For a detailed account of changes of the Estonian demographic makeup, see Tiit, E.-M. (2011) *Eesti rahvastik. Viis põlvkonda ja kümme loendust (Estonian Population. Five Generations and Ten Censuses)*, Tallinn: Statistikaamet.

2   Statistics provided on www.Estonia.eu (official website). For detailed overview of Estonian citizenship policies, see Järve, P. and Poleshchuk, V. (2013) *EUDO Citizenship Observatory Country Report: Estonia*, Florence: Robert Schuman Centre for Advanced Studies and Edinburgh University Law School.

3   According to the findings by Klara Hallik, in the Parliament functioning in 1995–99
    all mainstream parties were 'unanimous in the need to encourage non-Estonian out-
    migration … With only a few, though minor differences, all of the Estonian-based
    parties view[ed] the nation state as an ethnicity-based state and therefore none
    of their platforms [had] any plans to organize a political dialogue with the non-
    Estonians …'. Hallik, K. (1998) 'Rahvuspoliitilised seisukohad parteiprogrammides
    ja valimisplatvormides' ('Parties' Programs and Electoral Platforms on Ethnic
    Issues'), in M. Heidmets (ed.) *Vene küsimus ja Eesti valikud (The Russian Issues and
    Challenges for Estonia)*. Tallinn: Tallinna Pedagoogikaülikool, 95.

4   For comprehensive analysis of the early years of Estonian integration policy, see
    *Monitoring the EU Accession Process: Minority Protection, Volume I, An Assessment of
    Selected Polices in Candidate States*, Budapest: Open Society Institute, EU Accession
    Monitoring Program, 2002, 89–244.22,269 students out of all 112,883 in classes 1–9.
    Data of the Estonian Education Information System, EHIS, provided by the Ministry
    of Education and Research on the authors' request (31 January 2014).

5   This is 22,269 students out of all 112,883 in classes 1–9. Data of the Estonian
    Education Information System, EHIS, provided by the Ministry of Education and
    Research on the authors' request (31 January 2014).

6   According to the recent nation-wide pool conducted by Saar Poll (2013) 80 per cent
    of ethnic Estonians and only 24 per cent of ethnic non-Estonians believed that, all
    in all, the reform was useful for minority youth. Furthermore, both communities
    would rather share the opinion that the reform was inadequately prepared (50 per
    cent Estonians and 83 per cent ethnic minorities). The survey was commissioned
    by the Tallinn City Government and carried out in September–October 2013 by a
    standard representative sample for Estonia by the company Saar Poll. Altogether
    surveyed one thousand people (aged 15–74) were surveyed, and 31 per cent of
    them were people of ethnic minority origin. The results of the study have not been
    published yet. They are on file with the authors.

7   However, proficiency in Estonian still does not guarantee equal opportunities on
    the labour market. According to the results of the 2011 national census (provided by
    Statistics Estonia on pub.stat.ee), there are noticeable differences in unemployment
    rates of those who speak Estonian as a first or as a foreign (second) language.

8   For critical overview of Estonian law and policy, see Kochenov, D., Poleshchuk,
    V. and Dimitrovs, A. (2013). 'Do Professional Linguistic Requirements
    Discriminate?—A Legal Analysis: Estonia and Latvia in the Spotlight.' *European
    Yearbook of Minority Issues*, 10, 137–78.

9   There are sociological discussions that indicate in Estonian-language schools
    ordinary speakers of minority languages experience more problems in terms of
    academic success as compared with native-speakers. See e.g. Pulver, A. and Toomela,
    A. *Muukeelne laps Eesti koolis: Lõpparuanne (Non-Estonian Child in Estonian School.
    Final Report)*, Tallinn: Tallinna Ülikooli Psühholoogia Instituut, 2012, 10–11.

References

Jaakson, K. and Reino, A. (2013). 'The impact of Estonian research, development and education policies on perceived value conflicts in universities', in E. Saar and R. Mõttus (eds), *Higher Education at a Crossroad: The Case of Estonia*. Frankfurt am Main: Peter Lang, 217–46.

Kärner, A., Jürimäe, M., Jaani, J. and Kõiv, P. (2013). 'Principal steps towards curricular freedom in Estonia', in W. Kuipers and J. Berkvens (eds), Balancing Curriculum Regulation and Freedom across Europe. CIDREE yearbook 2013. Enschede, the Netherlands: Gildeprint, 21–38. Retrieved from http://www.cidree.org/publications/yearbook_2013.

Kiilo, T. and Kutsar, D. (2013). 'Dilemmas related to the professional self-identity of Russian-speaking teachers in Estonia: Adapting and accommodating to changes in the language-in-education domain'. *Journal of Baltic Studies*, 44, 475–502.

Koreinik, K. (2013). *The Võro Language in Estonia: ELDIA Case Specific Report*. Mainz, Germany: ELDIA.

Krull, E. and Trasberg, K. (2006). 'Changes in Estonian general education from the collapse of the Soviet Union to EU entry.' ERIC Online submission, Number: ED495353.

PISA Results in Focus. (2012). OECD. Retried from http://www.oecd.org/pisa/keyfindings/pisa-2012-results-overview.pdf.

Saar Poll. Social Market Research, Public Opinion and National Defence. Tallinn (2013). www.saarpoll.ee

Silova, I. and Eklof, B. (2013). 'Education in Eastern and Central Europe: Re-thinking post-socialism in the context of globalization', in R. F. Arnove and C. A. Torres (eds), *Comparative Education: The Dialectic Between the Global and the Local* (4th edition). New York: Rowman and Littlefield Publishers, 379–402.

Stevick, E. D. (2010). 'Education policy as normative discourse and negotiated meanings: Engaging the Holocaust in Estonia'. *Prospects: Quarterly Review of Comparative Education*, 39(2), 239–56.

6

Hungary: Vocational Education and New Developments, 1990–2014

Andrea Laczik

Introduction

This article presents the recent history, trends and some of the most important developments in Hungarian schools with a focus on vocational education and training. The article is divided into three parts. The first part offers a more general introduction to education in Hungary during the pre-1989 era and argues through examples that deviations from the highly controlled Soviet type of education had already started in the 1950s and spread and accumulated over time. The second and third parts focus on initial vocational education and training (VET) developments. Between 1989 and 2010, the tendencies of accelerated decentralization at a systemic level, then the opening to localized solutions and the preparation to EU accession, guided VET developments. It is argued and exemplified throughout these two sections that the national and EU demands concerning VET often coincide. The third section outlines some of the most recent (post-2010) major changes in school-based VET in Hungary. It is further argued that centralization is happening under the current new government, with a return to the pre-1998 VET system. The discussion in the second and third part is based on similar developments, such as the evolution of the National Qualifications Register, Vocational and Examination Requirements and employer engagement.

Transition before transition started: 1945–89

Hungary had developed an education system after the Second World War that demonstrated some common characteristics with other Eastern bloc countries allied with the Soviet Union. These include, for example, the monolith school system that supported the development of the 'communist person,' ultimately aiming towards the utopia of the communist society. Marxist and Leninist ideology was ingrained in the system, and education was highly centralized, controlled and planned by the single party. Education was a state monopoly, and the government made every effort to control schools to disseminate Marxist ideology and to include education into a centrally managed, planned economy. Through the means of the Communist Party's Youth Organization, a hegemony of interference in school matters was achieved (Grant, 1969). Although a Soviet type of education system operated in Hungary, it simultaneously shows distinct specificities. On the one hand, developments of the Hungarian education system demonstrated a non-linear progression over time in terms of its struggle with the party in power; on the other hand, developments during this period also showed a tendency towards decentralization. Whereas the political system required a tight control of education, and in this sense developments could be considered systematic, deviations from the mainstream system reflected the impact of continuous economic and societal changes during the pre-1989 era.

Kelemen (2003) discusses the reform attempts between 1945 and 1990 that shaped the education landscape in Hungary and the reasons behind these. In his article, he divides promising-looking and real reforms in education into four main periods framed around four significant events. Contemporary educationalists, however, are divided about the extent to which these reforms can be considered as real reforms that have led to a lasting impact. Even though these events and activities may not have reached their full potential in the socialist state of Hungary, they were the seeds of initiatives that have supported the progress of decentralization of education at the time and beyond. These four points of discussion are as follow:

1. 1945–1948—Unfinished or expropriated reform?
2. 1961—Pseudo-reform in the name of consolidation
3. 1972—Reform or anti-reform?
4. 1985—Outbreak attempt of reform values

1945–48: Unfinished or expropriated reform?

After the Second World War, the main political players shared some common ideas about desirable policy developments in education. They were aiming to diminish inequality in education, update and modernize education and democratize the system and content in education. Although, in general the coalition parties aimed at changing education that was led by democratic ideas, the strengthening of the Hungarian Communist Party (HCP) with its programme could already be detected. Undoubtedly, one of the main achievements of 1945 was the introduction of the eight years of basic education. This type of school was developed in line with the European model; it offered basic education for the masses, and it was free and compulsory and aimed to eliminate illiteracy. However, the impetus to establish basic schools lacked the political and professional consensus of the coalition. In 1948, the Law of Nationalisation of Education was accepted, which was in line with other West European countries where education was a state monopoly. The difference was that in Hungary this was followed by the takeover of a totalitarian political system that rejected liberalism, democracy and pluralism, in particular ideological and religious (Pukánszky-Németh, 2001), and promoted the power of the government. The development of the socialist education system had commenced (Hungarian on-line library, 1996–2000).

The second phase in the development of education, according to Kelemen (2003), was what he called *1961—Pseudo-reform in the name of consolidation.* The time leading up to 1961 was characterized by the elaboration and intensification of the Soviet type of political power. Education was to serve the Hungarian Socialist Workers' Party (HSWP, in power between 1956 and 1989), and the schools were 'the tools to raise obedient citizens' (Pukánszky-Németh, 2001, v–470). The 1961 III. Education Act legitimized and stabilized the new power relations in education and the monolithic school structure. Compulsory school attendance was raised to sixteen years, and differentiation of secondary education was legalized. However, secondary education provisions were overwhelmingly vocational in nature. The post–basic education provision from the age of 14 included two years of further training, three years of vocational training and three different types of four-year secondary education. These three types were the highly academic *gimnasiums* (similar to grammar schools), upper secondary vocational schools and polytechnics. This differentiation of secondary education strongly supported the development of the working class as the main pillar of the socialist system, and pushed intellectual and independent thinking into the background. However, it was soon discovered that making secondary education and polytechnics generally available without the supporting background and resources was an impossible task. In general, the politically infused reform ideas of the 1961 III. Education Act were not supported and later diminished, and specific clauses of the Act were overruled by the Party's own resolutions, as was typical of this time. Nevertheless, some of the initiatives that were strengthened by the Act have to be acknowledged, such as the unfolding of the upper secondary vocational schools and aligning vocational education to the system of secondary education. As part of the school reform, a new curriculum for basic (1963) and secondary (1965) education was developed, within which the modern scientific content was balanced with age differentiations, and some allowances were made to meet learners' individual interests (Hungarian on-line library, 1996–2000).

The late 1960s is considered by Kozma (2012) as the 'opening of education policy' following the 1956 international isolation, and was one of the 'most intense reform times'. It peaked in 1968 with the announcement of economic reforms which resulted, for example, in the easing of the planned economy and in the development of the labour market. Although economic reform was curtailed, it started irreversible processes, when new compromises were negotiated between those in power and society. This new situation also required an education which reacted better to the actual economic and societal needs that pertained at the time. In the early 1970s, there had been, for example, an increasing number of social science and educational research societies, and the Fifth Congress of Pedagogy was organized in 1970. This Congress aimed at the critical evaluation of education and at development of programmes based on real needs analysis of the new economic and societal developments (Kelemen, 2008). Despite the forward-thinking reform activities and promising processes, the resolution of the Central Committee of the HSWP in 1972 reverted to its ideologically led politics, strengthened the one-party state, and reinforced the approach where political decisions overrode professional decisions. Yet again, despite the many faceted reform activities and considerable achievements of these times, the Party resolution brought the reinstatement of previous power relations and reinforced the dictatorial mechanisms instead of the announcement of the awaited strategies of modernization. This battle between professional and party interests is the reason for Kelemen (2003) calling this era '*1972—Reform or Anti-Reform*'.

The 1985 Education Act is the most important milestone during the last and final episode before the collapse of the one-party state. Similarly to the previous three phases, the power negotiations between politics, economics and society are at the heart of it. Although the communist rhetoric was still present, fewer of the political elite, including educational policy makers, actually believed in the communist ideology (Halász, 2009). For the tenth anniversary of the 1972 Party Political resolution, the HSWP published a 'soft' education policy statement, asking the government to evolve and approve a new development programme for general and higher education. At the same time, the development of a new education act was also planned, and the 1985 Education Act reflects the necessary compromises that led to the final output. The old rhetoric about the socialist nature of upbringing can still be found in the document, though it is less frequent and is mixed with new content and style. The Act provided more independence to educational institutions and pedagogues and determined the rights and responsibilities of all involved in education, for example, learners, parents, teachers and the local community. On the basis of the above, the Act could be considered as a return to liberal and democratic traditions in education. Some of the reforms, however, could not be put into practice or were restricted due to lack of resources, supporting economic environment or the party state's conflicting interests. Hence, Kelemen (2003) calls it '*Outbreak attempt of reform value*'.

In summary, the period between 1945 and 1989 was a struggle between the one party state and a desire for a liberal and democratic education and living. The mismatch between the reality and utopia, and the demands of politics, economy and society were growing over time, and pushed at all times for new reforms. The one party state had been clinging to power until the very end, consciously or subconsciously allowing the natural economic and societal processes to happen. The 1985 Education Act started a 'radical decentralization process' (Halász, 2000a, 2000b), some clauses of which were kept even after the collapse of the socialist state. Therefore, Hungary may claim to have had the least rigid and autocratic, least centralized and bureaucratic, socialist past within the Eastern bloc countries.

The vocational education landscape after 1989: Preparation for EU accession

Post-1989 education and training developed in a radically different political, economic and societal environment from the previous fifty years. In Hungary, decentralization of education (and other sectors) has accelerated and new initiatives responded to local national needs that often coincided with European aims and priorities. This is the context within which the government tries to influence the system and introduce some measures and standards, such as the National Core Curriculum (NCC) for general education, and the National Qualifications Register (NQR) for vocational education.

The political changes in 1989, the rapid move towards a market economy and consequently changes in the society demanded real reforms also in education. In the 1990s changes in education were driven by similar underlying aims regardless of the nature of the parties in power and their political beliefs. It is often difficult to identify the precise impetus behind those changes, whether they happened because of the need to modernize education, because education had to be more responsive to market economy and societal demands or whether education had to respond to international influences. Similarly, it is debateable, which urge was stronger: the move away from the Soviet type of system and the rejection of its underpinning ideology and values, or the aim to achieve a more decentralized, personalized and democratic education. The aims of the changes show different combinations and a variety of reasons.

It had been initially argued that attempts had been made already within the socialist regime to enhance pluralism, democratization, and increase autonomy of schools and teachers during earlier reforms. The fundamentally new political situation in 1990, however, demanded immediate changes in education, and simultaneously medium and long term reform plans were outlined. The immediate changes were reflected in the rejection of the Soviet type of education and included, for example, the ceasing of Russian teaching in all educational establishments, offering optional religious education in schools, changes in the content of teaching and in the curriculum, in particular in History and Hungarian literature, and the possibilities to publish and use alternative school textbooks. The modification of the Education Act in 1990 reflects the shortage of time that was available to develop a fundamentally new Education Law and it focused on the most important aspects, such as the removal of all references to the communist ideology. It concentrated around secondary and higher education, free school choice and on establishment and maintenance of educational institutions.

The impact of the new political, economic and societal development after 1989 in Hungary, set huge challenges to vocational education and training (VET). Before 1989 VET prepared young people according to the planned economy and jobs were guaranteed after completion. After 1989, due to the collapse of the East European market, the collapse of large national enterprises, and due to free labour market forces, mass unemployment has appeared in Hungary. Between 1989 and 1992 1,174,000 jobs had disappeared (Farkas, 2013a, p. 35). Pre-1989 was characterized by learner numbers being centrally determined by school types and vocations. However, through the introduction of free school choice in the 1990 Education Act, learners and their families were able to make decisions about their own future careers according to their needs and desires signalling their preferred progression route. Further changes included the increasing of compulsory schooling from eight years to ten years, stressing the importance of general education. Consequently, career decisions of young people were shifted to a more mature age, and VET was only offered to post-16-year-olds as post-compulsory provision. These developments clearly impacted on the number of young people enrolling in the different types of secondary schools—vocational schools, upper secondary vocational schools and *Gimnasiums*—from the 1990s.

Drawing on statistics between 1980 and 2012, evidence shows that while the proportion of young people attending vocational schools have decreased from 44 per cent to 25 per cent between 1990/91 and 2010/11, the proportion of young people attending upper secondary education that may lead to higher education had increased. The most popular type of upper secondary educational establishment is the upper secondary vocational school. In 2011/2012, 41 per cent of young people choose this type of school which offers them the choice of continuing in higher education or pursuing post-secondary vocational programmes (Ministry of Human Resources, Hungary, 2012:,11). Clearly, there has been a drastic change in the demand of vocational educational provisions since the 1980s.

The new Education Laws of 1993 affected general, higher and vocational education. The new 1993 Education Act about VET sets out as the aim 'to develop a flexible and differentiated system of VET that adjusts to the societal changes to the national economic and labour market demands'. This Act, however, did not regulate the operations of VET establishments but the operations of the VET functions. According to Halász (2011) there were three particularly significant elements of this: (1) The state saved the VET educational establishments from collapsing together with the business sphere; (2) adult education has become a new significant target group for VET; and (3) enterprises have become influential partners through paying a unique, new tax-like contribution and so directly financing VET, and through sitting on a tripartite decision-making board. The 1993 Education Acts for General Education, Vocational Education and Training and Higher Education have gone through several modifications; nevertheless, the main characteristics of the institutional environments did not change until 2010 (Halász, 2011: 5).

In the early 1990s, longer-term plans in education included the development and introduction of a new National Core Curriculum (NCC) in general education by 1998, and the introduction of a two level school leaving examination (*Matura*) that was implemented in 2005. The development of the NCC was particularly important with respect to freedom in teaching: what to teach and how to teach. The NCC was interwoven with democratic, national and European values, and taught the problems faced by society. The main objective of the introduction of the NCC was to offer unrestricted mobility of learners between schools.

While the NCC was setting the standard for general education up to the age of sixteen years, the National Qualifications Register (NQR) that was first published in 1993 served the same purpose in VET for post-16-year-old young people and adults. The NQR contains a list of state-recognized vocational qualifications. In 1998, compulsory school attendance was raised to age 18 (from 2012, when it was reduced to age 16). Young people could start a vocational programme at age 16 (up from September 2013. at age 14), and up to the age of 23 young people could obtain their first accredited vocational qualification free of charge (from 2013 only up to the age of 21). The development of the NQR was one of the most significant changes of the modernization process that transformed the VET system in Hungary. It imposes the same requirements to all forms of VET. In 2004–6, the NQR was redeveloped into a modular and competence-based system that seeks to enable mobility by defining the links between different vocational qualifications and to ensure a flexible and quick reaction to changes in the labour market, thus adapting the content of qualifications accordingly. The aims of the renewed NQR were to (1) reduce the number of qualifications in the register, (2) shorten the length of training through developing a modular system that recognizes prior qualifications, (3) develop a competence-based qualifications system with appropriate assessment, (4) strengthen the links between education and training and the economy, and (5) promote lifelong learning by adjusting the NQR and VET outcome requirements to labour market demands.

Simultaneously with the NQR development, the related Vocational and Examination Requirements were developed for each qualification through the input of employers, who were offered the opportunity to impact on the processes and content of VET provision. The Vocational and Examination Requirements draws on the expertise of employers to ensure that it contains only those elements, activities and knowledge that are relevant to the particular occupation. Through analysis of occupations, competence profiles for each occupation were defined by teams of VET professionals and practical experts such as employers, VET teachers and the chambers of commerce. The National Institute of Vocational and

Adult Education co-ordinated the development process. The Vocational and Examination Requirements specify not only the professional knowledge and skills necessary to perform the various tasks involved in a given occupation or job but also the methodological (logical thinking, problem-solving), social (communication, cooperation and conflict-resolution) and personal (flexibility, creativity, independence) competences. The renewed NQR was generally introduced in all VET schools from 2008, and the NQR continues to be regularly updated (see next section). This reform initiative in VET was in line with those reforms of qualifications that could be observed in other European countries and were promoted by the European Union.

While the NQR has been a major development at national level, changes that reflect regional differences have also been pursued. One of these changes is represented through the development of Regional Integrated Vocational Training Centres based on the Dutch model and supported by ESF since 2005. They were developed to rationalize the overly fragmented VET system and to ensure that qualifications are region specific and have labour market relevance. Most Regional Integrated Vocational Centres are consortia of local VET schools. However, 20–25 per cent of Regional Integrated Vocational Centres have not been organized on a regional basis (ReferNet Hungary, 2011a, 2011b: 17), which present a major barrier to fulfilling their local role. The current government indicated that while the Regional Integrated Vocational Training Centres remain, their financing and training offer would be defined by the central government (Ministry for National Economy, Hungary, May 2011).

According to the 2006 amendment to the 1993 Act, local professional consultative bodies (RFKB) were set up in the regional integrated vocational training centres and in larger vocational training schools. These professional consultative bodies were set up to report skills needs at a local level to ensure that these match the actual local VET output. The RFKB is to encourage the training of young people in vocations that are underrepresented, at the same time reducing the number in those vocations where there is an oversupply in the labour market. However, in the current economic climate it has been increasingly difficult to predict skills demand and to be responsive to labour market demand. Often employers cannot see more than six months ahead, and therefore the prediction of skills demand has been increasingly difficult. In addition, the RFKB faced further difficulties because of the information they base their prediction on. Their recommendation for the following academic year is based on the information from the previous year; hence prediction could not be accurate. Inevitably, the RFKB's interference with VET schools' learner enrolment has developed some tension between VET schools and the RFKB. In addition to the potential inaccuracy of prediction, there is also a mismatch of interest. VET schools wish to continue to deliver programmes that have been on offer in their schools and attract learners, on the basis of which they receive funding. According to recent changes, VET schools only get state financial support if they offer the state-accredited NQR qualifications.

It has been widely accepted that VET changes post 1989 have been greatly influenced by international developmental programmes funded in particular by the World Bank and the European Union. The period leading up to the EU accession in 2004 was characterized by two main tendencies: first, the moving away from the one-party system, planned economy and the education infused by socialist ideology, and second, the preparations that aimed at fulfilling the criteria for European integration. These two objectives nevertheless moved the modernization processes in education in the same direction. Despite the changing of leading political parties in the 1990s, the development of the regulatory environment in education has been linear.

In 1995, the European Commission published the White Paper that outlines the criteria of EU accession for education and training, putting learning at the heart of the document. Learning is, however, key in other than the education sector, such as in employment. This multi-sectoral approach to learning may present a challenge to those new EU accession countries where learning has been the domain of the education sector only, and single-sector-based thinking has dominated. For example, education aims have been set that have direct relevance to employment. These include, for example the development of ICT, language and enterprising skills, linking the world of work and education, and other skills development. These areas of education activities suggest a close link to the economy and employment and support the realization of employment policies (Halász, 2003a, 2003b). Halász (2001) argues that the question for Hungary is not whether education and training are ready for the EU accession but (1) whether they could contribute to the preparation of Hungarian society and economics to EU integration, (2) whether education and training can sufficiently make use of the advantages and opportunities that EU integration offers and (3) whether the education system in Hungary is ready to face the challenges, tensions and difficulties occurring from being member of a bigger community (p. 1). Preparation for European integration clearly set new challenges and at the same time offered new opportunities.

As outlined earlier, new initiatives were implemented for both, to align with EU requirements and to utilize advantages and opportunities offered by

European integration. Halász (2000a, 2000b) pointed out that it was only in VET where the EU required legal harmonization for the mutual acceptance of VET qualifications. In the case of Hungary, this would not demand a fundamentally different approach to the regulations of occupations because of earlier international influences. Hungary has developed a regulatory framework that fits in with EU expectations. Some of the policy developments included the support of employer engagement in the training, introduction of a competence-based (outcome-oriented) curriculum in VET or the institutionalization of social partners' decision making in VET (Halász, 2000a, 2000b).

Preparation for integration opened up a number of desired aims—national and European—that needed action. These areas covered, for example adult education and lifelong learning, employer engagement, acknowledgment of prior learning, basic skills development, ICT and language skills development. Education also had to respond to regional differences; it had to support less developed and deprived regions and to support social cohesion. The European Union (Phare, Leonardo, Socrates projects), OECD, the World Bank and the Soros Foundation earmarked financial recourses that were realized as developmental projects in these priority areas.

Latest policy developments in the Hungarian VET system

In 2010, Fidesz, the Hungarian Civic Union, won the general election with 56 per cent of the votes and has an outright majority in the National Assembly. Therefore, power relations in Hungary have significantly changed, within which education policy is being formulated. In 2011, the new government introduced new Education Laws for general education, vocational education and higher education. The system of vocational education and training is undergoing yet again significant changes, and fundamentally new initiatives in the delivery of VET are being introduced. The interview with a Hungarian VET expert reflects the scale and speed of ongoing changes in the fall of 2011: '*A discussion about current developments [in vocational education] is difficult because changes are fluid and are happening many times a day*' (Interview, 2011).

However, Halász (2011) argues that the demand towards VET (and other education sectors) has remained the same: to contribute to economic competitiveness, to improve employability, and to integrate socially disadvantaged groups (p. 33). He also argues that for the time being the government will have exclusively EU funding for developmental projects in these priority areas, and therefore national aims will have to align with EU priorities. Following the change in government in 2010, Halász speculates on reforms that could potentially include, for example, the strengthening of direct operative controlling of education and bringing the training for specific vocational occupations to a younger age (p. 34). These speculations have now come to reality. VET programmes are starting now at the age of 14, and '*The previously decentralised education system is in the process of becoming increasingly centralised*' (Refernet, Hungary, 2012: 6).

According to the new Law on Vocational Education and Training (2011), the structure of school-based initial VET has changed. Young people may take up early vocational programmes already from the age of 14 (previously 16), and vocational schools now generally offer a new dual type of training programme that is three years long instead of four. This three-year VET programme in vocational schools offers young people general and vocational education, placing significantly more emphasis on practical training in the third year. Already since 2010, young people in eighty-six occupations were able to access early VET. Through these developments the government tries to reduce early school leaving and tries to supply enterprises with skilled workers.

From the academic year 2013/14, those young people who attend secondary vocational schools will also be entitled to full vocational training, including practical training from the very beginning of their secondary education at the age of 14. At the end of schooling, learners sit the secondary vocational school leaving examination that entitles them to apply for a university place. Alternatively, they may enter at least one occupation within which they have received their vocational training, or they can continue to complete an accredited vocational qualification. For those young people who successfully obtain the secondary vocational school leaving examination, the vocational programme will be shortened by one year.

The current VET system and the qualification types are very similar to what existed prior to 1998 (and 1989). It was only between 1998 and 2010 that IVET was longer and could only start at the age of 16. This was in accordance with the National Core Curriculum, a general education programme that was compulsory for all to follow.

Critics argue that young people in the new system will not have sufficient time to develop key skills (literacy, numeracy and ICT), therefore reducing their later opportunities in the labour market, and that it will further widen the gap between the graduates of vocational schools and of secondary vocational schools. It is yet to be seen what outcomes would be achieved through these policy initiatives.

The Hungarian initial VET system has been strongly school based, and practical vocational training has been provided mainly in a (school) workshop setting. Current policy changes, however, emphasize practical training and aim to ensure that young people receive more practical training as part of their initial vocational programme, in particular through more work-based training in real enterprises (ReferNet Hungary, 2012: 16). Practical training is offered in the school's workshops, or at enterprises based on a contract between the VET school and the enterprise, or between the enterprise and the young person. The latter contract refers to the newly introduced dual training in Hungary. Through these initiatives, the government is trying to compensate for one of the system's weak points, the lack of knowledge, skills and competencies that could be gained through work experience (Kabai et al., 2010). However, only a few businesses have been engaged in dual VET to date, and only 20–22 per cent of learners in initial VET are placed in company-based practical training (Farkas, 2013b). This percentage is expected to rise with the roll-out of dual training in September 2013.

According to the new law, young people have to engage in practical training in real enterprises as part of their initial VET programme. This places employers under increasing pressure and raises the question of viability of this initiative despite its desirability. There are a number of reasons that may act as barriers to offering real training opportunities to young people. The current economic climate restricts employers' possibilities; they have limited resources, and during these unpredictable times it is difficult for them to plan ahead. According to the Central Statistical Office (2011) just over 1 per cent of enterprises employ 250 or more people, and these large companies employ 26.5 per cent of all employees in Hungary. Almost 99 per cent are micro, small and medium-size enterprises, and 95 per cent employ a maximum of nine people. Consequently, it is not always easy to find a training placement. Critiques of introducing practical training at this scale argue that whereas the socialist era could operationalize such a system due to its large number of state-subsidized big companies, the demography and structure of current enterprises cannot sufficiently respond to such demand. However, as the dual training is now a general VET provision in all vocational schools, time will tell to what extent economic partners can respond to the demand set by the dual training.

The Hungarian Chamber of Commerce and Industry (HCCI) undertakes a quality-assurance role of the practical elements of VET that happen both at enterprises and in vocational schools, and accredits institutions that deliver vocational qualifications. The training of young people in particular in enterprises demands careful monitoring and preparation, such as an individual approach to training young people, quality assurance of training and quality assurance of employer trainers. All these elements have a direct impact on learners' experience and ultimately on the quality of their vocational qualification. In order to ensure that employer trainers are sufficiently experienced and qualified, they will have to obtain a master craftsman examination from 2015 (Education Act on VET, 2011). Master craftsman training will include the development of teaching skills, and master craftsman examinations will be organized by the HCCI. The Hungarian Association for Vocational Training, however, claims that the Hungarian small and medium enterprises (SMEs) do not have the capacity and resources to underpin that goal and to offer young people training that meets the quality requirements of VET (RefNet Hungary, 2011).

As argued before, vocational education and training has to support the economy and prepare young people for the world of work, for employment and for lifelong learning. Hence, encouraging employer engagement to support vocational education and training has been high on the agenda. Policy-level interventions clearly show the government's commitment to involve economic partners in VET and to offer young people extended practical training and relevant preparation for employment.

In November 2010, the HCCI and the government signed a framework agreement about VET, which is a clear indication of an enhanced role for economic partners in VET. HCCI has taken on the review of the content for 125 practice-heavy qualifications (about 25 per cent of all qualifications on the register). The HCCI was tasked to overview, update and rationalize the National Qualifications Register (Országos Képzési Jegyzék), to update the professional and examination requirements in terms of their structure and content; update the framework curricula; prepare the content of vocational examination tasks and the related assessment guidance; appoint the chairman for final examinations; organize/co-coordinate the benchmarking examinations; organize vocational competitions, including Worldskills and Euroskills; and to support the work in career advice and guidance (Parragh, 2011: 4–5).

The HCCI relied on its own professional knowledge and networks during the review of qualifications and of professional and examination requirements. Expert groups of four to eight people representing education (VET providers) and employers were invited to work together to negotiate the content of the qualifications and their modules. During the development process, inevitably these expert groups faced challenges. One challenge arose from the composition of the expert groups who demonstrated different experiences, expressed different views and emphasized different priorities. These groups consisted of educational practitioners/vocational teachers who taught young people, and employers who were to employ newly qualified professionals. Other challenges included, for example, the tendency of wishing to include more knowledge and skill development in a module than what was realistically possible. Experts had strong preferences of what to include or what to leave out. Qualifications development is a complex technical process and requires specialist knowledge. Therefore, consensus building among participating stakeholders was a key to success. There was also a challenge to reflect the needs of multi-national, large and small and medium-size companies simultaneously. The HCCI has co-ordinated this development work while the National Vocational and Adult Institute monitored it. The work was completed in the summer of 2012.

In early 2013, the HCCI started to develop the vocational framework curricula. Two hundred and ninety-two vocational framework curricula were developed and published by 31 March 2013. These have been fully implemented in vocationally oriented schools from 1 September 2013. Whereas previously the framework curricula were only guiding documents, now they are legal acts to comply with.

Since 2010, HCCI clearly has taken a key role in the shaping of VET policy and practice in Hungary. HCCI advocates multi-sectoral thinking about learning and training where vocational education and training is not only an issue for education policy and educational system administration but also an issue for employment, economic and social policies (Csaba, 2013).

Summary

Hungary was one of the Soviet bloc countries before 1989, and it shared some common characteristics with other education systems in the region. The Hungarian Communist Party pursued a highly centralized, controlled and monolithic education, and education was interwoven with communist ideology; education was to serve the development of the socialist country. During the period from 1945 to 1989, most secondary education provision was vocationally oriented, and VET operated as the supporter of the planned economy of socialist Hungary and the Comecon. At the time of the political changes in 1990/91, 77 per cent of young people still participated in full-time vocational education, either in a vocational school or in an upper secondary vocational school.

However, starting from the 1950s, attempts were made to break out of the tight political control, and seeds of developments towards a liberal, democratic and pluralistic education system started to grow. It was clear that developments in the economy and society demanded the adjustment of education. Gradually over time, the politics of the Hungarian Communist Party has lost its teeth. Some of the early achievements, nevertheless, must be acknowledged, such as the introduction of eight-year compulsory free basic education in the 1940s, raising the compulsory school attendance to sixteen years, the development of a differentiated—even if skewed towards vocational education—secondary education in the 1960s and a growing number of social science and educational research institutes in the 1970s. The 1985 Education Act was a forward-thinking educational policy development, legalising more autonomy of educational institutions and pedagogues and outlining the rights and responsibilities of all stakeholders in education. This Act survived the political change and was used with some modification until the 1993 Education Acts were developed.

In the 1990s, Hungary demonstrated a very decentralized public education system not only among the other East European countries, but worldwide (OECD, 1998; Halász and Lannert, 1996). Following the changes in politics in 1989, changes in economy, society and in education have accelerated. This has resulted in previously less known or unknown phenomena, such as self-employment, unemployment and competition.

The discussion of VET changes between 1989 and 2010 focused on aspects of modernization and decentralization of the system and provision and on the requirements for EU accession. It was argued that national aims often coincided with EU and international priorities. Developmental programmes, in particular in VET, have been financially supported by the EU and the World Bank since the mid-1990s. The new economic and societal environment demanded changes of the VET system and provisions. Some of these included the standardization of vocational qualifications, the development of the National Qualifications Register, the closely linked Vocational and Examination Requirements, the development of Regional Integrated Vocational Centres and the increased involvement of employers in VET. These initiatives include systemic changes in VET and also regional and local developments. VET has to provide a well-qualified, flexible, enterprising workforce and prepare young people for the world of work. During the 1990s and early 2000s, the role of the state in VET has been decreasing while the autonomy of the regional and local institutions has been increasing.

In 2010, the new government with 56 per cent of the votes has an outright majority in the National Assembly which suggests a different power relationship when it comes to policy developments. In 2011, the government developed Education Acts for general education, vocational education and higher education. They introduced significant changes in the VET system and in VET provision. The current government is said to be committed to improving VET provision to meet the labour market demand, to make VET more prestigious and attractive to young people and to reduce the dropout rate among VET learners. In order to achieve these aims, in 2012 compulsory school attendance age was reduced to 16 (previously 18), and young people can start vocational training at the age of 14 (previously 16). A new dual-type VET was rolled out in September 2013 in every vocational school as the only option, emphasising the importance of practical training in enterprises. The Hungarian Chamber of Commerce and Industry has taken on responsibilities concerning vocational qualifications and examinations, involving its networks of employers. The scale and the depth of changes in school-based VET in Hungary have been great, and there is a clear move to centralization of VET. It is yet to be seen whether these new developments fulfil the expectations of learners, schools, employers and the government.

References

(1993). évi LXVI. törvény (a szakképzésről).

(2011). évi CLXXXVII. törvény (a szakképzésről). Available at http://net.jogtar.hu/jr/ gen/hjegy_doc.cgidocid=a1100187.TV.

Csaba, E. (2013). 'Változások a szakképzésben kamarai szemmel' (Changes in vocational training through the lense of the Chamber of Commerce and Industry). Presentation to the Hungarian Association of Vocational Education and Training (13 February 2013).

European Commission. (1995). *Teaching and Learning: Towards a Learning Society.* White Paper, Brussels: European Commission.

Farkas, É. (2013a). *A láthatalan szakma. Tények és tendenciák a felnőttképzés 25 évéről (The invisible vocation. Facts and tendencies during the 25 years of adult education).* Pécs: Typiart Médiaműhely.

Farkas, É. (2013b). *Teaching and learning methods in initial vocational education and training.* Background study on Hungary. Unpublished manuscript.

Grant, N. (1969). *Society, Schools and Progress in Eastern Europe.* Oxford: Pergamon.

Halász, G. & Lannert, J. (eds). (1996). *Jelentés a magyar közoktatásról—1995.* Budapest: Országos Közoktatási Intézet.

Halász, G. (2000a). 'A magyar integrációs felkészülés kérdései'. *Új Pedagógiai Szemle*, 10, 110–21.

Halász, G. (2000b). 'Az oktatás és az európai integráció', in Blahó, András (szerk.), *Tanuljunk Európát*, Budapest: Budapesti Közgazdaságtudományi és Államigazgatási Egyetem, 297–340.

Halász, G. (2001). 'Konferencia: A magyar oktatás európai integrációja'. *Új Pedagógiai Szemle*, 1, 140–46.

Halász, G. (2003a). 'Educational change and social transition in Hungary', in Polyzoi-Fullan-Anchan (ed.), *Change Forces in Post-Communist Eastern Europe. Education in Transition*. London and New York: RoutledgeFalmer. 55–73. Available at http://www.see-educoop.net/education_in/pdf/halasz_edu_change_in_hungary1-oth-enl-t00.pdf.

Halász, G. (2003b). *Tanulás és európai integráció*. OKI konferencia előadás a Gyulai Felnőttoktatási Akadémián: A tanuló felnőtt—A felnőtt tanuló. Gyula, 2003. szeptember 10–12. (Learning and European integration. Based on the presentation at the Gyula Adult Education Academy: The learning adult—Adult learning. Gyula, 10–12 September 2003).

Halász, G. (2009). *A nyolcvanas évtized a magyar oktatásban* (Professional background study to support the Hungary 1989–2009 television programme about education). Manuscript.

Halász, G. (2011). Az oktatáspolitika két évtizede Magyarországon: 1990–2010 Kézirat. október. Készült a „Magyarország politikai évkönyve" c. kiadvány számára. Available at http://halaszg.ofi.hu/download/Policy_kotet.pdf.

Hungarian on-line library (1996–2000). 'Kultúrpolitika és közoktatásügy 1945–1989 között'. (Cultural politics and public education between 1945 and 1989.) In *Magyarország a XX. században*. (Hungary in the 20th century). Szekszárd: Babits Kiadó. Available at http://mek.oszk.hu/02100/02185/html/1369.html#1373.

Kabai, I. et al. (2010). *A gazdasági szereplől elvárásai a szakmai képyés átalakítására. Final Report*. Budapest: Zsigmond Király Főiskola. Társadalomtudományi Kutatóközpont.

Kelemen, E. (2003). 'Oktatáspolitikai irányvátozások Magyarországon a 20. század második felében (1945–1990).' (Changes in the educational policy in the second half of the 20th Century in Hungary (1945–1990). *Új Pedagógiai Szemle*, 53(9), 25–32.

Kozma, T (2012). Nyitás az oktatáspolitikában. Egy rendhagyó nyári egyetem. (Opening of Education Policy. An unconventional summer school.) Available at http://dragon.unideb.hu/~nevtud/Oktdolg/Kozma_Tamas/doc/keziratok/Nyitasazoktataspolitikaban.pdf (accessed on 15 March 2013).

Központi Statisztikai Hivatal, Hungary (2011). *Vállalkozások demográfiúja és struktúrája (2000–2011)*. (Office of National Statistics, Hungary: The demography and structure of enterprises (2000–2011)). Available at http://www.ksh.hu/thm/1/indi1_2_4.html.

Ministry for National Economy, Hungary. (May 2011). (*Koncepció a szakképzési rendszer átalakítására, a gazdasági igényekkel való összehangolására.* Concept for the development of vocational education and training, and for its alignment with the economic demand.). Budapest: Nemzetgazdasági Minisztérium.

Ministry of Human Resources, Hungary. (2012). *Oktatás-statisztikai évkönyv. 2011/2012.* (Statistical Yearbook of Education. 2011/2012.). Budapest: Nemzeti Erőforrás Minisztérium (Ministry of Human Resources).

OECD. (1998). *Education at a Glance.* Paris: OECD.

Parragh, L. (2011). 'Versenyképes gazdaság—Versenyképes szakképzés. A Magyar Kereskedelmi és Iparkamara törekvései a duális szakképzés kialakításában'. (Competitive economics—Competitive vocational training. The work of the Hungarian Chamber of Commerce and Industry to support the development of dual system in VET). *Szakoktatás.* 61(7), 2–6.

Pukánszky-Németh. (2001, *updated*). Neveléstörténet—12.1. Harc az iskoláért. in Neveléstörténet. I. Mészáros (ed.). http://magyarirodalom.elte.hu/ nevelestortenet/12.01.html (accessed on 26 March 2013).

ReferNet Hungary. (2011a). *Hungary—Restructuring VET to better meet labour market demands.* Available at http://www.cedefop.europa.eu/EN/articles/19185.aspx.

ReferNet Hungary. (2011b). *Hungary. VET in Europe—Country Report 2011.* Budapest: Refernet.

ReferNet, Hungary. (2012). *Hungary. VET in Europe—Country Report.* Budapest: Refernet. Available at libserver.cedefop.europa.eu/vetelib/2012/2012_CR_HU.pdf.

Further Reading

Balogh, L. (2001). 'Az iskolai Szerkezetvaltas tortenete'. *Új Pedagógiai Szemle*, 3, 13–30.

Benedek, A. (1997). 'Az európai integráció és a szakképzés'. *Új Pedagógiai Szemle*, 10, 24–33.

Bognár, A. (1997). 'Az idegen nyelvek oktatásának helye és szerepe az Európai Unióhoz való csatlakozásban'. *Új Pedagógiai Szemle*, 6, 60–73.

Csehné Papp, I. (2007). 'A munkaerőpiac és az oktatás problémáinak elemzése napjaink szakemberképzésének tükrében'. *Új Pedagógiai Szemle*, 3, 193–99.

Kelemen, E. (2000). 'Oktatásügyi változások közép-kelet európában az 1990-es években'. *Magyar Pedagógia*, 100(3), 315–30.

Kelemen, E. (2008). 'A magyar neveléstudományi kongresszusok története'. *Új Pedagógiai Szemle*, 2, http://www.ofi.hu/tudastar/kelemen-elemer-magyar (accessed on 15 February 2013).

Ladányi, A. (1998). 'Az európai integráció és a magyar felsőoktatás'. *Európai tükör*, 3, 61–72.

Magyar Elektronikus Konyvtar (?) *Kultúrpolitika és közoktatásügy 1945–1989 között.*
Available at http://mek.oszk.hu/02100/02185/html/1369.html (accessed on 26 March
2013)..

Matolcsy, Gy. (2012). *J/8112. számú jelentés a kis- és középvállalkozások 2009–2010.
évi helyzetéről, gazdálkodási feltételrendszeréről, a vállalkozásfejlesztés érdekében
megtett intézkedésekről, valamint a kis- és középvállalkozások részére nyújtott állami
támogatások eredményeiről.* Budapest: Hungarian Government. Available at http://
www.parlament.hu/irom39/08112/08112.pdf.

7

Latvia: Education and Post-Socialist Transformations

Iveta Silova

Introduction

Since regaining independence in 1991, Latvia has embarked on a series of major education reforms. Similar to other post-socialist countries of Eastern and Central Europe, the general spirit of these reforms has reflected a strong desire to disassociate with Soviet education policies and practices while adopting Western (European) ones. In Latvia, this process has been accelerated by the European Union (EU) accession process, which has offered mechanisms to realign the educational system with the EU standards. Latvia joined the Council of Europe in 1995 and the Bologna process in 1999, and finally became the member of the EU in 2004. Although most of the EU measures do not explicitly aim at regulation of national systems and policies, they nevertheless have had a tremendous impact on education policies and practices in the newly independent Latvia. The basic logic and the main objectives of the EU educational initiatives—promoting international cooperation, enhancing the quality of education, encouraging social integration and increasing employability of graduates—have generally corresponded to the national development goals, forming the cornerstone of education policies in independent Latvia.[1]

In the context of Latvia's EU accession, the catchwords of the new (post-socialist) education reforms have been 'democratization', 'liberalization', 'pluralism', 'multiculturalism' and 'humanization of learning' (Silova, 2009). Educational transformation processes have generally touched all areas of the education system, triggering profound changes in education governance, curriculum, textbooks, examination and assessment systems, teacher education and infrastructure. For example, school textbooks (especially in such subjects as history, geography and civic education) have been rewritten to remove Soviet ideological content and redefine national identity in terms of Latvian and European values. Similarly, curriculum content has been revised to democratize the teaching and learning process by shifting the emphasis from teacher-centred to learner-centred instruction. In other words, 'adopting the language of the new allies,' the European Union has become commonplace, signalling Latvia's desire to 'return' to and ultimately 'catch up' with Europe (Silova, 2004).

However, the Europeanization process has been complicated by the legacies of the socialist past. These socialist legacies have manifested themselves at different levels, including the more straightforward infrastructural and administrative-bureaucratic legacies and the more elusive political and cultural continuities (Barkey and von Hagen, 1997). The tensions between the socialist legacies and the European values have become most visible in Latvia's minority education reform. On the one hand, post-Soviet education reforms have deliberately pursued *Latvianization* strategies to ensure the protection of Latvian national rights and reverse the decades of *Russification* and Soviet assimilation processes. On the other hand, Latvia's determination to join the European Union has required redefinition of national education policies in terms of European values, which emphasize respect for pluralism, multiculturalism, human rights and tolerance as well as cultural and linguistic diversity. This chapter attempts to capture the complexity of creating a new European space—and the limits of multiculturalism it has encountered—by examining the complex interplay between the Western education reforms and the constraints imposed by the Soviet legacies in the area of minority education in post-Soviet Latvia.

The Soviet legacy of ethnolinguistically segregated schools

At the time of the collapse of the Soviet Union in 1991, Latvia had the largest Russian minority of the Baltic states and the second largest in the former Soviet Union.[2] Since Latvia's annexation by the Soviet Union in 1940, the proportion of Russians in the country more than tripled, reaching 34 per cent by the end of the 1980s (Vebers, 1994). At the same time, the Latvian population decreased from 77 per cent in 1935 to 52 per cent in 1989, nearly reaching the point of 'demographic minorization' of ethnic Latvians (Karklins, 2004). Although the share of Russian speakers has declined since the collapse of the Soviet Union, ethnic Latvians still comprise only 59.5 per cent of the country's population (Central Statistical Bureau of Latvia, 2011). Given the inherited complexity of the demographic situation, combined with the highly politicized nature of the issue, the reconciliation of ethnic relationships has become the main focus of political debates in post-Soviet Latvia.

In the education sphere, the debate has revolved around the Soviet legacy of two parallel school structures—one using Russian language instruction and the other using Latvian. Established during the Soviet period (1940–91), these schools differed not only in their language of instruction but also in curricula, value systems and teaching staff. They were used by the Soviet regime as mechanisms to institutionalize a dual notion of nationhood among the Russian and indigenous populations. As Karklins (1998) explains, students attending Latvian schools associated themselves with Latvia and were usually bilingual, whereas students attending Russian schools typically had a 'strong Russian orientation' and spoke Latvian relatively poorly.[3] In addition to strict control over school curricula, separate schools for Russian- and Latvian-speaking students enabled policing of unwanted nationalistic sentiments and ensured surveillance of students' behaviours and attitudes, inside and outside the classroom, while maintaining a privileged position of students attending Russian schools.

In the post-Soviet context, the segregated school system has remained, although the number of students attending Russian-language schools has been gradually decreasing (see Table 7.1). For example, the percentage of students attending Russian-language schools fell from 47 per cent in the 1990/91 academic year to 27 per cent in the 2012/13 academic year. Meanwhile, the percentage of students attending Latvian language schools increased from 53 per cent in the 1990/91 academic year to 72 per cent in the 2012/13 academic year. The percentage of students attending other minority schools has remained below 1 per cent through the last two decades.

Although the proportion of students attending Russian language schools has been gradually decreasing, the segregation of schools along ethnolinguistic lines has been seriously questioned both nationally and internationally. In Latvia, some nationalistically oriented political parties (e.g. 'Fatherland and Freedom' is a conservative political party) declared Russian language schools an 'unwanted' phenomenon that symbolized the legacy of Soviet occupation and continued to 'nurture Soviet colonizers.'[4] In the early 1990s, Russian schools were increasingly perceived by some policy makers as a threat to rebuilding an independent Latvian nation. Meanwhile, any mention of closing Russian-language schools and/or merging them with Latvian-language schools into one unified system were perceived by the Russian-speaking population as a discrimination against minorities. Policy debates about the future of Russian-language schools thus increased the already existing ethnic tensions among the Latvian- and Russian-speaking groups in Latvia. Internationally, the problem was quickly reframed as one of impeding Latvian accession into the European Union. According to various international agencies,[5] development of a cohesive, multicultural society—free of ethnic tensions and institutional segregation—was a necessary prerequisite for joining the European Union. In this context, separate schools for Latvian- and Russian-speaking students were perceived as an obstacle to reaching this goal, undermining the European values of cohesion, integration, and multiculturalism.

Although different policy options were discussed with regard to the future of Russian schools—ranging from closing Russian schools to diversifying the education system through the establishment of various minority schools—it was decided by the end of the 1990s to leave separate educational structures intact. Instead of institutional integration, education reform efforts focused on promoting ethnic integration through school curricula and extracurricular activities. In 1999, the government approved the national programme 'Integration of Society in Latvia', which identified a wide range of components, including loyalty to the state; acceptance of Latvian as the state language; shared basic values such as an independent and democratic Latvian state; common universal human and European cultural values; respect for Latvian as well as minority

Table 7.1 Number of students by language of instruction (1990–2013)

Academic year	Latvian language instruction		Russian language instruction		Other language schools		Total	
	Number	Per cent	Number	Per cent	Number	Per cent	Number	Per cent
1990/91	176,054	53.2	154,912	46.78	87	0.02	331,053	100
1992/92	176,513	55.1	143,340	44.8	322	0.1	320,175	100
1995/96	197,598	60.3	128,430	39.2	1539	0.5	327,567	100
1996/97	210,385	61.9	127,784	37.6	1664	0.5	339,833	100
2000/1	225,768	67.4	107,470	32.2	1334	0.4	334,572	100
2003/4	230,212	70.3	95,841	29.3	1305	0.4	327,358	100
2012/13	138,549	71.8	52,447	27.2	1,794	0.9	192,790	100

Note. From *Demographic Yearbook of Latvia* (p. 40), by Central Statistical Bureau of Latvia (2000) and United Nations Human Development Report (1997: 59); for the 2003/4 academic year, data from Ministry of Education and Science (2005); for the 2012/13 academic year, data from Central Statistical Bureau of Latvia (2014).

languages and cultures; the right for non-Latvians to preserve their language and culture; mutual enrichment and trust; cooperation among individuals, social and ethnic groups; civic participation; and individual responsibility of each person to contribute knowledge, initiative and good intentions to Latvian society.[6] In other words, the programme defined integration as a two-way process that would require both Latvian- and Russian-speaking groups to actively participate in building a more cohesive society.

To ensure implementation of the programme, a new Secretariat of Minister of Special Assignments for Society Integration Affairs was established in November 2002, although it was handed over to the Ministry of Culture and the Ministry of Interior in 2010. Furthermore, the Law on the Society Integration Foundation (SIF) was adopted by the Saeima (Parliament) on 5 July 2001 to promote society integration in Latvia through the provision of financial support to various programmes, activities and events.[7]

Notwithstanding the conceptual breadth of the national programme 'Integration of Society in Latvia' and the financial resources available for its implementation, education policies had primarily focused on the Latvian language learning issues, promoting Latvianization (rather than integration) of the society. Meanwhile, other integration goals, such as diversity, multiculturalism and tolerance, began to gradually fade away from the education policy narratives. Thus, two decades after the collapse of the Soviet Union, schools had continued to reproduce divisions along ethnolinguistic lines through schools textbooks, curriculum and the broader institutional culture.

Reframing 'integration' in education: The focus on Latvianization policies

When the concept of ethnic integration was translated into education policy, Latvian language was presented as the main mechanism of integrating Russian and other minority students into Latvian society. Not only did such reframing narrow down the original definition of 'integration', neglecting its focus on multiculturalism, but it also signalled a continuation of a long-term education policy trend of Latvianizing the education system. Since the early 1990s, one of the main goals of state educational reform was to restore the status of the Latvian language in state educational institutions. The use of Latvian language increased much faster in higher education institutions than in primary and secondary schools. For example, the Language Law of 1992 established that in state-financed higher educational institutions, studies must take place in Latvian after the second year of study. As a result, four-fifths of all students received instruction in the Latvian language in the 1994/95 academic year (UNDP, 1995). The remaining one-fifth of the students attended private higher education institutions, which provided instruction in Russian language (UNDP, 1996). This policy triggered the establishment of parallel higher education institutions in Latvia—public higher education institutions in the Latvian language and private higher education institutions in the Russian language. Interestingly, this also reflects the situation in the employment sector, where the majority of Latvian speakers are employed by the state sector, whereas the majority of Russian speakers are employed by the private business sector (Silova, 2006).

At the school level, reform initiatives included increasing the number of Latvian language classes in non-Latvian schools, introducing obligatory Latvian language exams for high school graduates, requiring all teachers to pass the highest level of the state language test and introducing Latvian as the only language of instruction in state-financed higher education institutions, as well as prohibiting the use of textbooks published outside of Latvia (Silova, 2006). In particular, the Education Law (Ministry of Education and Science, 1998) was amended in August 1995, requiring that two subjects in minority primary schools (grades 1–9) and three subjects in minority secondary schools (grades 10–12) were to be taught in the Latvian language beginning September 1996.[8] In December 1996, the Ministry of Education and Science (MoES) issued another regulation, which envisaged Latvian language certification at the highest level for educators in Russian and minority schools, regardless of the level of Latvian language needed for the fulfilment of their professional duties.[9] Although one and a half years was given for preparation for the certification exam, many teachers thought that they did not have enough time to adequately prepare for the exam, and nearly a hundred teachers were fired for failing the examination.

At the end of the 1998, the Latvianization trend became more apparent as the new Education Law (1998) stated that 'at state and municipal education institutions instruction shall be in the state language.' At the same time, the next paragraph of the Law stated 'instruction may be provided in other languages' at (1) private education institutions, (2) state or municipal education institutions which implement minority education programmes and (3) other education institutions as prescribed by other laws. Furthermore, the new Education Law (Ministry of Education, 1998) announced that state-financed secondary education would only be available in the Latvian language starting from 2004,[10] and primary education would be reformed through the introduction of transitional bilingual education programmes in minority schools. In the Language Law (Saiema, 1999), the initial goal of bilingual education policy was explicitly introduced as a mechanism of integration, stating that it would 'facilitate the integration in the society by improving the Latvian language skills among the inhabitants of Latvia.'

Although officially introduced under the umbrella of integration reforms, bilingual education was geared towards Russian-language schools only and did not require participation of Latvian-language schools. In particular, the Ministry of Education developed four models of transitional bilingual education programmes, also referred to as 'minority education programmes'. These models differed by the suggested proportion of classes held in the minority and Latvian languages. For example, the first model was based on a rapid increase of the Latvian language and was meant for students with high level of Latvian language knowledge, whereas the fourth model was a more gradual transition to studying in Latvian language and was more appropriate for students with no previous Latvian language skills. In addition, the Ministry of Education provided an opportunity for schools to also elaborate their own transitional bilingual education models, which would then require an approval by the Ministry officials.

The idea of Latvianizing Russian schools through bilingual education programmes triggered strong opposition from NGOs representing Russian-speaking and other minority communities in Latvia. Some critics openly argued that the introduction of bilingual education was not 'a value in itself, but a cover-up of a gradual establishment of education in Latvian language only' (Arshavskaya et al., 2000: 7). Moreover, a Declaration of Public Organizations (1999), signed by the representatives of the Latvian Human Rights Committee, the Russian Community of Latvia, the Baltic Slavic Society for Cultural Development and other NGOs, appealed to the international community by stating that the Latvianization of Russian schools involved 'a threat to assimilation' and therefore contradicted Hague recommendations regarding minority education. Critics were also concerned about the potential decrease of education quality in Russian-language schools if students would be unable to study in their mother tongue. Another concern was insufficient teacher training in both Latvian language and bilingual education.

Some of these criticisms were addressed by subsequent policy changes. For example, the government has offered some support for teacher training through the National Program for Latvian Language Training (NPLLT), which was established in 1996 and was supported by United National Development

Program (UNDP). The programme lasted for ten years and provided language courses and methodological training for teachers in Latvian as a second language and, since 1999, bilingual education. Another positive initiative was the 1998 decision to offer a salary bonus for teachers teaching in Latvian or bilingually. However, reflecting on this 'carrot and stick' approach, critics argued that there was too much reliance on the 'stick'—coercive measures and large amounts of legislation and regulations—rather than positive involvement and assistance (Brands Kehris and Landes, 2008: 14).

Reflecting on the outcomes of these integration reforms, it is important to consider three questions: Did Latvian language proficiency increase among students from Russian-language schools? How then did the introduction of bilingual education affect student achievement? And, more importantly, how did the bilingual education reform affect integration of Russian- and Latvian-speaking students? Answers to the first two questions suggest that the bilingual education reform has been fairly successful. In particular, research shows that the knowledge of Latvian language among young non-Latvian students has considerably improved since the implementation of reform (Priedite, 2005; Zepa et al., 2006; Grabane, 2012). In 1999, slightly more than a half (54 per cent) of the surveyed 15- to 24-year-olds whose native language was not Latvian evaluated their Latvian language skills as poor; however, this percentage decreased to 30 per cent in 2003 and 25 per cent in 2006 (Zepa et al., 2006). Similarly, more recent annual studies on state language acquisition and use among Russian speakers suggest that the number of young people with good Latvian language proficiency has increased from about 40 per cent in 1996 to 73 per cent in 2008 (Zepa, 2010).

Meanwhile, the results of the Program for International Student Assessment (PISA) study reveal that there are practically no differences between the average achievement of students studying in Russian-language schools (and implementing bilingual education programmes) and those in Latvian language schools (Geske et al., 2006; Lindermann, 2011).[11] In fact, the findings illustrate that students in Latvian language schools had slightly better average results in 2000 and 2003, but the difference in student achievement levels had disappeared in 2006.[12] As some scholars emphasize, these findings demonstrate the success and effectiveness of bilingual education reform (Zepa, 2010; Jurgena et al., 2012).

However, other studies point to the ethnic gap in university admissions and tertiary attainment. For example, Hazans et al. (2010) found that ethnic minorities in Latvia, on average, lag behind titular population by 5–6 per cent points in tertiary enrolment of all 17- to 24-year-olds, and by 10 per cent points in tertiary enrolment of secondary graduates of the same age. The study also argues that the titular (Latvian-speaking) population is attaining tertiary education at a higher rate than minorities and that, among those with higher education, the titular population is more actively pursuing graduate degrees than its minority counterparts (Hazans et al., 2010).

The answers to the third question—whether and to what extent bilingual education reform promoted ethnic integration among different groups—is perhaps less optimistic. For example, Curika's (2010) research shows that there is a very low interaction ratio between Latvian- and Russian-speaking students. In particular, about 90 per cent of students from 'Russian' as well as from 'Latvian' schools make the majority of their friends inside their ethnolinguistic group (p. 76). As Curika (2010) concludes, this lack of connection between students from different ethnolinguistic groups in real life may potentially lead to prejudiced opinions about each other. Similarly, another study, *Integration of Minority Youth in the Society of Latvia in the Context of the Education Reform*, found a growing trend among the Latvian and Russian-speaking populations towards separation and mutual isolation as a result of the education reform (Zepa, 2010). In other words, bilingual education reform may have improved the Latvian language skills among minority students in Latvia, but it has not contributed to ethnic integration among Latvian- and Russian-speaking students in any meaningful ways.

Subverting 'integration': Official and hidden curriculum

By focusing on language issues almost exclusively, ethnic integration policy efforts in Latvia have not sufficiently addressed such important aspects of education reform as curricula and extracurricular activities. This is reflected in both official school curriculum (e.g. textbooks) and the 'hidden curriculum'—lessons which are learned (but not officially intended) through the transmission of norms, values and beliefs in the classroom and the overall school environment (Giroux and Purpel, 1983). Several studies confirm that school textbooks and curricula do not reflect the multicultural nature of Latvian society, thus contributing to institutional segregation in the educational system along ethnolinguistic lines (Krupnikova, 2004; Grigule and Pavula, 1998; Silova, 1996). Drawing on the analysis of nearly ninety school textbooks,[13] Krupnikova's (2004) study confirmed that both Latvian- and Russian-language textbooks are ethnocentric in their disregard of other ethnicities present in Latvia, and the social and cultural contributions to the development of Latvia's society that these different groups make. Alarmingly, this textbook analysis study suggests that the 'textbook reality' of Latvian- and Russian-language textbooks is overtly separated. Latvian-language textbooks create a monocultural information space, absent of minority representatives, whereas in Russian-language textbooks Russian characters are detached from the Latvian social context. As Krupnikova (2004) explains:

> Those studying with the Latvian-language textbooks could get the impression that Latvia is a monocultural state, populated exclusively by ethnic Latvians; while Russian-language textbooks mainly describe another state's reality (Russia), with occasional returns to Latvia, exclusive of its Latvian population. Reading Latvian textbooks, it is hard to believe that in real life all these Kristaps, Lienes, Marutas and Nikolays, Olgas and Ivans actually live in the same country, walk the same streets, play in the same backyards and go to the same cinemas (p. 74)

Furthermore, Krupnikova (2004) states that the textbooks' authors often take an ethnocentric viewpoint to describe countries of the Third World and its inhabitants, present non–Christian religions by emphasizing their fundamentalist aspects and address migration issues exclusively from a negative perspective. Perhaps the most striking example is from an early literacy textbook (ABC) published and approved by the Ministry of Education in 2005—a year after Latvia's accession into the European Union—which contains a page of alphabet letters with illustrations accompanying each letter. These illustrations contain images of different objects (e.g. moon, dog, eggs, fish, nuts) and only two images of human beings. One image is used to illustrate the letter *N* and features a half-naked black man—here *N* stands for 'negro.' And the other image of a human being illustrates the letter *I* and shows a half-naked, dark-skinned man wearing feathers on his head—here *I* stands for [American] 'Indian.' This is only one example of a prejudiced portrayal of 'the other' in a Latvian textbook. Even though all textbooks are centrally evaluated to meet specific criteria (including sensitivity to diversity),[14] similar examples could be easily found in other textbooks whose audiences range from elementary grades to high schools.

Not only do textbooks contain prejudiced messages about 'us' and 'them', but they also make explicit comments about the value of different languages in a Latvian society. For example, several textbooks (used in different grades) contain a poem that aims at teaching students to cherish and protect their (Latvian) language from the 'negative' influences of other languages. A short version of the poem, authored by Mara Cielena and featured in a first-grade textbook (Paegle, 1997) says:

Wash your feet, and wash your mouth,
And brush your teeth really well.
But this is not all—
Before going to bed, we will clean your language.
Let the words picked up in a rush
Fall off like a thistle:
'Kurtka', 'samosvals', 'bante', 'davai',[15]
Which do shame to your one and only Latvian language. (p. 44)

A longer version of the same poem also appears in a third-grade textbook and contains more derogatory messages, which compare foreign words— such as jacket, dump truck and bow—to 'dirt'. A conclusion at the end of the poem confirms that Latvian language has words that are 'unwanted', and 'if a speaker uses foreign words instead of Latvian words in his/her speech, then that person's speech is ugly' (p. 45). Poems like this send very clear messages to children about the value of diversity and multiculturalism in a society, seriously complicating ethnic integration efforts. As Krupnikova (2004) suggests, 'After being introduced to the Russian language in such a way, [children] would be right to conclude that there are "good" and "bad" languages, those which make you a good girl or boy, and those which make you a bad one' (p. 66).

Furthermore, many textbooks invoke a strong tautology that 'Latvians' exist as a result of their birth in the space of 'Latvia', a homeland always formulated as such because it has always been home to 'Latvians'. The notion of 'homeland' thus suggests a perfect correspondence between the national identity and the national space (nation-state), which is further cemented by references to the national language, always neatly coinciding with the national borders (whether real or imagined) (Mead and Silova, 2013). For example, one first-grade Latvian textbook explicitly claims: 'Latvians speak Latvian. Latvians live in Latvia' (Cimdina et al., 1993: 88). Following this text, a fill-in-the-blank activity is presented for children in which the following prompts are given: 'Russians live in … What [language] do Russians speak?' And 'Poles live in … What [language] do Poles speak?' (88–89). Given the possible responses listed (Russian and Polish), the intended answers are obvious—the children are expected to unquestionably complete the phrases with those languages corresponding directly with the nation-states and nationalities given (i.e. 'Russians live in Russia and speak *Russian*. The Poles live in Poland and speak *Polish*.'). Thus, the text reinforces the naturalization (and illusion) of the formula in which language is naturally (and unproblematically) mapped onto the pairing of people and placed in a one-to-one correspondence. Any deviation from this formula—whether birth place or language skills—questions one's belonging to a Latvian homeland.

In other words, research reveals that the ethnocentric nature of textbooks used in Latvian, Russian, and other minority-language schools reinforces the already existing divide between separate schools for different ethnolinguistic groups. Teachers confirm these findings, too. In particular, Golubeva and Austers (2011) surveyed teachers of majority and minority schools who were asked to assess teacher perceptions regarding the presence of ethnic stereotypes in curriculum in general, and the fairness of representation of minority and majority groups in history curriculum in particular. Their findings reveal that more than 50 per cent of minority-school teachers feel that school textbooks and curricula contain stereotypes about major ethnic groups. Furthermore, 37 per cent of teachers in Russian-language schools disagree with the statement that 'Official policies concerning non-discrimination are implemented in everyday [school] school life' (Golubeva and Austers, 2011). The study also revealed that the trust towards the fairness of the official history curriculum among the teachers of Russian-language schools is very low: only 5 per cent agree that the representation of Latvians and Russians in history textbooks is balanced and fair (Golubeva and Austers, 2011: 59).

What is more alarming is that this school divide is generally perceived as 'normal' by many Russian- and Latvian-speaking students. In particular, the majority of Latvian- and Russian-speaking students—63.9 per cent in Latvian language schools and 78.9 per cent in Russian language schools—think that the separate schooling system is good (Curika, 2010). Similarly, the findings of the study *Divided Education, Divided Citizens* (Golubeva and Austers, 2011) found that 42 per cent of Latvians and 56 per cent of Russian-speakers claimed that they would not want to learn in one class with those belonging to the 'other' group. In other words, institutional segregation reproduces social divide within the Latvian society through official curriculum, textbooks and the overall school culture, all of which affect identity and civil participation among students of different ethnolinguistic groups.

Reconciling Soviet legacies with European values:
The limits of multiculturalism

Since regaining independence in 1991, Latvia has been undergoing complex education transformation processes aimed at repositioning itself within the European education space. Although the European Union has become a particularly influential context for education reform, it has also highlighted some of the tensions in reconciling 'Western' ideas with the Soviet legacies and local realities. The EU integration efforts have been generally welcomed (e.g. as reflected in Latvia's participation in various EU programmes and its ultimate accession into the European Union in 2004), but they have also released tensions between the European dimension on the one hand, and the socialist legacies and national identities on the other (Silova, 2009). In Latvia, these tensions have become most visible in the implementation of minority education reform, especially in the government's efforts to integrate the Russian- and Latvian-speaking populations. Although they embraced the EU rhetoric on ethnic integration, the policy makers placed a strong emphasis on bilingual education for minority schools while underplaying other reforms aspects such as curricula reforms, textbooks revision, teacher education and extracurricular activities.

More than two decades since the collapse of the Soviet Union, Latvia's desire to 'catch up' with Europe—including its values of pluralism, multiculturalism and human rights—has thus resulted in mixed outcomes. As Muižneiks (2010) points out, 'the overall picture and recent trends are very contradictory', with elements of separation, marginalization, and integration simultaneously present in all aspects of political, economic and social life. In education, the progress towards ethnic integration could be observed in the improved knowledge of the Latvian language skills among minority groups, which was primarily achieved through the introduction of bilingual education programmes. On a positive note, too, academic achievement of students in Russian- and Latvian-language schools seemed to have been generally unaffected by the reforms. At the same time, however, institutional segregation has continued to reproduce the existing divide among different ethnolinguistic groups in Latvia through textbooks, curriculum and the overall school culture, complicating integration processes and institutionalizing ethnocentrism and prejudice towards minorities. Missing from the ethnic integration reform efforts have been such important aspects as the development of shared cultural values, mutual enrichment and trust and civic participation as well as cooperation among individuals and social and ethnic groups.

As this chapter has illustrated, the EU accession process has triggered major educational changes in Latvia, drawing selectively on ideas, values and reforms borrowed from the European Union. In this context, the patterns of global, national and local discourses have shaped new power/knowledge relationships that have had differential effects of inclusion and exclusion. In the Latvian case, the application of 'new' ethnic integration discourses to the 'old' education structures inherited from the socialist past has contributed simultaneously to the production of new ways of reasoning and new power dynamics in a society. While semantically repositioning Latvia within the European education space, ethnic integration reforms have resulted in the hybridity of education policies and practices as they have faced the Soviet structural and institutional legacies, thus ultimately setting the limits of multiculturalism in newly independent Latvia.

Notes

1   The many educational changes that have occurred cannot be separated from programmes such as Tempus (higher education) and Phare (vocational education), as well as from the flow of information and exchanges originating in meetings, seminars and publications of the Council of Europe and the Organization for Economic Cooperation and Development (OECD) and from bilateral schemes sponsored by numerous Western governments as well as private foundations (Cerych, 1997).

2   The only larger Russian population in terms of percentage of the overall population in the former Soviet Union is Kazakhstan (Open Society Institute, 1997).

3   According to the census data of 1989, 71 per cent of Latvians in cities and 57 per cent in the countryside spoke Russian as a second language, whereas only 22 per cent of the Russian nationals and 18 per cent of other non-Latvians spoke Latvian, resulting in 'asymmetric bilingualism' between Latvian- and Russian-speaking groups (Vebers, 1994).

4   For a more detailed discussion, see Silova (2006).

5   OSCE, Council of Europe, USIA, IHF, and UN agencies. Although some international organizations attempted to influence the development of a 'multicultural society' indirectly through small grants to local NGOs and

individuals, as in the case of UNESCO and USIA, other international agencies, particularly the OSCE and the Council of Europe, aimed to directly intervene in policy development and implementation regarding such issues as citizenship, language and education.

6   For a more detailed discussion, see Silova (2006).

7   Between 2001 and 2009, the Fund had financed 1,483 projects, including 880 projects for promoting ethnic and social integration for the total amount of LVL20 (USD39) million (Ministry of Foreign Affairs of the Republic of Latvia, 2014).

8   See Ministry of Education and Science regulation # 1-14-2.

9   See Ministry of Education and Science regulation # 175.

10 In February 2004, the *Education Law* was amended, allowing secondary education minority schools to teach 3/5 of all subjects in the Latvian language and 2/5 in minority languages (section 9, part 3).

11 The Latvian sample included 4,719 students (114 Latvian, 46 Russian, and 16 mixed schools).

12 However, children from both Latvian and Russian schools in the countryside had significantly lower educational attainment compared to children in the cities, particularly in Riga (Geske et al., 2006).

13 This study analysed a selection of eighty-one textbooks for grades 1–9, published in Latvia, to determine (1) whether they reflect the multi-ethnic nature of Latvian society, (2) whether the multiculturalism principles are observed (i.e. whether ethnic minorities are proportionally represented along with the majority), (3) whether the balance between the cultural heritage of the Latvian nation and those of the national minorities has been achieved and (4) whether the textbooks contain ethnic, cultural and religious stereotypes.

14 The existing textbook evaluation criteria include broad statements pertaining to social integration and minority rights. For example, the general textbook evaluation criteria says: 'The Latvian Republic's Constitution and other legislation stressing human rights have been respected in the textbook, including the basic principles of children's rights, race, nationality and gender equality …' (Ministry of Education and Science, 2003). However, there are no specific indicators developed and incorporated into textbook development standards for each subject, thus allowing for very broad and vague interpretations (Krupnikova, 2004).

15 *Kurtka*—jacket (Russian), *samosvals*—dump truck (Russian), *bante*—bow (Russian; German), *davai*—let's (Russian). Interestingly, mostly Russian words are used as examples of 'foreign' words in this poem, with the possible exception of '*bante*', which can also have German roots.

References

Arshavskaya, T., Gushin, V., Pimenov, I. (2000, June). 'Obrazovanie na russkom yazike v Latvii: Analiz situacii [Education in Russian language in Latvia: Situation analysis]', *Obrazovanie i Karjera*, 12(063), 7–8.

Barkey, K. & von Hagen, M. (eds). (1997). *After Empire: Multiethnic Societies and Nation-Building*. Boulder, CO: Westview Press.

Brands Kehris, I. & Landes, X. (2008). *Multicultural Education in Latvia*. Riga, Latvia: Latvian Centre for Human Rights and Ethnic Studies.

Central Statistical Bureau of Latvia. (2000). *Demographic Yearbook of Latvia*. Riga, Latvia: Central Statistical Bureau of Latvia.

Central Statistical Bureau of Latvia. (2011). *Demographic Yearbook of Latvia*. Riga, Latvia: Central Statistical Bureau of Latvia.

Central Statistical Bureau of Latvia. (2014). Education statistics. [Online]. Available at http://data.csb.gov.lv/ (accessed on 10 May 2014).

Cerych, L. (1997). 'Educational reforms in Central and Eastern Europe: Processes and outcomes'. *European Journal of Education*, 32(1): 75–97.

Cimdina, R., Lanka, A., Krustkalna, L. (1993). Riti raiti, valodina: Latviesu valodas macibgramata cittautiesiem [Latvian language textbook for speakers of other languages]. Riga: Zvaigzne.

Curika, L. (2010). 'Civic attitudes in separate schools in Latvia', in M. Golubeva (ed.), *Inclusion Unaffordable? The Uncertain Fate of Integration Policies in Europe*. Riga, Latvia: Providus, 75–78.

Declaration of public organizations: Framework document concerning a national program of integration of society in Latvia (1999). [Online]. Available at http://www.lhrc.lv/integr.html (accessed on 10 May 2014).

Geske, A., Grīnfelds, A., Kangro, A. & Kiseļova, R. (2006). *Kompetence dabaszinātnēs, matemātikā un lasīšanā—Ieguldījums nākotnei* [Competences in science, mathematics, and reading: Investment into the future]. Riga, Latvia: University of Latvia.

Golubeva, M. & Austers, I. (2011). 'Alternative civil enculturation: Political disenchantment and civic attitudes in minority schools in Estonia, Latvia, and Slovakia'. *European Education*, 42(4): 49–68.

Giroux, H. & Purpel, D. (eds), (1983). *The Hidden Curriculum and Moral Education*. Berkeley, CA: McCutchan Publishing Corporation.

Grabane, S. (2012). Bilingual education in Latvia: Current trends and future developments. *The Annual of Language & Politics and Politics of Identity*, 6: 1–10.

Grigule, L. & Pavula, I. (1998). *The integration of students in the family, school, and society: The role of teachers*. Paper delivered at a conference organized by the Riga University of Pedagogy and Educational Leadership, Riga, Latvia.

Hazans, M., Trapeznikova, I. & Rastrigina, O. (2010). 'Ethnic and parental effects on schooling outcomes before and during the transition: Evidence from the Baltic countries'. *Journal of Population Economics*, 21(3): 719–49.

Jurgena, I., Mikainis, Z. & Kevisa, I. (2012). 'The potential for bilingual education to help integrate ethnic minority communities within Latvian multicultural society', in P. Cunningham & N. Fretwell (eds), *Creating Communities: Local, National and Global*. London: CiCe, 145–52.

Karklins, R. (1998). 'Ethnic integration and school policies in Latvia'. *Nationalities Papers*, 26(2): 283–302.

Karklins, R. (2004). *Ethnopolitics and Transition to Democracy: The Collapse of the USSR and Latvia*. Washington, DC: Woodrow Wilson Center Press.

Krupnikova, M. (2004). *Diversity in Latvian Textbooks*. Riga, Latvia: Latvian Center for Human Rights and Ethnic Studies.

Language Law (1999). Translated by Translation and Terminology Centre. Available at www.valoda.lv (accessed on 10 May 2014).

Lindemann, K. (2011). *School Performance in Linguistically Divided Educational Systems: A Study of the Russian-Speaking Minority in Estonia and Latvia* [Working Paper Nr. 143]. Mannheim: Mannheimer Zentrum für Europäische Sozialforschung (MZES).

Mead, M. A. & Silova, I. (2013). 'Literacies of (post)socialist childhood: Alternative readings of socialist upbringings and neoliberal regimes'. *Globalization, Societies, Education*, 11(2): 194–222.

Ministry of Education and Science of the Republic of Latvia. (1998). *Education Law*. Riga, Latvia: Ministry of Education and Science.

Ministry of Education and Science of the Republic of Latvia. (2003). *Valsts pamatizglītības standartam un valsts vispārējās vidējās izglītības standartam atbilstošu mācību līdzekļu—Mācību grāmatu apstiprināšanas nolikums. [Policy regarding state general education standards and guidelines for school textbook evaluation based on the state standards]*. Approved on May 12, 2003, decision Nr. 213. Riga, Latvia: Ministry of Education and Science.

Ministry of Education and Science. (2005). *General education: Statistical data*. Riga, Latvia: Ministry of Education and Science. [Online]. Available at www.izm.lv.

Ministry of Foreign Affairs of the Republic of Latvia. (2014). *Social Integration Fund*. [Online]. Available at http://www.mfa.gov.lv/en/policy/4641/4642/4649/fund/ (accessed on 10 May 2014).

Muižnieks N. (ed.). (2010). *How Integrated is Latvian Society? An Audit of Achievements, Failures and Challenges*. Riga, Latvia: University of Latvia Press.

National program "Integration of Society in Latvia" (1999). [Online]. Available at http://www.am.gov.lv/en/?id=4645 (accessed on 10 May 2014).

Open Society Institute. (1997). *Estonia and Latvia: Citizenship, language and conflict prevention* [A special Report by the Forced Migration Projects]. New York, NY: Open Society Institute.

Paegle, Dz. (1997). *Vards: Lasama gramata un ievadijums valodas maciba 1*. klasei [Word: A reading book and an introduction to language learning for the first grade]. Riga: Zvaigzne.

Priedite, A. (2005). 'Surveying language attitudes and practices in Latvia'. *Journal of Multilingual and Multicultural Development*, 26(5), 409–24.

Saiema (1999). *State language law*. [Online]. Available at http://www.minelres.lv/ NationalLegislation/Latvia/Latvia_Language_English.htm (accessed on 10 May 2014).

Silova, I. (1996). 'De-Sovietization of Latvian textbooks made visible'. *European Journal of Intercultural Studies*, 7(2), 35–46.

Silova, I. (2004). 'Adopting the language of the new allies', in G. Steiner-Khamsi (ed.), *The Global Politics of Educational Borrowing*. New York, NY: Teachers College Press, 75–87.

Silova, I. (2006). *From Sites of Occupation to Symbols of Multiculturalism: Re-conceptualizing Minority Education in Post-Soviet Latvia*. Greenwich, CT: Information Age Publishing.

Silova, I. (2009). 'Varieties of educational transformation: The post-socialist states of Central/Southeastern Europe and the former Soviet Union', in R. Cowen & A. Kazamias (eds), *International Handbook of Comparative Education*. the Netherlands: Springer Publishers, 295–320.

UNDP (1995). *Latvia Human Development Report*. Riga, Latvia: United Nations Development Program.

UNDP (1996). *Latvia Human Development Report*. Riga, Latvia: United Nations Development Program.

Vēbers, El. (1994). *The Ethnic Situation in Latvia: Facts and Commentary*. Riga, Latvia: Ethnic Study Center, Institute of Philosophy and Sociology.

Zepa, B. (2010). 'Education for social integration', in N. Muižnieks (ed.), *How Integrated is Latvian Society? An Audit of Achievements, Failures and Challenges*. Riga, Latvia: University of Latvia Press, 189–222.

Zepa, B., Lāce, I., Kļave, E., Šūpule, I. (2006). *The Aspect of Culture in the Social Inclusion of Ethnic Minorities: Final Report Latvia*. Flensburg, Germany: European Centre for Minority Issues (ECMI).

8

Lithuania: Education Policy and Reforms, 1988–2014

Rimantas Zelvys

Introduction

At the time of the Soviet rule, opportunities for the independent policy making in Lithuanian education were practically non-existent. The turning point appeared to be the years when the Soviet President M. Gorbachev initiated the so-called *perestroika* movement in the Soviet Union. Orientation towards democratization of society and loosening ideological restraints stimulated the first practical attempts to renovate Lithuanian education. The newly emerging Lithuanian education policy was marked by 'The Concept of the National School', which was developed in 1988. Thus the year 1988 can be considered as the starting point of educational transformations in the country. Lithuania claimed full independence from the Soviet Union in 1990, and in 1991 the first Law on Education in newly independent Lithuania was adopted. Sociopolitical and economical transformations of late 1980s and early 1990s were rapid, and the course of educational reforms was hasty and rather unpredictable. Initial attempts of national policy makers were aimed at de-ideologization and gradual decentralization of education.

During the early stages of educational changes, the search for new landmarks of newly emerging education policy has taken two main directions: 'returning to the roots' and 'borrowing from abroad'. Adoption of the 'General Concept of Education in Lithuania' in 1992 marked the end of the initial period of spontaneous transformations and the start of the first phase of systemic educational reform, which was mainly focused on changes in structure and contents of studies. The priorities of the second phase of the educational reform, which started in 1998, were much more pragmatic and economically grounded. During the second phase, such important initiatives as optimization of the school network, introduction of a national examination, formula funding of schools, reforming of the non-university sector of higher education, and so on, have been launched. The next phase was adoption of the strategy for the development of Lithuanian education system for the years 2003–12. After Lithuania joined the European Union in 2004, implementation of the Lisbon Strategy and the detailed work programme on the follow-up of the objectives of education and training systems in Europe evoked new developments of educational policy. Perhaps the most significant changes during the recent years happened in higher education, with the increased participation in the Bologna process, adoption of a new Law on Studies and Research in 2009 and introduction of the principle 'money follows the student' in Lithuanian higher education sector. The newly elected parliament on December 2012 approved a new government programme where further changes, for example reforming the principles of formula funding for schools and partial revision of funding higher education, are envisaged. The National Innovation Development Programme 2014-2020 issued by the Ministry of Education and Science in December 2013 set out a programme of modernisation of education policy and practice and represents a new direction for Lithuanian society by determining educational change in the country for the next decade.

Development of education policy in Lithuania

An independent state before the Second World War, Lithuania lost its independence in 1940, and since then its national education has continued to exist as an integral part of a unified and highly centralized Soviet educational system. All major decisions concerning changes in curriculum, assessment and examination, educational legislation, teacher training and educational structure were made by the central Soviet government, outside of the national education system. The national education system had a rather limited autonomy, which was manifested mainly by using the Lithuanian language of instruction in national schools and having an eleven-year-long general secondary education (whereas in Russia general secondary education lasted ten years). The extra year was needed because of the expanded curriculum, which included additional teaching of the national language, history, arts and literature. Under these circumstances, opportunities for independent policy making in Lithuanian education were practically non-existent: even the curricula of national language had to be approved in Moscow. Centralization and unification of the educational system was even more reinforced by the strict ideological control.

However, historical and cultural differences that distinguished the Baltic states from the rest of the Soviet Union were evident in many areas of social life, including education. Lithuanian institutions of higher education, which, differently from most of the other Soviet republics, maintained Lithuanian language as the main language of instruction, were always more liberal and West oriented, especially in the field of social sciences and humanities. University libraries were continuously updated thanks to numerous donations of the Lithuanians living abroad, mainly in the United States. Peculiarities of Lithuanian history were rather openly discussed in general secondary schools, as many teachers and parents of the older generation still remembered the years of independence and Soviet occupation in 1940. When economical hardships struck the Soviet Union in the early 1980s, the need for change was increasingly evident in all three Baltic states.

The turning point appeared to be the year 1985, when M. Gorbachev initiated the so-called perestroika movement in the Soviet Union. Attempts at democratization and loosening of ideological restraints stimulated the first practical attempts to renovate Lithuanian education. At the beginning, the newly emerging Lithuanian policy makers of the perestroika era dreamed about a greater autonomy within the reformed Union of Soviet Republics. The most prominent policy paper of that time was 'The Concept of the National School' (Pedagogikos Mokslinio Tyrimo Institutas, 1989). The main purpose of this initiative was further preservation of national language and culture; therefore, the leading theme of the document was an independent national curriculum and moderate decentralization of management of the national education systems within the existing federal state. The Concept was first presented in Moscow and met a mainly negative response from central Soviet educational authorities. However, the situation was changing very rapidly. The Concept of the National School in the newly reformed Soviet Union soon lost its relevance, as Lithuania claimed full independence on 11 March 1990. Later this year, the newly established Ministry of Education and Culture started the process of transformation of the national education system.

Initial attempts of national policy makers were aimed at de-ideologization of education as well as gradual decentralization and liberalization of the educational system. The first significant changes in education management were reflected in the Law on Education, adopted in 1991. The law granted educational institutions and local educational authorities more rights and introduced bodies of self-government, which were practically non-existent in Lithuanian schools during the Soviet times. The Law also introduced an element of choice by allowing a variety of state-owned schools (e.g. general secondary schools and gymnasiums) as well as private educational institutions.

The period 1988–90 comprised the initial phase of development of an independent educational policy. During that time, the necessary preparatory steps were taken to define a theoretical and conceptual framework for education reform; the years 1990–92 mark the first practical steps towards implementing these changes. The first reform efforts mainly correspond to what Birzea (1996) calls corrective reforms, which imply an immediate correction of the most visible characteristics of the Soviet-type education. In addition to corrective reforms, reforms of curriculum content started to gain momentum, mainly with the assistance of the foreign partners.

An extremely important step was the adoption of the General Concept of Education in Lithuania in 1992 (Ministry of Culture and Education of the Republic of Lithuania, 1994). This Concept partially retained the ideas of the Concept of the National School; however, now its main aim was not securing the autonomy of the national culture, but creating a modern school in a newly independent state. The Concept declared the main principles of Lithuanian education to be humanism, democracy, renewal, commitment to Lithuanian culture and the preservation of its identity and historic continuity. It also described the structure of the educational system, the system of teacher training, and principles of governing and financing as well as maintenance of the educational process. Finally, the Concept also specified aims and objectives for the educational reform until the end of the year 1997.

The General Concept of Education in Lithuania was a substantial step forward when compared with the Concept of the National School, as it was a much more forward-looking and mature policy document. The OECD experts who reviewed Lithuania's national policy in education acknowledged that it was by far the most important and influential document from the early stages of reform: 'The Concept has proven remarkably robust and remains the foundation of education reform and legislation' (OECD, 2002: 40). However, embedded in the Concept were also certain contradictions which posed further challenges for successful implementation of educational policy in Lithuania, namely:

• The Concept was approved later than the Law on Education. In order to implement ideas reflected in the Concept, the Law on Education had to undergo a number of amendments in 1993, 1994, 1995 and 1998.

- The Concept set landmarks for further development of general, vocational and higher education; however, the Law on Research and Higher Education was adopted in 1991, which granted wide autonomy to institutions of higher education. The further development of higher education sector went on independently and not always in accordance with ideas reflected in the Concept.

- The Concept mainly described the structure of new educational system; in this sense the Concept was promoting and encouraging structural changes in education. Priorities, main directions of educational policy and implementation strategies were not clearly defined. This led to different interpretations of the Concept during the stages of its practical implementation.

During the early stages of educational reform the search for new landmarks of newly emerging educational policy, like in many other Central and Eastern European countries, has taken two main directions: 'returning to the roots' and 'borrowing from abroad' (Anweiler, 1992). The first was directed towards restoration of the pre-communist system of education that existed before the Second World War. The other tried to copy separate segments of the currently existing education systems of the Western countries. It was to a certain extent an expression of the 'national' and 'cosmopolitan' orientations of policy makers. Perhaps the most vivid example of the first direction was the attempts made to restore elite gymnasiums and introduce the system of early differentiation and selection. The tendency was noticeable throughout the whole of Eastern and Central Europe. In particular, Phillips and Kaser (1992), in their review of the initial stage of reforms in post-communist countries, pointed out the nostalgic attachment of Eastern European politicians to the 'old Austrian Gymnasium'. Examples of the second direction were manifested by borrowing ready-made models of schools from other countries (e.g. the idea of youth schools for students with low learning motivation was 'imported' from Denmark; the dual system of general and vocational schools, from Germany, etc.). However, this tendency was most evident during the first half of the last decade. Eventually, the education policy became more independent both from historical sentiments and contemporary foreign influences.

On the other hand, the initial ideas of decentralizing and liberalizing education started to lose momentum. In 1994, a new administrative reform was carried out, dividing the country into ten regions and establishing regional educational authorities. The policy makers in education had to decide which functions to delegate to these authorities. There were basically two ways to approach this task. The first was to transfer a part of the functions that had earlier belonged to the central authorities to the regional level, thereby further decentralizing control over education. The second was to hand over certain functions of local educational authorities to the regional level. The policy makers at that time were not ready for a more fundamental decentralization and chose the second option. A new administrative reform was the turning point, leading in fact to a partial re-centralization of education. This did not go unnoticed by international researchers, who wrote about transformations in Central and Eastern Europe: 'It can happen, that a country starts to move to one direction and at a point shifts to another one. This was the case in Lithuania, where in 1994 the results of the initial decentralization to the municipal level were reversed, and educational management was concentrated to regions, in which autonomy is constrained' (Rado, 2001: 66–67).

In the fall of 1995, the OECD experts on education visited Lithuania as well as a number of other Central and Eastern European countries. Indeed, these visits constituted the first thorough external outlook at the processes going on in Lithuanian education after the fall of communism. Experts stated, 'There is a strong conceptual foundation for reforms, but a continuing gap exists between concepts and the reality of implementation' (OECD, 1996: 81). According to the OECD team, the country faced the 'challenge of implementing nation-wide policies … across regions and schools with widely varying sizes, economic conditions and availability of qualified teachers' (OECD, 1996: 81). Experts stressed a need for a new system of standards and assessment in order to evaluate the status of educational attainment from a comparative perspective and to assess individual student performance and certification. They also acknowledged a need to strengthen the general secondary education system, including gymnasiums, in a period of stable if not declining enrolment— including achieving more effective economies of scale in secondary schools. Experts admitted, '… efficient administration, using modern financial and management procedures, is required' (OECD, 1996: 81). They warned that slow reforms in pre-service teacher education appeared to have a dampening effect on the changes in curriculum and in teacher preparation for changes at the general secondary level. Most of the observations of the OECD experts revealed just the shortcomings of which the reformers in Lithuania were well aware themselves. Many of the recommended developments were already under way. However, the OECD report provided an additional impetus for change, as it showed that Lithuanian reformers are basically on the right track.

The accomplishments of the 1997 reforms

The end of the first phase of the reform in 1997 highlighted both successes and shortcomings of the national education policy during the initial period of transformations. A number of changes can undoubtedly be named as positive consequences of the initial phase of the reform, namely:

1. Revised and renewed curriculum.

Renovating curriculum and rewriting of the textbooks was one of the first challenges which educational leaders had to face after political changes, especially in the field of social sciences and humanities. An opportunity opened to update curriculum contents and, what is even more important, to offer students and educators the possibility of choice. Curriculum reform enabled teachers to create individual syllabi and granted the schools the right to develop school-based curriculum while also following the core curriculum decided at the national level. At the same time, alternative textbooks for the same subject in the same grades emerged—both those written by national authors and those translated from foreign languages. The processes of integrating and differentiating curriculum began to take place. Interdisciplinary integration allowed students to gain a more holistic view of the field of studies, while also differentiating among curriculum contents enabled to meet the individual needs of students in a more effective way. Students with special needs gained an opportunity to study in the mainstream schools, and the rest of the students were granted a chance to study the taught subjects at different levels—B (basic), A (advanced) and S (specialized).

2. Diversified and, to a certain extent, decentralized the system of education.

As a result of the changes, the traditional unified secondary schools were transformed into a variety of different types and models of schools. To mention just a few of them, some primary (grades 1–4) schools and gymnasiums (grades 9–12) emerged as separate structural entities. Youth schools for students with low learning motivation were established. Because of the declining number of students (especially in the countryside), some secondary schools were transformed into basic schools (grades 1–10). Some specialized gymnasiums were opened by institutions of higher education (technical university, pedagogical university, etc.). A number of non-state (private and denominational) schools were established. New schools for national minorities emerged. Besides the already existing schools with predominantly Russian and Polish language of instruction, other schools such as schools for Byelorussian, German and Jewish children, started to operate. As a result of partial decentralization, schools received greater autonomy. Schools boards were established that included representation on equal grounds of students, parents and teachers. School boards make decisions concerning school-based curriculum, resource allocation and so on. School principals also acquired more decision-making powers. Schools gained a possibility to have an account in the bank and to manage their own resources. Students and parents were granted a right to choose a school they would like to attend.

3. New principles of assessing student achievement.

There were several major changes in this field. First of all, it was decided to give up grading in primary school (grades 1–4). Instead, teachers provide parents with more detailed information about strengths and weaknesses of their children's learning and the scope of their progress. Second, students in basic and upper secondary grades were assessed according to a 10-point scale. Third, which is perhaps the most important part of the assessment reform, a system of national examinations was initiated. According to the project, students were supposed to take two centrally administered national exams (Lithuanian language and mathematics) while finishing basic school (grade 10). Those wishing to continue studies in institutions of higher education were to take up to five national exams by the end of the upper secondary school. One of these (Lithuanian language) was an obligatory one, whereas the other exams were optional. These exams were acknowledged by institutions of higher education as entrance exams. Students who were not interested in continuation of their studies in universities could take school-based exams, which were administered locally (Bethel and Zabulionis, 2000).

4. Reformed system of teacher training and appraisal.

Initial teacher training was partially decentralized, and a number of universities started training teachers, although Vilnius Pedagogical University has retained its leading position as the main teacher training institution. The contents and the structure of studies were revised, and the two-level model of studies was introduced (four years of study for the bachelor's degree and up to two years for a master's). The master's degree is usually considered an advantage if teachers wish to work in upper secondary education. The former highly centralized system of in-service training with just one National In-Service Teacher Training Institute was dismantled, and a number of in-service training centres were opened by universities, local and regional educational authorities, non-governmental organizations and so on. A new system of teacher and head-teacher appraisal was introduced. Teachers and school heads who acquired higher qualifications could get a certain increase in salary and were in a more favourable situation when competing for vacant teaching positions.

Negative aspects of reform

However, large-scale transformations almost inevitably have non-predicted, contradictory or just straightforwardly negative consequences. Lithuanian education is no exception in this case. During the first phase of the reform a number of negative aspects of educational transformation emerged:

1. The number of dropouts during the last decade increased radically.

Because of the less centralized and more liberal system of education, a number of students for various reasons did not come to school or left school in the early stages of education. About 97 per cent of students who entered the first grade finished the primary school, but only 77 per cent of the students received the school-leaving certificate from the basic (ten-year) school (Lietuvos Respublikos Svietimo ir Mokslo Ministerija, 2001). Rather vague possibilities existed for dropouts to continue their studies later on in order to get secondary and higher education. However, some opportunities to continue education were provided by youth schools and schools for adult learners.

2. Social stratification of post-communist society reflected itself in further differentiation of educational institutions.

A number of prestigious academically oriented upper secondary schools (i.e. gymnasiums) emerged, especially in larger cities. Although usually there were no formal selection procedures to enter gymnasiums, it was evident that informal selection was taking place. The social status and economic capabilities of families started to play a considerable role in the process of informal selection. Private educational institutions, which required payment of fees, also added to the further social stratification of the young generation. In contrast to private schools and academic gymnasiums, general and vocational schools in the underprivileged city areas and in the countryside started to decline in quality.

3. Because of the economic difficulties of the transitory period, the shortage of
   resources started to influence the quality of education.

Building of new schools slowed down considerably, and renovation of the
existing ones became a real problem. Funds for teaching materials and textbooks
were not sufficient, so parents often have to buy textbooks for their children
and donate money for upkeep of the school as well as for teaching equipment.
Computerization of schools was still another challenge, with schools trailing far
below the average for the European Union and even some of the neighbouring
countries in transition. For example, in 1996, the national average was one
computer for ninety-nine students in general secondary schools (in 2002, it
was one computer for twenty-five students) (Lietuvos Respublikos Svietimo ir
Mokslo Ministerija, 2003).

4. Social transformations affected the teaching force of the country.

Because of the relatively low teachers' salaries part of qualified specialists have
left for better-paid jobs. Most clearly this tendency showed up in such fields
as foreign languages and computer science. Young people did not consider
teaching profession as an attractive career opportunity, therefore from 30 per
cent to 60 percent of graduates of pedagogical university and pedagogical
faculties of other institutions of higher education found other jobs outside the
system of education (Mokslo ir Studiju Departamentas prie Svietimo ir Mokslo
Ministerijos, 2002). On the other hand, because of weak social guarantees and
low retirement pensions, old teachers were reluctant to leave their working
places, so in general the teaching force was getting older each year. As a rule the
older teachers were computer illiterate and were not aware of modern methods
of teaching and learning.

5. The declining birth rate raised the problem of effectiveness of the existing
   school network.

It became increasingly expensive to maintain small rural schools with
constantly declining number of students. Some of the schools inevitably had to
be closed down. However, it raised a number of technical problems, for example
transporting children to other schools, as well as social ones, for example
teachers and supporting staff losing their jobs. Local communities were arguing
strongly in favour of keeping the schools open, as the school quite often is the
only source of cultural activity in rural areas. Similar problems arose with
national minority schools. Schools with Russian language instruction began

to lose a considerable number of students as many Russian-speaking families favoured Lithuanian schools for their children. However, closing down national minority schools inevitably becomes politically sensitive, and politicians were extremely reluctant to make such decisions, so the number of students in Russian schools continued to decline even as the Lithuanian schools became overcrowded.

Those and other problems forced a rethinking of main policy directions and highlighted new educational priorities. In 1998, after the first phase of the reform came to an end, the Ministry of Education and Science worked out new landmarks for educational policy and pointed out three major priorities for the second phase of the reform:

- Modernization of studies and instruction and raising the quality of education
- Improvement of social and pedagogical conditions of learning and instruction
- Harmonization of the educational system

These priorities inspired the main policy steps taken from the year 1998 onwards. Educational researchers (Rimkeviciene, 1998) admit that priorities of the second phase of the reform are much more pragmatic and economically grounded when compared with highly inspirational visions of the 1992 General Concept of Education. Although during the period of 1992–98 reforms mainly concentrated on changes of structures and contents of education, the years 1998–2003 may be seen as the start of a truly systemic reform, which, according to Guthrie and Koppich (1993), is meant to evoke shifts in key areas of the education system. At least several reasons can be named for such change in educational policy:

- The 1998 Russian economic crisis, which heavily affected Lithuanian economy and forced to cut state funding for the social sector;
- Recommendations from international organizations, namely, the OECD and the World Bank, whose experts warned that Lithuania is still running an extensive and not cost-effective education system;
- Increased participation in international educational programmes and projects, which usually imply accurate budgeting procedures; and
- The growing pragmatism and economic awareness of national policy makers.

International influences

The priority of modernising and raising the quality of education implied the creation of national educational standards, further development of curriculum and textbooks, establishment of a national examination centre and introduction of national *Matura* examinations, participation in international comparatives studies (e.g. Trends in International Mathematics and Science Study (TIMMS)), creating the system of monitoring education, modernization of school libraries, computerization of schools and so on.

The priority of improving social and pedagogical conditions implied creating better access to secondary and higher education for students with special needs, representatives of national minorities, children from socially vulnerable families, young people in military service, adult learners and so forth.

The priority of harmonization of educational system implied strengthening links between general and vocational education as well as general and higher education, creating a more effective system of financing education, optimizing the school network, encouraging self-governance of educational institutions, assuring greater involvement of NGOs in the education sector, expanding international cooperation and so on.

Major reforms were initiated in several main directions. The most important reform steps undertaken were the following:

- Reform of the national examination system;
- Reform of educational financing and introducing the policy 'money follows the student';
- Differentiation of learning in upper secondary education by introducing optional educational profiles (sciences, humanities, arts, technology);
- Structural reform of general secondary education by introducing a ten-year basic education and structurally separating primary, basic and upper secondary schools (gymnasiums); and
- Optimization of the school network by closing down or consolidating schools with diminishing numbers of students and launching a programme of school buses.

In the midst of the new wave of the reforms, in the fall of 1999 the second OECD team undertook a mission to Lithuania. It produced the most comprehensive so far, Review of National Policies for Education in Lithuania (OECD, 2002). The review in general was positive. Experts admitted that 'Lithuania has

made significant progress in education reform since regaining independence'
(OECD, 2002: 265). They also stated that 'progress has been greatly aided by
broad consensus agreed [upon] among the country's leaders about the basic
goals of the 1992 General Concept of Education' (OECD, 2002; 265). Experts
supported most of the reform steps undertaken by Lithuanian policy makers
but at the same time warned about existing potential dangers. In particular,
they pointed out that changing to a policy of 'money follows the student' would
not alone be sufficient to provide the incentives and support for necessary
changes. The experts did not endorse an approach to optimization of the school
network that emphasizes only the efficiencies to be achieved without giving
full consideration to the educational implications and the potential impact on
people and communities. They also recommended a review of the implications
of profiling, especially the feasibility of introducing it in small rural schools
and the risk that even in the large urban schools students might find that
they cannot choose subjects 'across profiles'. Perhaps the most positive aspect
was the experts' evaluation of national examination reform. They stated that
the 'National Examination Center has done a remarkable job in improving
the reliability, validity and comparability of examinations, especially at the
important school/university interface' (OECD, 2002: 109). However, they
also pointed out the necessity of ensuring further support to the National
Examination Centre in order to safeguard its sustainability and ability to cope
with new demands.

One of the main concerns expressed in the report was about management
of education. Experts admitted that since Soviet times Lithuania has made
significant progress in decentralizing the education system. However, they
recommended that the state continue to realign the roles and responsibilities
at all levels of the education system to support a more decentralized, responsive
and accountable school and institutional network. Experts urged eliminating
the centralized inspection and control of the Soviet times, and to move
towards monitoring and supporting schools and holding schools and teachers
accountable for performance. They also acknowledged the need for increasing
the leadership and management skills at the level of schools and institutions
to assume increased responsibility. The OECD experts based their conclusions
and recommendations on the fact that the Ministry of Education and Science
remains the key state institution responsible for education policy in Lithuania.
Currently the Ministry is increasingly focusing on overall policy, standards
and monitoring, whereas oversight and management functions are gradually
delegated to the counties and municipalities. County educational authorities

bear responsibility for inspection and monitoring quality, in-service training and teacher appraisal, and local educational authorities are responsible for preschool and general secondary education. The system of national monitoring is in the final stages of development, and concise reports on education are published each year (Ministry of Education and Science of the Republic of Lithuania, 2003). After completion of the overall monitoring system, the Ministry claimed to delegate more of its powers to local and school levels. The Ministry's Department of Educational Strategy intends to play an increasingly important role in coordinating the activities of a more autonomous system of educational institutions. However, the process was moving more slowly than education policy makers had expected.

National policy makers took into account recommendations expressed in the second OECD review. Reforms underwent certain amendments as well as improvements, and by the summer 2002 the national examination and the differentiation, or 'profiling', reforms were more or less successfully implemented. The 'money follows the student' reform underwent a long preparation phase and at last started on January 2002. It was partially modified, and currently the money for the process of learning (teachers' salaries, textbooks, in-service training, etc.) is distributed according to the system 'money follows the student', whereas funding of the learning environment (school maintenance, heating, electricity, etc.) is still allocated in a traditional way. Structural reforms started but slowed down because of a lack of school premises as well as because of parental dissatisfaction. The most painful was the process of optimizing the school network. Closing down or consolidating small schools, especially in the countryside, is always a very sensitive political issue. Local politicians usually try to avoid making such unpopular decisions, so the optimization process seems to have become a complicated and long-lasting endeavour.

Development in the education sector gradually became one of the priorities of state policy. Educational researchers, in particular Rado (2001), observe that Lithuania is one of the few Central and Eastern European countries where educational funding eventually increased. Public expenditure on education as a percentage of gross domestic product (GDP) in Lithuania presented a rather stable tendency towards growth during the previous decade (from 5.6 per cent in 1994 to 6.5 percent in 1999). It decreased slightly during the 2000s and currently is about 5.9 per cent (Statistics Lithuania, 2012). The indicator is higher than the EU average, which is about 5 per cent.

Developments after 2000

With the start of the new millennium, the need for a new Education Law became ever more evident, as it was becoming increasingly difficult to institutionalize rapid changes that are going on in education by just making further amendments to the old Law. The project of the new Law on Education was prepared in the fall of the year 2001, and after public discussions, was adopted by the Parliament on June 2003. The new Law could have provided expanded possibilities and given additional impetus for further reforming management of the education system. However, from this author's viewpoint, the project hasn't seemed to evoke significant developments. Both local and international experts, who made an evaluation of the Law at the request of the Open Society Fund–Lithuania (Budiene et al., 2002), have agreed with this conclusion. A new Law doesn't foresee any decisive steps towards further decentralization. On the contrary, it frames Lithuanian education as a relatively centralized system where most powers are concentrated on a national level, state inspection is strong and schools are granted a rather limited freedom of managing resources and curriculum. In fact the new Law continues the administrative policy which started in 1994 and is aimed more at legalizing the changes that have already occurred than at inspiring the new ways of managing schools.

In this sense, a much more provocative policy document is a strategy for the development of the Lithuanian education system for the years 2003–12. The strategy was prepared by the working group formed by the president of the Republic of Lithuania in 1999. OECD experts acknowledged during their mission in 1999 that the presidential institution plays a special role in developing national educational policy. President Valdas Adamkus closely followed developments in education, and his adviser for social policy was the former first Minister of Education of the newly independent Lithuanian Republic. By this the president strived to secure the continuity and sustainability of educational reform. Though originally the working group was supposed to present a draft strategy by the end of 1999, eventually it took more than three years, and finally the strategy was presented to the public in October 2002. At last the strategy was approved by the Parliament on July 2003. The initial intention of the presidential group was first to develop a strategy and then to proceed to a new Education Law. Contrary to expectations, the development of the strategy document took more time than was expected, and therefore the situation of 1991–92 was repeated again: first came the Law and then the strategy.

The strategy aimed at further decentralization of Lithuanian education. It urged the Ministry of Education and science to delegate responsibility to regional and local educational authorities not only for general education but also for special, vocational and adult education. The strategy also invited to start a reform of educational inspection. Inspection should be gradually replaced by external audit, information analysis and consulting systems. On the other hand, Ministry of Education and Science was encouraged to concentrate on:

- Improving management and leadership;
- Setting the standards and requirements for general, vocational and higher education;
- Ensuring access and equity in education; and
- Quality assurance and public relations.

In 2004, Lithuania became a member of the European Union. Though the strategy for the development of the Lithuanian education system for the years 2003–12 was mainly developed as a response to the recommendations of the OECD experts, its realization eventually had also to be adjusted to the common European policy goals. In this respect, the implementation of the Lisbon strategy and the detailed work programme on the follow-up of the objectives of education and training systems in Europe became on of the landmarks of Lithuanian education policy. The Ministry of Education and Science tried to follow both tracks and concentrated on monitoring of the implementation of both strategies. Thus in 2008, an intermediate report was published about a proposed strategy to be implemented within five years. The authors of the report linked recommendations of the OECD experts with the goals of the strategy and demonstrated that reforms in general were implemented along the strategy lines. Simultaneously, the report about the implementation of the detailed work programme on the follow-up of the objectives of education and training systems in Europe was presented. The report stated that the 2003–12 strategy incorporated all the landmarks and indicators of the detailed work programme, namely, reducing the number of early school dropouts, increasing the number of students in the area of science and technologies and the persons with secondary education, improving literacy skills, ensuring the lifelong learning of the working-age population. Bologna process was yet another development which influenced Lithuanian education policy. In 2004, the Minister of Education and Science formed a working group for the implementation of Bologna process. The work towards implementation of the Bologna goals resulted in adoption of a new law on study and research in 2009, where all the Bologna principles were finally legitimized. Lithuania continued to take active participation in international comparative studies. The results of the studies are also considered as important landmarks for further development of Lithuanian education policy.

The major political challenge was the higher education reform, which started in 2009 with the adoption of the new Law on Studies and Research. The reform was aimed at changing the legal status of higher educational institutions, governance of universities and principles of funding. Although changing the legal status from state enterprise to public enterprise did not evoke many contradictions, changes in university governance inspired more heated discussions. According to the new Law, most of the powers, including the power to elect Rectors, were transferred from the internal Senate to the partially external university board. There aim was to make universities more open and accountable to the public; however, there were fears that partially external boards will become agents of political influence imposed on universities. The first years of the reform showed that the governance reform did not change the life of academic communities as much as it was expected. The most contradictory was the funding reform as it introduced the principle 'money follows the student'. With the new system, school graduates, who, according to the results of the national examination, are entitled to state funding, may choose the higher education institution and the study programme, and thus the funding of institutions depends on the number of students they manage to attract. If a student decides to change institution, the money also follows the student. The rationale was that higher education institutions will have to compete for students and thus will make more efforts to increase the quality of the studies. However, the first years of reform showed that students prefer to choose the most popular, and not necessarily the highest quality, programmes in the universities of big cities. The victims of the reform were regional universities and specialized higher education institutions, which had no attractive programmes to offer, for example agricultural universities, veterinary academies or academies of physical training. Currently, the model is being modified by introducing state grants for the most needed, but not popular, specialties.

A new version of the Education Law was adopted by the Parliament in 2011; however, the Law did not introduce any significant changes in the area of general secondary education. The results of the implementation of the 2003–12 strategy are still under discussion. The prevailing opinion is that, in general, the strategic goals were achieved, though some of the priorities were reconsidered or lost their actuality. Political changes in the country also led to certain amendments to the process of implementation strategy. In December 2012, the newly elected Parliament approved a new government programme where further changes, for example reforming the principles of formula funding for schools, are envisaged. The task of the new government will also be to approve the Lithuanian education strategy for the years 2013–22.

Concluding remarks

Lithuanian education policy underwent an extremely intense phase of development during the last quarter of the century. Almost non-existent during the Soviet years, it started from the Concept of the National School in 1988, which claimed greater autonomy within the reformed Soviet Union. The 1992 General Concept of Education marked the end of the first phase of the education reform and was in fact the first strategic policy document of the newly independent state. It was strongly focused on structural transformations and promoted values of a newly emerging post-totalitarian society: humanism, democracy and renewal. However, the process of transition evoked economical difficulties as well as non-predicted educational changes. The ongoing educational reform succeeded in revising curriculum and improving the system of assessment, diversifying education and renewing the training of teachers. On the other hand, the new socio-economical situation in the country increased the number of school dropouts and encouraged social stratification and differentiation of educational institutions; a shortage of resources and the quality of the teaching force started to raise serious concerns. The process of decentralization slowed down, and new priorities of educational policy had to be formulated. Priorities indicated for the second phase of the reform, which started in 1998, were the following: modernization and raising the quality of education, improving social and pedagogical conditions of learning and instruction, and harmonization of the educational system. The reform acquired a much more systemic nature, and the priorities of 1998 were formulated in a more pragmatic and economically grounded way than the highly inspirational Concept of 1992. Education gradually became one of the real priorities of the state, which is expressed by the growth of the percentage of GDP allocated to education. The percentage increased from 5.6 per cent in 1994 to 6.5 per cent in 1999, and currently is about 6 per cent. The strategy for the development of the Lithuanian education system for the years 2003–12 marked a new phase of development of Lithuanian education. Together with the Lisbon Strategy and the Bologna process, it framed a very clear landmark for further development. After formally accepting the Bologna principles as well as the indicators and standards worked out during the Lisbon Strategy, not very much room is left for local politicians to change the course of educational development. On the other hand, there are new interesting initiatives in the areas of funding and governance of higher education. Lithuanian education strategy for the years 2013–22 seems to be the most important document which will determine the development of the education policy of the country for the next decade.

References

Anweiler, O. (1992). 'Some Historical Aspects of Educational Change in the Former Soviet Union and Eastern Europe', in D. Phillips and M. Kaser (eds), *Education and Economic Change in Eastern Europe and Former Soviet Union*. Wallingford: Triangle Books, pp 29–39.

Bethel, G. and Zabulionis, A. (2000). *Examination Reform in Lithuania: Background, Strategies and Achievements*. Vilnius: National Examination Centre.

Birzea (1996). 'Educational reform and power struggle in Romania'. *European Journal of Education*, 31(1), 97–107.

Budiene, V. et al. (2002). *Svietimo Politikos Monitoringas: Lietuvos Respublikos Svietimo Istatymo Projekto Ekspertinis Vertinimas*. Vilnius: Knygiai.

Guthrie, J. W. and Koppich, J. E. (1993). 'Ready, A. I. M., reform: Building a model of education reform and "High Politics"', in H. Beare and W. L. Boyd (eds), *Restructuring Schools*. London: Falmer Press, 12–27.

Lietuvos Respublikos Svietimo ir Mokslo Ministerija. (2001). *Lietuvos svietimas 2000*. Vilnius: Pedagogu Profesines Raidos Centras.

Lietuvos Respublikos Svietimo ir Mokslo Ministerija. (2003). *Lietuvos svietimas 2002*. Vilnius: Zara.

Ministry of Culture and Education of the Republic of Lithuania. (1994). *General Concept of Education in Lithuania*. Vilnius: Leidybos Centras.

Ministry of Education and Science of the Republic of Lithuania. (2003). *Education in Lithuania 2001. Figures and Trends*. Vilnius: Svietimo Aprupinimo Centras.

Mokslo Ir Studiju Departamentas Prie Svietimo Ir Mokslo Ministerijos. (2002). *Pedagogu rengimo kokybe Lietuvos aukstosiose mokyklose ir ju isidarbinimo galimybes*. Vilnius: Mokslo ir Studiju Departamentas.

OECD. (1996). *Secondary Education Systems in PHARE Countries: Survey and Project Proposals*. Paris: OECD Publications.

OECD. (2002). *Reviews of National Policies for Education*. Lithuania, Paris: OECD Publications.

Pedagogikos Mokslinio Tyrimo Institutas. (1989). *Tautine mokykla (Mokyklu tipu koncepciju metmenys)*, 1 d. Kaunas: Sviesa.

Phillips, D. and Kaser, M. (1992). *Education and Economic Change in Eastern Europe and the Former Soviet Union*. Wallingford: Triangle Books.

Rado, P. (2012). *Transition in Education*. Budapest: The Open Society Institute.

Rimkeviciene, V. (1998). 'Education', in *Lithuanian Human Development Report*. Vilnius: UNDP, 89–100.

Statistics Lithuania. (2012). *Education 2011*. Vilnius: Statistics Lithuania.

World Bank. (2000). *Hidden Challenges to Education Systems in Transition Economies*. Washington, DC: The World Bank.

Zelvys, R. (1999). *Managing Education in a Period of Change*. Oslo: ELI Publishing.

9

Malta: An Overview of European Influences on Educational Reforms

Carmel Borg and Peter Mayo

Introduction

The islands forming the Maltese archipelago that together constitute the Republic of Malta have a long history of foreign domination and colonization. Malta achieved its formal independence from Britain in 1964, became a republic in 1974, witnessed the closure of the British military bases in 1979 and joined the European Union in 2004. Typical of small states (Bacchus, 2010: 143), its economy is a tertiary one, largely dependent on tourism and other services. Like other countries in Southern Europe, it has been experiencing the transition from having been a country of emigration to one of immigration. Malta is very much a frontier island with respect to North Africa and especially Libya, from where many migrants (many from Sub-Saharan Africa) have been attempting to cross over to Europe in search of a better life. As regards education, mass public provision was introduced after the Compulsory Education Ordinance of 1946 (Zammit Mangion, 1992). There were schools before this period, but they were not available to everyone.

This chapter reviews the preschool and compulsory educational provision and how the secondary and post-secondary education sectors have developed in recent years. It then outlines the development of adult and higher educational provisions and their expansion and enhancement, not least through European initiatives such as the Nice and Bologna Agreements.

Childcare centres

Growth in this sector is directly related to changes in the social and economic patterns of the country and, in the context of a growing welfare gap, to government's drive to encourage more women to join the workforce. Government childcare services are offered to children aged three months to three years. These centres offer a daily programme aimed at providing a holistic development for the child through a repertoire of play activities. The aforementioned centres also include personalized programmes for children at risk of social exclusion. Parents are means-tested, and fees are set according to income and frequency of use of service. The newly elected Labour Government has pledged universal, free day care to all prekindergarten children. Government childcare centres are managed by the Foundation for Educational Services (FES), a semi-autonomous, public institution charged with providing non-formal educational services. Government childcare centres and similar, privately owned facilities, conform to the National Standards for Child Day Care Facilities established in 2006.

Educational provision: Kindergarten education

Although the Catholic Church in Malta provided sporadic early childhood education as early as the late nineteenth century, the history of universal early-childhood and kindergarten education provision in Malta is relatively recent. In 1975, the then Labour government, acting on an electoral manifesto which promised universal, free kindergarten education on a voluntary basis from age 3 years 9 months to 5 years, opened kindergarten centres in every town and village in the Maltese islands. This political project, which started with kindergarten provision for 4-year-olds, was completed by the Nationalist Party, elected in 1987, with the provision of universal kindergarten education for 3-year-old children, starting from 1988. Around 94 per cent of kindergarten-age children are sent voluntarily, mainly to government-supported kindergarten centres and also to other fee-paying centres run by the private independent sector and by faith-based, mainly Catholic institutions.

With a few exceptions, most state kindergarten centres are located within the community and are generally attached to the local primary school. In the private sector, early-childhood spaces range from large private houses catering for kindergarten-aged children only to schools that provide early childhood and primary education and educational complexes that provide early childhood education as part of a comprehensive provision that includes secondary education.

Private, kindergarten and compulsory education provision increased significantly between 1987 and 1997, mainly because, as in 1984, Church schools introduced a ballot system that challenged the quasi-exclusive nature of the child population within the Catholic school system. Upwardly mobile parents seeking distinction pushed for private provision to avoid sending their children to public institutions.

Compulsory education

Compulsory education starts at age 5 years and ends at age 16. Free access to compulsory education is provided by the government through a college system. Led by a principal and administered through a College of Heads, each of the ten colleges is organized around a cluster of co-ed primary schools that feeds two gender-segregated, secondary schools. The college system was mainly introduced as part of a strategy to eliminate an elitist education system which streamed pupils as young as 9 years old. In addition to the elimination of early streaming, within the present, college-based system, benchmarking replaces the 11+ exam, and setting replaces the segregationist approach to secondary education, which was characterized by the physical separation of students through a tripartite secondary school system. The latter system rested on an 11+ exam as a gatekeeper.

Compulsory education is also provided by the Catholic Church, which offers this education for a voluntary donation, and by a private, independent-school sector which offers a comprehensive package against a fee.

Popularly perceived as the better of the three systems, the Catholic-school system follows the national curriculum framework, is largely segregationist in its gender policy and adopts a ballot system as a way of gatekeeping the huge demand for its services. Following the surrender of most of the Church's property, the Catholic-school system has been largely sponsored by the state.

The private-school system mostly provides alternative access to that of the Church and is generally co-educational in nature. Parents benefit from generous tax breaks. The private fee-paying sector receives a grant of 3 million Euros and state aid for support services in return for its adherence to the National Curriculum Framework

National curriculum framework

The Education Act of 1988 provided for a National Minimum Curriculum (Borg and Mayo, 2006). Two National Minimum Curriculum documents were published in 1989 and 1999 respectively. Recently, the Ministry of Education and

Employment published a 'National Curriculum Framework for All' (NCF). The December 2012 document is a 'policy instrument' covering implementation, monitoring and evaluation. It provides a 'reference' to centralized as well as school-based curricular action. It constitutes a 'living framework' that allows for ongoing adjustments during its implementation.

In the words of the same document, the NCF aims at: encouraging collaboration; sustaining 'individual attention'; providing quality time for social interaction and non-formal learning; helping educational leaders to rationalize content to ensure quality more than quantity; guaranteeing basic entitlement for all, defined as mastery of Maltese, English, Mathematics, a Science subject and Digital Literacy; promoting social justice and solidarity as key values in the development of Maltese society; guaranteeing the acquisition of formal qualifications; supporting educational leaders in implementing targets at classroom level; promoting excellence, commitment, responsibility, flexibility and entrepreneurship as key competencies for a reliable and competitive workforce; nurturing innovation; promoting cross-curricular, thematic, interdisciplinary and collaborative approaches to combat fragmentation and compartmentalization; promoting diverse pathways to learning; and privileging assessment procedures that value and assesses both the processes and the products of learning.

The NCF provides for three cycles of education: an Early Years Cycle (KG1, KG2, Yr.1 and Yr.2); the Junior School Years Cycle (Yr. 3 to Yr. 6); and the Secondary School Years Cycle (Yr. 7–Yr. 11). The Secondary School Years Cycle is further subdivided into a Lower Secondary Years Cycle (Yr. 7–Yr. 8) and a Senior Secondary School Years Cycle (Yr. 9–Yr. 11).

Based on pedagogies that promote observation, experimentation, trial and error, exposure to stimulating environments and highly contextualized settings, the curriculum experience of the Early Years Cycle is informed by a number of broad outcomes that foreground the development of: a strong sense of identity; positive self-image; social competence; effective communication; positive attitude towards learning; and engaged and confident learners. At the end of the Early Years cycle, all children's holistic development will be profiled.

Building on the experience acquired within the Early Years Cycle, the Junior Years Cycle aims to provide an integrated, cross-curricular experience that helps students develop their full potential as lifelong learners, through personal development, social engagement and economic productivity.

The learning areas of the Junior Year cycle include: Languages (Maltese and English); Mathematics; Science and Technology; Religious and Ethical Education;

Humanities; Education for Democracy; Visual and Performing Arts; and Health and Physical Education. The NCF specifies how much time is to be dedicated to each area – 30.0 per cent languages, 15.0 per cent Mathematics, 15.0 per cent Science and Technology, 5.0 per cent Health and Physical Education, 5.0 per cent Religious and Ethics Education, 10.0 per cent Humanities and Education for Democracy, 5.0 per cent Visual and Performing Arts, and 15.0 per cent School-Based choices. The percentages indicate a strong statement in favour of the traditional basic subjects (English, Maltese and Mathematics), a strong presence of Science and Technology, the confirmation of Catholic Religion as the supreme religion of the country, the low esteem accorded to the Visual and Performing Arts and the relative autonomy given to schools in curriculum development.

The Secondary Years Cycle confirms the core curriculum developed in the Junior Years. At the Lower Secondary level, curricular time is organized as follows: 30 per cent languages; 12.5 per cent Mathematics; 12.5 per cent Science and Technology; 5.0 per cent Health and Physical Education; 5.0 per cent Religious and Ethics Education; 10.0 per cent Humanities and Education for Democracy; 5.0 per cent Visual and Performing Arts; and 20.0 per cent School-Based Choices. At the Senior Secondary level, the percentage distribution of curriculum time remains largely the same, with minor adjustments – 30 per cent of the time languages, 12.5 per cent Mathematics, 12.5 per cent Science and Technology, 10.0 per cent Health and Physical Education, 10.0 per cent Religious and Ethics Education, Humanities and Education for Democracy and Visual and Performing Arts, and 25.0 per cent School-Based Choices.

At Secondary level, school-based curricular choices include a wide repertoire of subjects that schools are encouraged to offer—Accounts, Art, Business Studies, Computing, Design and Technology, Drama, Economics, Graphical Communication, Environmental Studies, European Studies, Geography, History, Home Economics, Foreign Languages, Life Sciences, Materials Science, Music, Physical Education, Physical Sciences, Social Studies, Textile Studies and Vocational Subjects.

While assessment of and for learning is ongoing, at the end of the Secondary Cycles, students are entitled to the Secondary School Certificate and Profile. This new certificate documents students' secondary-level journey. In addition, at the end of the Secondary Cycle, students are expected to sit for the Secondary Education Certificate (SEC) examination (equivalent to the GCSE exams) organized locally by the Matriculation and Secondary Education Certificate (MATSEC) Board.

Post-secondary education

In Malta, Post-Secondary Education is generally understood as a two-year, pre-university phase in one's educational life. Various institutions – government, Church and private – cater for this phase. Access to this phase is dependent on obtaining the Secondary Education certification. Those who fail to obtain such a certificate may continue their journey in one of the institutions that helps students prepare for such certificate as well as for the MATSEC Certificate (Malta's equivalent to the A levels). Post-Secondary courses lead to the Malta Matriculation Certificate and to entry to university. Malta has set the following targets for 2025/26:

- Per cent of 19-year-old students participating in further and higher education, excluding post-secondary education—40 per cent
- Per cent of 17-year-old-students participating in further and higher education—90 per cent (2012: 80+ per cent)
- Per cent rate of students who obtain 1 to 5 grade in SEC in any five subjects—75 per cent (2012: 66.3 per cent)
- Per cent of early school leavers—10 per cent (2012: 30 per cent)
- PISA Literacy (Levels 2 to 6)—85 per cent (2009+: 63.7 per cent)
- PISA Mathematical Literacy (Levels 2 to 6)—80 per cent (2009+: 66.4 per cent)
- PISA Scientific Literacy (Levels 2 to 6)—80 per cent (2009+: 67.5 per cent)

Adult education

State-sponsored adult education had existed well before the introduction of mass compulsory education in 1946. It can be traced, through documentation, at least to 1850 (Wain and Mayo, 1992). Given the predominance of Roman Catholicism, the Catholic Church, some of its priests and connected organizations have been and continue to be important players in adult education (Mayo, 2007).

Adult Education means different things to different people in Malta. It was traditionally associated with adult literacy and basic education in the late 19th and first half of the twentieth century at a time when there was no mass public education. It was linked, for the most part, with emigration and involved literacy especially in English. The main purpose was to assist emigrants in settling in former British colonies of settlement such as the United States, Canada and Australia. Vocational education, often with a strong agricultural bias, was also instrumental in this regard (the receiving countries preferred country to city dwellers). Adult education was also associated with religious instruction and with social development. Social development was initially often promoted by institutions that followed the social teachings of the Catholic Church. One can mention the Catechesis Secretariat, based at the Catholic Institute, Floriana, whose work dates back to the mid-1960s. The Secretariat organizes adult catechesis education groups in various parishes throughout Malta, which helps to give gives importance to the teaching of adults.

Politics of adult education

The church is of course not the only player. Hardly surprising, the major player is the state. Through its annual budget allocations, the state provides funding for services rendered by state institutions in the areas of general adult education, health promotion and vocational education. The European Union, through its various actions and other sources, notably the European Social Fund (ESF), is increasingly becoming a key provider of funds for adult education. Corporations such as the Employment & Training Corporation (ETC) benefit from ESF funding (Mayo, 2007: 35).

State-sponsored training for adults

The Employment & Training Corporation, which was launched in the autumn of 1989, involves a partnership between state and industry. The idea of such a partnership makes sense in a micro-state where the state must shoulder a substantial part of the responsibility for the vocational preparation of adults. Small companies do not enjoy the necessary 'economies of scale' to render in-house training a viable option. They also face the danger of 'poaching'. The ETC acted in partnership with the then Education Department (and also the Jesuit-run community adult education NGO, the Paulo Freire Institute and the University's Literacy Unit) to provide literacy courses for the unemployed, a number of whom lack literacy skills—more than 80 per cent of ETC registrants have up to secondary level education, with a percentage of them hardly having attained ordinary level standard; about 20 per cent of those registering for work are functionally illiterate.[1] Basic Skills is also another area which attracts a large number of participants for these reasons. But the ETC has provided programmes in a variety of 'non-trade' areas, including office skills, small business management, and computers and marketing (ETC Annual Report, 1994/5).

Other and more recent areas tackled by the ETC include European Computer Driving Licence (ECDL) courses, a Dangerous Goods certificate course and a whole range of courses ranging from those in Hospitality to Basic Management skills. The ETC also provided a number of courses (many being IT related) through the Night Institute for Further Technical Education (NIFTE), which was set up in 1998 through collaboration with the Ministry of Education, the Malta Development Corporation (now Malta Enterprise), the Federation of Industries and the Israeli organization ORT-Union College for Sciences and Advanced Technologies (Cardona, 2000). The original intention was to involve several sectors of Maltese industry in offering their sites and facilities for the further technical training of adults. At first, no charge was involved, but expenses are now being charged on a cost recovery basis. The Corporation also provides a training subsidy scheme for employees in micro-enterprises and sponsors the participation of registrants in courses offered by other organizations, including private ones. In addition, the ETC has introduced a system of short flexible traineeships with and tailored to the needs of industry (involving on-the-job and off-the-job training) and, as expected, has been bidding for ESF-funded projects. It was successful with 6 out of the 30 bids submitted in 2003.[2]

Other state-sponsored agencies such as the Foundation for Educational Services have been tapping ESF funds. It was through these funds that the FES sought to implement the provision in the Maritime and Security Training Centre (MSSTC) document regarding the development of schools as community learning centres. Funding for this project was subsequently and inexplicably stopped (Mayo, 2007: 29). We will later comment on other state-funded institutions involved in adult education, notably the higher education institutions.

Sporadic political initiatives were also to be found in the early part of the twentieth century, particularly through the efforts of Manwel Dimech (Zammit Marmara', 1996). Socialist and labour-oriented adult education made its mark in the 1980s with the emergence of NGOs connected with the Labour Party and the General Workers' Union. Prior to that, we saw the emergence of an academy connected with Christian Democratic politics, strongly linked to the Nationalist Party. Other initiatives such as the Centre for Labour Studies emerged at the University in the early 1980s primarily because of the experiments in self-management introduced in a number of firms, including the Dockyard. Links between local adult education providers and German foundations (*stiftungs*) and other agencies began to occur, especially with regard to adult education providers connected with the Church, unions or the main political parties (Caruana and

Mayo, 2004: 62). Once Malta joined the European Union, however, the Friedrich Ebert Stiftung closed its Malta offices. Maltese adult education agencies have little else on which to draw (Mayo, 2007). And yet it is agencies such as these that are often relied upon to uphold the view of adult education as a public good, and not a consumption good.

Private sector

Viewing education as a 'consumer positional good' is very much the case with the emerging private higher education market, which caters for adult learners by offering a variety of programmes (intended towards certification provided by foreign universities, mainly British) not found in the public university, where evening undergraduate courses for adults are very limited (Mayo, 2007; Darmanin, 2009). The idea of education as a consumer good applies to the booming quangos of Human Resources Development (HRD), ICT and the English language (this last, to foreigners).

The kind of adult education provided by the above institutions is mainly social purpose oriented. Nevertheless, the country has its fair share of commercially oriented provision of adult education, as indicated earlier on, especially in the introductory part of this volume. One of the growth areas as far as commercially oriented adult education goes is that of teaching English as a foreign language to adults and youngsters. Many of the schools involved in this enterprise have been organized within a federation (Federation of English Language Teaching Organisations of Malta [FELTOM]). Others continue to emerge, with a number operating outside the Federation. The success of this industry can be gauged from the following statement by Deputy Head of Mission at the German Embassy in Malta, Helmut Domas (2004), who stated in 2003:

> The largest group of these students, about 15,000 in number, arrive yearly from Germany. Hence Malta has overtaken the UK as the most favoured destination for studying English as a foreign language, at least as far as German students are concerned.

The growth of this veritable industry over the years has led to efforts being made by the more serious institutions in the preparation of adult educators involved. The degree of preparation of educators involved serves to separate the wheat from the chaff as far as the language schools are concerned (Borg and Marsh, 1997).

Trade unions

Trade unions also refined their provisions in adult education, establishing their own foundations. The major union, the General Workers' Union (GWU), provides a more general education via the Reggie Miller Foundation, with a focus on trade union and a broad cultural education. The Foundation is located at the Workers' Memorial Building in Valletta, the Union's main premises, and consists of ten schools that cater to teaching Languages, Music, Art and Crafts, Theatre and Drama, Information Technology, Health and Safety, Leadership, academic subjects, general courses and courses held abroad, mainly in the United Kingdom. Priority is given to the education of shop stewards, and the Foundation was set up primarily for this purpose. With a complement of around one hundred educators and around twenty-five hundred participants a year (excluding participants in seminars held outside the premises), the Reggie Miller Foundation is undoubtedly one of the largest adult education agencies in Malta.

The Unjoni Haddiema Maghqudin (UHM), set up in 2003, operates the Salvinu Spiteri Foundation in honour of the first UHM president, Salvinu Spiteri (1926–1996). Its main aim is as stated here:

> The furtherance and the promotion of the development of human resources in Malta in the light of the following motivations: (a) that Malta's richest resource is its people and that its economic and social development is highly dependent on its ability to nurture and utilize the abilities, skills and motivation at work; (b) that, in order to further these abilities and skills, and to encourage higher motivation, it is necessary to create and enhance an awareness of the need to develop and to provide workers with adequate and directed training on a continuing basis. This will enable them to meet the present and future challenges in a changing and increasingly competitive international environment; (c) that the need is felt to retrain workers for future requirements in the use of modern technology in a world where production systems are changing radically; and (d) that investment of energies in the provision of such services in the upgrading of human resources is in the prime interest of the workers of Malta.

The embracing of HRD by the trade union is very much in evidence in the above quote from UHM's official website. It seems to be a reflection of the times (an age characterized by the intensification of globalization) in which unions are operating. Nowadays, the concern to attract investment and jobs seems to take precedence over the traditional trade union concern regarding employees gaining greater control at their place of work through a broad workers' education programme, unless the term HRD is being redefined and recast to incorporate these latter concerns. In this case, one would be subverting the dominant discourse to obtain support for programmes which include a strong trade union rather than simply a utilitarian management agenda.

It is heartening to see that education constitutes an important element in the setup of the larger unions. There are, however, barriers arising through the traditional inability of unions to press for paid educational leave in their negotiations with employers, although the current political climate, in this period of hegemonic Neoliberal globalization, had put the unions on the back foot. They are likely to press for opportunities for retooling labour skills and vocational reorientation courses in a time when people are working beyond age 60.

There is also the alarming prospect of pensions becoming an individual rather than a social responsibility. This will lead many to continue seeking work in old age. The emphasis in their education, during that period, would likely continue to be on 'employability'. Older adult workers become further victims of an often illusory discourse, especially in an age when there is a global scramble for few middle-class jobs (the market value of which is lowered through the massive presence of a qualified labour pool from places such as China and India), which will leave so many qualified and experienced people disappointed, including youngsters, let alone older adults.

Learning in later life

Demographic trends in Malta are similar to those in the rest of the Western Hemisphere. In twenty-four years, between 1985 and 2009, the percentage of aged 60+ and aged 75+ adults went up from 14.3 and 3.8 per cent to 22 and 6 per cent respectively (Formosa, 2012). Life expectancy for men and women increased from 70.8 and 76.0 years in 1985 to 77.7 and 81.4 years in 2009. Projections estimate that in the year 2025 the percentage of older persons aged 60+ will rise to 26.5 per cent (Formosa, 2012). In Malta, older adults, more than their younger counterparts, are frequent users of health and care services. Together with single parents, they constitute a most vulnerable category, with 22 per cent risking poverty (Eurostat, 2010). Despite the tax-oriented incentives, post-retirement-age employment is very low. In 2009, only 1 per cent of the aged 65+ cohort was in employment (Formosa, 2012). Educationally, in 2009, 80 per cent of the aged 60+ group held no educational qualifications (Formosa, 2012).

The demographic trends indicate an ageing population that is relatively healthy, albeit economically challenged, and that has access to free health care and a range of social services. Educationally, Malta is still a long way from providing a comprehensive and socially inclusive programme for late-life learners. To date, the country does not have a policy on education for older adults. The absence of such a policy and of a national strategy, combined with limited educational qualifications, may account for the weak presence of the aged 60+ adults in institutions of formal learning. In fact, despite the fact that the Higher Education Act provides for the maturity clause which exempts older persons from presenting prior qualifications, statistics for 2009 indicate that in the three main institutions of higher learning—University of Malta, Malta College of Arts, Science and Technology and Institute of Tourism Studies—the rate of participation is 0.6, 0.8 and 0.8 per cent, respectively (Formosa, 2012). Overall, only 2 per cent of older adults age 60+ avail themselves of formal learning sites (Formosa, 2012).

In the absence of a strategy for lifelong learning and of a line budget for adult education in the community, non-formal provision at the level of local councils is weak and inconsistent. Formosa (2012) reports that out of sixty-eight local councils, only two claimed to be providing learning courses for aged 60+ adults. Many local councils do not keep a record of the ages of the participants, which may account for the poor tally of aged 60+ participants attending local council courses.

In the voluntary sector, the Catholic Church is a major player in non-formal adult education provision, including provision for the aged 60+ cohort of participants. Parish priests or their delegates usually chair the sessions, which are mainly religious in content, attended mostly by Catholic women, and when not dealing with transcendental issues, normally address personal issues that range from health to isolation, loneliness and widowhood.

The annual reports of the Employment & Training Corporation (ETC), the national agency responsible for equitable access to training programmes and employment services, show that the despite the rhetoric of active economic ageing, the rate of aged 60+ participants attending its courses are low. Formosa (2012) argues that this fact is 'not surprising considering ETC's policy of not providing educational services to citizens who qualify for the national statutory pension' (p. 279).

The University of Malta subsidizes the local University of the Third Age (UTA). Set up in 1993, UTA is the only voluntary institution in Malta that caters exclusively to the learning interests of older adults. Formosa (2012) challenges

UTA's democratic credentials, describing it as an institution which privileges female, middle-class, urban older persons. Formosa's assertion is based on statistical research provided by the National Statistics Office (NSO) which reveals that only one member of the 2005/6 UTA participants listed her past work as elementary, while 29 per cent held professional roles. Formosa's conclusion is that, rather than being socially inclusive, the UTA reproduces the status quo by appealing almost exclusively to participants with high cultural and social capital.

Older adults living in residential homes constitute a growing sector of the local population and a potential growth area in adult education. In the absence of an outreach programme, home or institution-bound elderly people are perhaps the most marginalized and the least catered to educationally. Unfortunately, the opening of institutions is not premised on the provision of in-house or outreach educational programmes. As a result, the provision is inconsistent where available.

EU impact and 'employability-oriented' adult education

Following Malta's EU accession, agencies and individuals began to compete for Grundtvig and Leonardo funding. Other adult education initiatives began to emerge, relying for the most part on ESF (European Social Fund) funding. The early 1990s also saw the establishment of the Employment & Training Corporation (ETC), and the last decade saw the re-emergence of the Malta College of Arts, Science and Technology (MCAST), which also attaches importance to adult vocational education. This brings us to the higher education sector which not only plays an important role in adult continuing education but also covers most of the post-16-year-old and post-18-year-old spectrum.

The University and its incorporation of other institutions

Higher education, and especially university education, has a long history in Malta which dates back to at least 1592. In fact, the University of Malta traces its origins to a Jesuit-run college, the *Collegium Melitense*, established at the time when the Order of St John ruled Malta. This college was set up by direct papal intervention on 12th November 1592 (see University of Malta, 2001: 8; Fiorini, 2001: 34). A 1578 Bull of Pope Gregory XIII and other enactments, which permitted the Jesuits to confer degrees in certain areas, allowed the College to act as a degree-granting institution (University of Malta, 2001: 8; Fiorini, 2001: 37).

This college was the forerunner of Malta's only university, which was established after the Jesuits were expelled from the islands in 1768, and their lands, including the Collegium, were confiscated by the Grand Master of the time.

The University became known as the Royal University of Malta, under British rule in 1937. In 1974, the institution became known as the University of Malta as a result of a change in the Constitution which rendered Malta a republic. Apart from the University, we also saw the setting up of teacher education colleges in Malta. They too formed part of Malta's higher education setup. A training college for female teachers was opened in 1944 under the auspices of the nuns belonging to the Society of the Sacred Heart. In 1947, St Michael's College was opened for prospective male teachers, first at Pembroke and subsequently, through Colonial Development and Welfare funds, at Ta' Giorni, where a building replete with all the accoutrements for a residential college was erected. In both cases, the training was carried out by the De La Salle brothers.

The 1960s saw the establishment, through UK and UN funding and expertise, of the Malta College of Arts, Science and Technology, which came into its own, after a slow start, in the late 1960s and which provided a degree course in engineering (the degree was granted by the University of Malta) (Zammit Mangion, 1992: 83, 84) and non-degree courses in a variety of areas, including Business Studies, Secretarial Studies, Catering and Accountancy. Since its inception, MCAST was not a fee-charging institution, although students paid fees to the foreign bodies who provided the examinations and certification in certain areas (e.g. Association of Chartered Certified Accountants [ACCA]). In 1971, the Nationalist government, on the eve of a general election, abolished tuition fees for full-time courses for Maltese students at the University (Zammit Mangion, 1992: 83). In 1975, the teacher education programme became part of MCAST; the building housing the College of Education was sold to the Libyan government to become a residential college for Libyan students. The teacher education programme (both the three-year certificate course and the one-year Post-Graduate Certificate of Education [PGCE] course) was housed within MCAST's newly established Department of Educational Studies. This new structure for teacher education in Malta lasted only three years.

In 1978, the Labour government, headed by Dom Mintoff, introduced a number of higher education reforms. These reforms, although leading to the institution of new faculties such as those of Education (comprising the above-mentioned teacher education programmes) and Management, led to the abolition of the Faculties of Arts, Science and Theology. They also led to the amalgamation of MCAST (temporarily transformed into the New University, lasting only for a two-year period) with the University of Malta (Mayo, 2007).

The 1978 Higher Education Reforms involved a 'Worker-Student' Scheme (Bonavita et al., 1977; Schembri, 1982; Spiteri Campbell, 1984).[3] In this scheme, the university student alternated five and a half months of work with five and a half months of study at the University. Students were provided with a basic wage throughout the year, paid monthly at the same rate during both the study and work phases (Baldacchino, 1999; Mayo, 2003) as well as during the one-month vacation period. Salaried employees were also allowed to join the scheme, with the possibility of retaining their salary while carrying out their studies under conditions similar to those for mainstream students.

The Nationalist Party won the 1987 General Elections and, on assuming office, the newly elected government lost no time in re-establishing the Faculties of Arts, Science and Theology at the University, all offering full-time courses. The new government abolished the Worker-Student Scheme; it also introduced a stipend to be paid to students enrolled full time at the University and brought to an end the Worker-Student Scheme that was at the heart of the 1978 reforms concerning full-time university education.

Statistics of growth

The stipend system served to increase the numbers of people attending the University. Although only 250 students graduated in 1988, 1,250 graduated in 1995 (Baldacchino, 1999: 209). By 1996, the university student population had grown to 6,500 (ibid.). The numbers continued to rise to reach an estimated population of 9,970 around 2008[4] as the University went through and continues to go through a process of 'massification'. There are approximately 11,000 students, at present, including over 650 foreign/exchange students from seventy-seven different countries, following full-time or part-time degree, certificate and diploma courses, many of them run on the modular or credit system (www.um.edu.mt). There are a further 2,800 pre-tertiary students at the Junior College which also falls under the University. A basic Foundation Studies Course enables international high school students, who have completed their secondary or high school education overseas but who do not have the necessary entry requirements, to qualify for admission to an undergraduate degree course at the University of Malta (www.um.edu.mt). Almost 3,000 students graduate in various disciplines annually.

Organizational setup

The University has fourteen faculties—Arts, Built Environment, Dental Surgery, Economics, Management & Accountancy, Education, Engineering, Health Sciences, Information & Communication Technology, Laws, Media and Knowledge Sciences, Medicine & Surgery, Science, Theology, and Social Wellbeing (www.um.edu.mt).

The University of Malta's Gozo Campus, on Malta's sister-island, Gozo, is a venue for part-time evening degree courses in Arts and Commerce and holds short courses and seminars. There is now also a resource centre located in the southern part of the island, the Cottonera region, from whence access to the University has historically been low.

Associated with the University is the Mediterranean Academy of Diplomatic Studies, which was established by special agreement with the Graduate Institute of International Studies, Geneva. The University's main campus is also home to the International Maritime organization (IMO), International Maritime Law Institute (IMLI) and the International Ocean Institute Malta Operational Centre (IOI-MOC).

Priority areas

There are a number of fields which the University has identified as priority areas. Chief among these are relations with industry and the strengthening of the engineering departments; the further development of information technology, computer science and artificial intelligence; the University's contribution to the improvement of primary and secondary education and the forging of inter-university links to stimulate international educational exchange (www.um.edu.mt).

Administration

The administrative setup of the University of Malta involves a number of academic, administrative and technical staff members who are appointed or elected to the various governing bodies of the University. The principal officers of the University are the chancellor, the pro-chancellor, the rector, the pro-rectors (four at the moment, including one for the Gozo Centre), the registrar, and the deans of the faculties as well as the finance officer and the librarian. The main governing bodies are the Council, the Senate and the Faculty Boards.

As the supreme governing body of the University, the Council is responsible for its general administration. Faculties group together departments concerned with a major area of knowledge, whereas institutes are of an interdisciplinary nature. The Council is also responsible for appointing new staff members, both local and foreign, to the various academic posts.

The Senate is largely responsible for the academic matters of the University, primarily regulating studies, research, documentation and examinations. The Senate also establishes the entry regulations.

The Faculty Board directs the academic tasks of the Faculty. The Board presents plans and proposals to the Senate and the Council. In addition, it determines the studies, teaching and research within the Faculty.

MCAST and other institutions

Despite the massive increase in university courses over the years, it was felt that other institutions were necessary to provide studies pitched at different levels from basic education to degree-level courses. The year 1987 saw the setting up of the Institute of Tourism Studies, which runs a variety of courses, some developing into honours degrees courses at the University, such as the one in hospitality management. It virtually comprises the old catering school which previously formed part of the old MCAST but has expanded its remit. Students are sent on placements abroad and even gain practice at the Institute's much frequented and highly regarded restaurant. It comprises the following centres: Centre for E-Learning Technologies; Centre for Cultural & Heritage Studies; The Science Centre; The Centre for the Future Foresight in Tourism; Centre for Cleaning Science; and The Chocolate Academy.

The idea of a vocational college that will cater for full-time and evening courses in a whole range of subjects not provided by the University and other institutions was moot in the mid-1990s. Discussions were held under different ministers, and plans were put forward for the establishment of a vocational college. This turned out to be the Malta College of Arts, Science and Technology which was once again resurrected in 2001, thirteen years after its demise. It is run by a Board of Governors which includes experienced educational administrators and many representatives from the industrial sector. MCAST comprises virtually ten institutes, including the Gozo Centre. The other nine are the Institute of Agribusiness, the Institute of Building and Construction Engineering, the Institute of Community Services, the Institute of ICT, the Institute of Mechanical Engineering, the Institute of Art and Design, the Institute of Business and Commerce, the Institute of Electrical and Electronics Engineering and the Maritime Institute. A number of these institutes had previously been part of the old MCAST or the former Technical Institute, or they existed as separate schools in their own right. MCAST's mission is 'to provide a universally accessible vocational and professional education with an international dimension, responsive to the needs of the individual and the economy'.[5]

MCAST also provides numerous evening training programmes in various skills, and anyone over sixteen years of age can register for these programmes. There is no limit to the age of participants beyond age 16. The motivations for attending evening courses are various. People take evening courses provided by MCAST for a variety of reasons. Some take them up for their continuing professional development; others follow such courses for vocational reorientation, and there are also those who enrol in such courses to develop the sort of skills that represent an alternative to those employed in their daily work.

Many of the evening courses lead to certificates of attendance, but a number of them are geared towards formal foreign certification (*City & Guilds* and *B. Tec*). Courses are also tailor- made to the needs of enterprises and firms that seek to upgrade the qualifications of their personnel in certain areas, for example technicians, welders and hairdressers. They avail themselves of MCAST's considerable economies of scale in the use of facilities, and its ability to tap into the required teaching expertise, to obtain such a service for which MCAST provides the funding. A Training for Industry programme exists for this purpose which also includes programmes of re-skilling. Then there are also market-driven 'mass courses' in a variety of areas, including Interior Design, which attracts around eighty to one hundred applicants each term.[6]

Private higher education institutions

Apart from these predominantly publicly funded institutions, the country has experienced the emergence of private institutions which provide courses leading to degrees, diplomas and certificates provided by foreign universities. St Martin's Institute of Technology offers University of London degree courses in Computing and in Business Management.

The European Institute of Education, through its head office in Malta, also offers courses in a variety of areas, leading to credentials awarded by different institutions, most prominently the University of Leicester's distance learning programmes, but there are awards provided by the University of Sunderland and the University Institute Kurt Bosch in Switzerland. There are courses in language, educational administration, European law, journalism, business administration, marketing, public policy and management. More recently St Catherine's High School, in collaboration with the University of Sheffield, is offering postgraduate degree courses run by the English university, notably an MA in Early Childhood Education and a PhD in Education.

Regulation in education

The Education Act (ACT No. XIII of 2006) led to the establishment of a National Council for Higher Education. This is not the first time a body providing guidelines for the development of Higher Education in Malta was established. In 1957, a Royal University Commission was in place. This was subsequently replaced, during the first Labour administration of the 1970s, by a Commission for the Development of Higher Education whose first chairperson was the distinguished German sociologist and politician Ralph Dahrendorf, then Director of the London School of Economics. The more recent National Council for Higher Education has the following responsibilities:

- Promoting structured dialogue between all further and higher education institutions;
- Supporting all stakeholders with research, data and information about the sector;
- Maintaining a register of authorized and accredited institutions and programmes available in Malta;
- Developing a national strategy for further and higher education; and
- Preparing key performance indicators and benchmarking the sector against international developments.[7]

Malta Qualifications Council

Finally, the latest landmark in the development of Higher Education in Malta and Gozo is the setting up of the Malta Qualifications Council (MQC) in December 2005. The overall objective of the Malta Qualifications Council, as specified in Legal Notice 347/2005,[8] is to 'steer the development of the National Qualifications Framework for Lifelong Learning[9] and to oversee the training and certification leading to qualifications within the Framework and which are not already provided for at compulsory education institutions or degree awarding bodies.'[10]

The MQC is meant to define 'the levels of qualifications and competences within the NQF and for establishing standards related to qualifications within the Framework. Malta's Qualifications Framework is at the forefront of European developments, achieving as it does, the inclusion of qualifications across compulsory, vocational and academic sectors into a single framework.'[11]

Conclusion: Lifelong learning as an all-embracing concept

The reference to lifelong learning in the MQC goals and the existence of a national qualifications framework in this regard would suggest the existence of a national strategy encompassing this master concept for education throughout the European Union. It is the sort of strategy that would embrace the whole area of Education in Malta. A working group was set up at the start of the new millennium to develop a draft strategy meant to be placed in the public domain. By 2004, this draft strategy was completed and presented to a Faculty of Education (University of Malta) at the end of the first semester staff seminar. For some reason, the draft document was not placed in the public domain. One of the present authors queried whether financial considerations had much to do with this or whether the draft strayed significantly from the economism of the Lisbon objectives (Mayo, 2007). At the time of writing, the country had witnessed a change of government as the Labour Party won the general elections by a landslide. This brought to an end an almost twenty-four-year period of government by the Nationalist Party, excluding the two-year interlude in 1996–98 when Labour governed but gave way to a snap election which returned the Nationalists to power. No drastic changes are being envisaged in the short term, though there have been pre-electoral promises of a sabbatical for schoolteachers and an attempt to decrease the level of bureaucratization of teaching. There have been discussions concerning possible foreign investment in higher education and, as a result, the setting up of additional universities or university institutions. There has been the promise, by the ruling party in its electoral manifesto, of setting up a Polytechnic of the Mediterranean. It is early days yet, and one envisages gradual rather than sudden changes, the latter approach having characterized Labour governments between 1971 and 1987.

Notes

1   Information obtained from taped interview with Mr Joe Cutajar, ETC's Training Services Senior Manager, held at the ETC's Valletta office on 5th December 2003.
2   Taped interview with Mr Joseph Cutajar, 5th December 2003.
3   Act XX1-1978 (Act to amend the 1974 Education Act), *Government Gazette* No. 13,508, 7th July 1978.
4   Information provided by Registrar's Office, University of Malta, 28 October, 2008.
5   See http://www.mcast.edu.mt/downloads/quicklinks/strategic_plan.pdf (accessed on 30 December 2006).
6   Ibid.
7   From the website of the NCHE https://www.nche.gov.mt/page.aspx?pageid=12 (accessed on 23 December 2010).
8   Malta Government Gazette supplement No. 17,834, 28 October, 2005. *Section B* pdf available on MQC website http://www.mqc.gov.mt/about-us?l=1 (accessed on 23 December 2010).
9   See pdf available on MQC website http://www.mqc.gov.mt/about-us?l=1 (accessed on 23 December 2010).
10 MQC website http://www.mqc.gov.mt/about-us?l=1 (accessed on 23 December 2010).
11 Ibid.

References

Bacchus, M. K. (2010). 'The education challenges facing small nation states in the increasingly competitive global economy of the twenty-first century', in P. Mayo (ed.), *Education and Small States. Global Imperatives, Regional Initiatives and Local Dilemmas*. London and New York: Routledge.

Baldacchino, G. (1999). 'Recent developments in higher education in Malta'. *Mediterranean Journal of Educational Studies*, 4(1): 205–14.

Borg, S. and Marsh, A. (1997). 'Teaching EFL to adults: the development of professional practitioners', in P. Mayo and G. Baldachinno (eds), *Beyond Schooling: Adult Education in Malta* (pp. 175–198). Msida: Mireva.

Borg, C. and Mayo, P. (2006). *Learning and Social Difference. Challenges for Public Education and Critical Pedagogy*. Lanham: Paradigm.

Cardona, M. (2000).,'Il Tema della Learning Region. Il Caso di Malta' (The Learning Region Theme: The Case of Malta), unpublished thesis, laurea course in Scienze dell'Educazione, Universita' degli Studi di Roma III.

Caruana, D. (2004). 'Adult education in Malta', in D. Caruana and P. Mayo (eds), *Perspectives on Lifelong Learning in the Mediterranean*. Bonn: IIZ-DVV.

Darmanin, M. (2009). 'Further and higher education markets' cushions: Portability of policy and potential to pay'. *International Studies in Sociology of Education*, 19(3): 175–201.

European Commission. (2010). http://ec.europa.eu/eurostat.

Fiorini, S. (2001). 'The *Collegium Melitense* and the *Universitas Studiorum* to 1798´, in R. G. Sultana (ed.), *Yesterday's Schools. Readings in Maltese Educational History*. Malta: PEG.

Formosa, M. (2012). 'Education for older adults in Malta: Current trends and future visions'. *International Review of Education*, 58: 271–92.

Mayo, P. (2002). 'University continuing education in Malta'. *Journal of Maltese Education Research*, 1(1): 23–43. www.educ.um.edu.mt/jmer/.

Mayo, P. (2007). *Adult Education in Malta*. Bonn: DVV-International.

Mayo, P. (2009a). 'Competitiveness, diversification and the international higher education cash flow: The EU's higher education discourse amidst the challenges of globalisation'. *International Studies in Sociology of Education*, 19(2): 87–103.

Schembri, C. (1982). 'The Development of the Worker-Student Scheme in Malta.' unpublished dissertation (B. Educ.), University of Malta.

Spiteri Campbell, E. (1984). 'The Student-Worker Scheme at the University of Malta.' Department of Adult and Higher Education Occasional papers, Manchester: University of Manchester.

Sultana, R. G. (2002). *Education and National Development in Malta*. Malta: Mireva.

University of Malta (2001). *University of Malta Calendar 2001/2002*. Malta: University of Malta.

Vella Bonavita, R., et al. (1977). *Draft Report on Some Restructuring Implications in Tertiary Education of the Student-worker Concept*. Malta: Ghaqda Ghalliema Universita.

Zammit Mangion, J. (1992). *Education in Malta*. Malta: Studia Editions.

Zammit Marmara', D. (1996). 'Manwel Dimech's Search for Enlightenment', in G. Baldacchino and P. Mayo (eds), *Beyond Schooling. Adult Education in Malta*. Malta: Mireva.

Wain, K. and Mayo, P. (1992). 'Malta', in P. Jarvis (ed.), *Perspectives on Adult Education and Training in Europe*. Leicester: NIACE.

10

Poland: Education Transitions and the Emergence of European Influences, 1989–2014

Ryszard Kucha and Ewa Frankiewicz

Introduction

Contemporary Poles have, for years, been particularly involved in the history of their own nation and state. On the one hand, this comprises the memory of the grandeur of the Commonwealth of Both Nations, in particular the Jagiellonian age, the time of the Four-Year Sejm and the Commission for National Education. On the other hand, it is also an awareness of the Partitions period, when Poland was erased from the map of Europe for 123 years; the defeat of two national uprisings; and emigrations of many generations 'for bread' to Western Europe and to North and South America. It includes also the memory of splendid achievements of Polish culture and literature that heartened the Polish population in the territories captured by the three partitioning powers: Austria, Prussia and Tsarist Russia.

Poland's venerated memories also include the open struggle for national liberation during the First World War and the Polish-Soviet War (1919–21), the time of building Polish independence during the interwar decades between 1918 and 1939, and the collapse of the Polish state invaded by the Third Reich and the Stalinist Soviet Union in September 1939. Nor do the Poles forget about the Polish independence underground and the armed struggle of the Polish Army on many fronts against Nazi Germany.

A significant part of Polish national awareness was influenced by the years after the Second World War, when history allowed us to enjoy the euphoria of victories and inflicted the tragedy of the Yalta Agreement, which subordinated Poland to the Stalinist Soviet Union and collapsed in disgrace only after 1989. This was the time of both forced political emigration, many bitter reminiscences in the aftermath of the post–Second World War changes of state frontiers, and also the period of arduous restoration of the country after war damage. The period from 1944 to 1989 cannot be closed, as some do, by statements like 'Between hope, resentment, fear, and discouragement'. These feelings and anxieties must not be disregarded when trying to define Poland's road to membership of the European Union and the North-Atlantic Alliance (Kucha 1997: 9–10).

The year 1989 inaugurated the processes of political-system transformation in Poland, accompanied by many political, cultural, economic and educational turbulences connected with the redefinition of the previous hierarchy of ethical norms and the rules of conduct in social and professional life. These changes affected the moral and intellectual authorities who had been dominant in the country's sociopolitical life before 1989 (Szołtysek, 1995: 101). 'The only correct ideological and political attitudes' built in Poland after the Second World War and promoted by the media, literature and school at that time lost their raison d'être in the new social circumstances. The whole state-based system of education, health care and social welfare and culture and of economy was thus undermined (Krąpiec, 1993: 269).

The Polish pedagogical science, the 'child of the times and system' after Poland was occupied by the Red Army, was prepared for many years to perform an ancillary role for the authoritarian state and political system, which meant attempts to perfect all instruments for effectively moulding the minds of the Poles, the worldview and competencies to suit the education and upbringing objectives created outside of them by the Marxist-Leninist ideology (Kwieciński, 1994: 15). As a result, as Kwieciński concluded, the formative turning point of the early 1990s found the Poles ill-prepared to meet its challenges to build a new democratic order and a modern, efficient economy created by the people rather than by political structures (Kwieciński, 1994: 15–16). The time of settling scores with the past then began, which was necessary to better understand our collective fates. This, however, required matter-of-fact, substantive arguments and assessments rather than superficial, fragmentary judgements and mere distancing oneself from the recent daily reality of Poland's population of almost forty million (Muszyński, 1994: 36 et seq.).

Integration—Yes, but what kind of integration?

Socio-economic transformations initiated in Poland in 1989 posed many difficult questions and problems that needed to be solved quickly: Where are we going and what are we striving after as the state and society? What kind of political system would we like to build? What could be the future consequences of our choice? The answer to those questions was apparently simple because we wanted almost everything at that time. While naming all the demands at one go, we paid absolutely no attention to their ideological or social context. It was not, therefore, a coherent sociopolitical programme, but a set of wishes and expectations voiced by the Poles (Banach, 1992: 292).

The foregoing list of Polish hopes and expectations did not mean at all that as a country we would be able, even minimally, to fulfil the vast programme of longed-for reforms. It may even be assumed that few Poles were aware of what the programme of the expected reforms to integrate with Europe required from the Poles. Poland did not produce its vast European movement for building European awareness with specifically Polish features. On the contrary, the wish to join the European Community as soon as possible first of all triggered a desire to imitate the European consumption patterns, attitudes and behaviours. For this reason, it should be emphasized that because it was not until 1989 that Poland regained real political independence from Moscow, it was simply not possible to fully prepare Polish society for European integration (Krukowski, 1995: 83–84).

However, endeavours to integrate Poland with Europe also caused reluctance or even resistance from some circles who, being afraid of losing their monopolistic position as the guardian of Polish national values, began to disseminate views about 'a threat to the country's thousand-year-old national identity', whose sources supposedly originated from the Roman Catholic doctrine of Mieszko I and Boleslaus the Brave. References were also made to 'the principle of identity in the doctrinal-genetic and historical-cultural aspects'. It was even assumed that 'throughout the history of Poland's existence, Roman Catholic religion was a kind of niche in which the Polish nation organized themselves, united, strengthened and acted, and in which they found shelter during national disasters' (Krąpiec, 1993: 269).

For the followers of the foregoing option, of significant importance are the mechanisms of the West European market economy, accepted by the Poles. However, the supporters justify their criticism by the civic demands of Polish society, based on the answer to the question as to whether Poland's economy should join the free market economy system in Europe or whether it should rather depend on human work aimed to increase common welfare. They believe that a hierarchy of values based on competition and profit, typical values of the liberal rule-of-law state, does not meet the expectations of the Poles brought up on the principles of Catholic doctrine. A hasty argument was also advanced that the Poles wanted to create a state that would be worth living in, but not one easy to live in (Szołtysek, 1995: 115).

We should not be surprised therefore by the view that there are contradictions between economic efficiency and a personal hierarchy of values which was then promoted by some part of the Polish political right with strong ties to the Catholic Church. This fact would indicate an attempt to defend the privileged sociopolitical position of this Church, and show the fear of losing it if the Poles adopted Western models of civic behaviours. However, the immense role of education and upbringing in this field should be emphasized because if our openness to integration processes proves to be genuine and permanent on the scale of the Continent, this will mean that it stems from the empowerment and cultural identity of all community members in observing their common rights and duties (Łomny, 1995: 7). Yet the awareness of inevitability of the expected integration processes in no way alters the fact that we try to accomplish the resultant objectives with both hope and fear and with a huge amount of national phobias, prejudices and uncertainties. That is why many representatives of some—especially political—circles may find it extremely difficult to note that the European Community is first of all an area of voluntary organization of work and coexistence based on mutual dialogue and understanding, and on economic cooperation and mutual assistance connected with observance of the law and principles of tolerance, interpenetration of cultures and mutual trust, concern with the natural environment, rejection of violence and hatred and Polish national xenophobia (Kucha, 1997: 12).

Quo vadis Polish education?

It is an undeniable fact that both the organization and content of upbringing and education curricula at schools in the European countries arose and developed under the influence of sociopolitical transformations on the European continent over the last two centuries. It should be thus assumed that both the structure and teaching content in the future school will depend first of all on the evolution of systems inherited from the past years. It should also be agreed upon that the development of education and upbringing in Europe will largely be a supranational process. Can it therefore be assumed that Europe will in the future achieve the organizational unification of the educational system and contents previously taught in individual countries (Hamilton, 1994: 5–11; Lawn, 1994: 13–20)?

How does the image of the contemporary Polish system of education and upbringing look like in the context of the question? Heavily burdened by the complex legacy of the past, the Polish school shows clear signs of stagnation, although certain symptoms of recovery are also discernible. In Poland, we still notice the negative impact of outdated infrastructure and insufficient funds on the general situation of the school as well as its teachers and students. Nevertheless, some social and systemic changes took place at all tiers and types of schools, and the network of private and community schools and individual programme classes was expanded. The process of gradual communitization of public education was thus initiated (Kucha and Misiak, 1996: 49–54).

The vocational education system also began to be reorganized, assuming that it would take several generations. Furthermore, some signs of recovery in the field of teacher training system are discernible in Poland. Kwieciński believes that these measures should lead to devising such a reform of the education and upbringing system that 'would not stem from ideological premises but from objective development needs of the new generations of Polish society, from our (i.e. Poland's) due position in the common Europe, and from civilizational challenges of the coming century' (Kwieciński, 1990: 6, 9). This opinion has not lost its relevance, even if we are in the mid-2010s. Directions of reform should not, however, depend on the education policy of the political camp in power at a particular time, but on recognition of education as a truly national, social and European priority. That is why the most difficult task facing reformers will be to change the consciousness of the Poles and societies in the neighbouring countries and to try to give up the unjustified feeling of superiority and national egoism for openness, partnership or even altruism (Kucha, 1997: 13).

The extremely critical social and pedagogical thought at the close of the last century levelled very harsh criticism at both the pedagogical theory and educational practice of socialist democracy of the period. It might be worth trying, nevertheless, to be more objective in this criticism—those who galloped their horses towards liberation from the fetters of Soviet totalitarianism at the end of the twentieth century must have drunk too much elixir of courage because their steeds tended to suddenly bolt from time to time. They may have bolted hearing the tiger's roar from the Siberian taiga, which made their hearts tremble with apprehension. What about the riders who abused the substances fortifying the heroic attitude? It is almost certain that their ambitions must have secured their lasting position in the history of human and social revolutions on the European continent (Frąckowiak, 1997: 15). Therefore, in the circumstances when the emerging new does not know where it is going while the old has a constant advantage both in thinking and in daily action, the Polish national phobias and superstitions create our *teatrum ceremoniale* expressed in the question: Is our educational egalitarianism of the present day an illusion without any future because it remains a pipe dream or even an abstract utopia? All these doubts made the Polish reality of educational revival embrace the idea of a democracy not conducive to emancipation (Frąckowiak, 1997: 17). In this way, it was possible to formally and institutionally legalize educational diversification and inequalities as a form of obstructing the realization of concrete democracy. Underlying this process was most often the old-style thinking coupled with the absence of a valuable strategy for the development of the Polish education system. Moreover, if young democracy behaves like a raft on the ocean, with each passenger rowing in different—his or her own—direction, it may soon turn out that bureaucracy will easily build its own hierarchies of power, ruling, respectability and affluence, subordination and even humiliation and poverty (Frąckowiak, 1997: 25).

Political and civilizational changes, which began to take place in Poland in 1989 and still continue, shook the foundations of the educational system and all its organizational and curricular levels. However, a basic question arises as to whether the quality of the initiated transformations is consistent with the quality of those connected with market economy in Western Europe. Elżbieta Górnikowska-Zwolak and Andrzej Radziewicz-Winnicki listed several significant obstacles present in science and education in Poland that hinder the desired transformation process. These are, according to the two authors, the rules of creating a specific tradition in Poland that significantly diverge from Western European conditions and traditions, the problem of transformation of particular values between generations, civilizational incompetence of many decision makers, and the lack of tried and tested instruments and funds ensuring effective subsidization for education (Górnikowska-Zwolak and Radziewicz-Winnicki, 1997: 28–38). For the foregoing reasons, the structures of new interrelations between social, economic and political mechanisms are still developing in Poland. It should be remembered that between 1944 and 1989, specific thinking and action habits developed in the social consciousness, whereas they are no longer applicable today, and new rules of thinking and action need to be learned (Mańka and Roter, 1997: 39). This may lead, the two authors contend, to long-lasting destabilizing situations and even to organizational and curricular chaos (Mańka and Roter, 1997: 40 et seq.).

What present-day Polish society essentially needs nowadays is the strongest possible motivation for development. Hence, the process of individuals' development should be treated as a process of the autonomous evolution of society: a strong and resilient organism with its own individuality and sense of unity, one that also meets the criteria for a post-industrial (i.e. postmodern) society.

Attempted education reforms in Poland before 1989

Educational systems of all countries, in particular schools of all types and educational levels as the main element of these systems, almost constantly come under fire of criticism and are the object of more or less inventive restructuring and reforming attempts. The second half of the last century was uniquely special when de-scholarization and the removal of school from social life as an almost anachronistic institution was even demanded. Attempts to remove school failed, however, and no one thinks of such measures today; instead, this triggered an extensive development called a 'school explosion'. Poland, in its People's Poland period, also prepared appropriate expert opinions between 1973 and 2005, and in only three cases, complete draft reforms of the school system (Kupisiewicz, 2006a: s. 7).

After Edward Gierek took power in People's Poland in December 1970, the preparation of an educational reform was initiated because the existing education system was recognized as entirely inefficient in terms of curricula and organization. The development of a suitable draft for the thorough restructuring of the country's educational system was assigned to a special expert team consisting of eminent theorists and practitioners in education and teaching, who were headed by Prof. Jan Szczepański. Setting up the expert team was a departure from the previous practice of creating similar bodies not only in Poland but also in the other former Soviet bloc countries. In May 1973, after two years of intensive work, the in-depth *Report on the State of Education in People's Poland*, edited by Jan Szczepański, was published in Warsaw. It should be added that work on the report was based on the decisions of the then Party and state authorities concerning extensive provision of secondary education and resolutions demanding that Poland's socio-economic development be significantly accelerated. Consequently, the twenty-four-member Committee of Experts worked on such forms of the school system as 'would ensure the minimum form of secondary education and at the same time it sought to construct a model … of the educational system comprising all institutions and organizations that impacted the development of personalities of Poland's citizens so that they received the upbringing and education allowing them to work optimally in all spheres of life activity' (Szczepański, 1973: 13). A new meaning also had to be given to patriotic education and personality formation because people were expected to get accustomed to the rational organization of their own daily life and concern for health (Szczepański, 1973: 24).

The need to start the educational reforms was justified by the Committee in their five propositions of exceptional importance and practical significance: (1) Upbringing is not and cannot be the task of only the family and school, although the two institutions play a significant role in it; (2) at present, we learn not only during childhood but also later, that is, during our mature years and until advanced old age; (3) if training and self-education should take place always and everywhere, then the selection of the content of these processes is becoming more important than ever; (4) the educational process should be democratized, that is, it is necessary to provide children, teenagers and adults with equal opportunities of educational start and promotion; (5) the level of vocational education should be improved by basing it on broad general-education foundations; (6) implementation of the foregoing theses requires well-prepared teachers. It was clear that teachers should be guaranteed such training via modern higher education (Kupisiewicz, 2006a: 11–18).

The justification for the published theses was not questioned by the education administration at that time, yet the authorities did not implement educational policy directions consistent with the content of the propositions. It also happened that this bureaucracy acted against the widely accepted theses, which is evidenced by the division of the Polish primary school system into two separate segments: primary school and gymnasium (*gimnazjum*, lower secondary school). Although the *Report on the State of Education in People's Poland* was highly assessed by specialists, there were no politicians who were ready to start radical education reforms in this country (Kupisiewicz, 2006a: 20).

In 1979, the *Expert Evaluation of the Situation and Development of Education in People's Poland* was published. It was a joint study by a five-member team of Warsaw University professors, headed by Prof. Suchodolski (1979). This small team formulated and expanded five theses concerning teachers, complete democratization of the school system, essential restructuring of schools, the system of continuing and parallel education as the main directive on the thorough restructuring of education, and building an educating society. We should add that the authors of the *Expert Evaluation* ... did not voice explicitly negative opinions on the intention of the political and educational bureaucracy to base the functioning of Polish school on the ten-year school concept as its main foundation. Therefore, along with valid theses, there was no firm protest against the adoption of the ten-year school as the mainstay of Poland's educational system (Kupisiewicz, 2006a: 27). In addition, the form and way of presenting the problem by the authors allowed the educational bureaucracy in Poland to adduce the recommendations and theses of the *Expert Evaluation ...*, which the administration simply did not respect in practice (Kupisiewicz, 2006a: 28–29).

Scientific reflections and directives also abounded in the years after 1987, when the then Prime Minister appointed the thirty-four-member Committee of Experts for National Education. The Committee was assigned the task of preparing a diagnosis of the existing system of national education and showing the main directions of restructuring it with a particular emphasis on school institutions of different types and different teaching levels. Consequently, there were comparative analyses and studies and forecasts of the country's socio-economic development, and materials were utilized which were collected for the key problem 'Modernization of the Educational System of People's Poland' and for other studies. The final result of the Committee's work were two reports: *Education—A National Priority. Report on the State and Directions of Development of Education in People's Poland* (Kupisiewicz, 1989) and *Education in Conditions of Risk* (Kupisiewicz, 1990). It should be added that the final report was presented to Prime Minister Tadeusz Mazowiecki, with Henryk Samsonowicz being the then Minister for Education. Did the political bureaucracy and the Education Ministry, which accepted the report *Education—A National Priority ...*, manage to take appropriate reform measures? Neither the Tadeusz Mazowiecki government nor those of Jan Krzysztof Bielecki or Jan Olszewski or Hanna Suchocka did (Kupisiewicz, 2006a: 45–48).

Nevertheless, it is necessary to appreciate the consistency and perseverance of one of the most eminent experts on the issues of Polish visions of educational reforms, Prof. Czesław Kupisiewicz, the author of the 'Synthetic Report on the Need and Directions of School Reform', published in the *Głos Nauczycielski* weekly in May 1996. The paper emphasized the need for a turning point in attitudes towards science and education, without which Poland would stand no chance of keeping up with the Western world in socio-economic and civilizational fields. The author of the report contended that a comprehensive education reform was the need of the hour. This was signalled, according to the author, by the low rate of provision of education, insufficient permeability of the school system, structural and curricular/methodological incompatibility of school education with the principle of continuing education, poor quality of teaching and educational work, curricular backwardness of the teaching content, low professional and general qualifications of vast numbers of working teachers, and the under-invested school system and university education (Kupisiewicz, 2006a: 50–68).

Finally, in 1998, the draft reform of the educational system in Poland, developed by the Ministry of National Education, was published as a book by Wydawnictwa Szkolne i Pedagogiczne in Warsaw. The cover letter by the then Minister of National Education, Prof. Dr Hab. Mirosław Handke, read:

> Between 25 and 27 May 1998, in Krakow and in Tarnów, the Draft Reform of the Educational System will be presented during the meeting with university presidents, schools superintendents, and with members of local governments. It is an extension of the Preliminary Concept of Reform of the Educational System presented on 28 January 1998 in Poznan. We used the time between the two presentations to consult with those interested, owing to which we learned the opinions on the reform. The present draft contains a detailed elaboration of the preliminary concept …
>
> We present the draft reform and request your opinions once again. We are doing this because we are aware of how great and responsible is the work of education reform. We would like the reform to be one that will allow schools to create conditions for development of the best character traits and talents of the students, will assist families and facilitate cooperation between parents and teachers. We would like a reform that would make schools a strong foundation of the development of the Republic of Poland'. (Reforma systemu edukacji. Projekt, 1998: 5–6)

These were fine words showing that the authorities were aware of the importance of the proposed education reform and expectations associated with its implementation. The authorities therefore decided to carry it out without consulting with teachers about the decision: thus, the latter did not take part in the execution work with the conviction and personal involvement expected of them by the Ministry. Of significance was the known fact that the reform was insufficiently prepared in terms of its concept, personnel, funds, infrastructure and organization, which did not guarantee a complete success to the reformers (Kupisiewicz, 2006a: 85). And yet the introduced reform changed a lot, although it also resulted in new errors and proved the fallibility of the bureaucratic reformers.

Parallel, as it were, to the education reform controlled by education bureaucrats, the evaluation of 'the conceptual and organizational achievements' of the educational transformation in Poland continued. When the Polish Academy of Sciences 'Poland 2000 Plus' Forecast Committee published a two-volume *Strategy for Poland's Development until 2020* in 2000, the study recommended the idea of long-term repair measures in Poland, explicitly suggesting that the activities of society, the state and local governments be focused on education, housing construction, science, and innovation and development (Kupisiewicz, 2006a: 88). These issues were also debated during the next meeting of the Polish Academy of Sciences General Assembly in Warsaw on 24 and 25 May 2001. In his introductory report, the chairman of the 'Poland 2000 Plus' Forecast Committee explicitly stated: 'For all its unquestionable successes in teaching at all levels, the past century never fully satisfied anyone. According to Profs. Kupisiewicz and Banach, despite tremendous efforts and expenditure ... education does not meet either the present-day requirements of democracy, or the growing needs of society, or expectations of individuals, in particular those with heightened educational and life aspirations. This is so because not only the goals, tasks and contents implemented at school, but also the methods, organization and ways of teaching and educating fall considerably short of these needs and expectations' (Kupisiewicz, 2006a: 88).

The same chairman explicitly stressed in his speech: 'In recent years there have been many attempts to remedy the situation. They brought a considerable increase in the secondary education coverage and a threefold increase in the number of university students over the decade. Regrettably, the restructuring of the school system initiated by the Education Ministry in 1998 was unsuccessful. No one denies the need for a radical change of the whole educational system but the projects that are ill-prepared in terms of concept, personnel and funds should not be tolerated. Such actions undermine the idea of necessary reform and discourage both students and parents from it' (Kupisiewicz, 2006a: 88).

In education in the late twentieth and early twenty-first century, the reform policies were thus not too successful, both in international and domestic terms. The 1998 assessment in the Memorandum of the Polish Academy of Sciences 21st Century Forecast Committee did not, regrettably, lose its relevance. It read: 'There has been a deep crisis of education and a decline in its material base. Cuts in preschool education provision and extracurricular and non-school classes as well as weakening of primary education reduce the opportunities of many social groups. The uncontrolled and chaotic commercialization of higher education institutions is disturbing, the more so that it is accompanied by a drastic fall in the quality of higher education' (Społeczeństwo polskie wobec wyzwań transformacji systemowej, 1998: 47).

The main assumptions and directions of development of Polish education by 2020

According to the eminent expert on Polish education and the school system, Czesław Kupisiewicz, educational policy should take into account several major objectives of this development. The first objective is, unquestionably, to provide an equal school start and equal educational opportunities to children and teenagers, and to guarantee the upper secondary education coverage to at least 80 per cent of students every year, and the higher education coverage (bachelor's and master's degrees) to at least 40 per cent. The second objective is to build an educating and, at the same time, knowledge-based society. The third objective is to adjust the school system to the constantly changing economic, social, and cultural needs; and the fourth objective should be the development of science and expansion of higher education as a factor guaranteeing the achievement of the other objectives.

In order to accomplish this overall goal it is necessary to provide an equal school start and equal educational opportunities to children and teenagers already at the preschool level, increase the number of people with secondary and university education, improve the professional competence of a large part of teachers, expand school infrastructure first of all in rural areas, and amend the reform introduced by the Education Ministry in 1998, particularly emphasizing the strengthening of the social functions of the school (Kupisiewicz, 2006a: 96–97).

In the years after the initiation of the 1998 reform, it became possible to introduce some organizational and curricular solutions. It should be observed, however, that many of them were only begun, and they are, as Czesław Kupisiewicz notes, still *in statu nascendi* (Kupisiewicz, 2006b: 116–17).

All the documents and studies, both those preceding the publication of *The Draft Reform of the Educational System* in 1998 and other documents, were not able to create a complete vision of the reform because they did not take into sufficient account the processes resulting from complex tasks of the political-system transformation and from European and global integration, or they neglected the processes of the development of information society and knowledge-based economy. Furthermore, the decision-making centres of the educational system failed to adequately utilize social and pedagogical sciences in specifying the goals and directions of the reform and in correctly assessing qualitative and quantitative changes in primary, secondary and higher education. It was only in 1999 that the Central Examination Board and its regional agencies were set up in order to develop requirement standards and a new form of secondary school-leaving examinations (*Matura*). The work on the new *Matura* (upper secondary school examinations and certificate) thus continued to produce the next cases of social tensions and understandable discontent of parents, teachers and students (Banach, 2005: 59). An in-depth analysis is needed to assess the actual state of implementing the structure of the educational system. Attention should focus first of all on how the gymnasium (*gimnazjum*, lower secondary school) performs its anticipated and actual role, and the educational effects achieved so far in the educational system under reform as a whole should be verified (Banach, 2005: 60).

We should now be reminded, not only all the Poles but mainly the reformers and the educational bureaucracy, that the 1998 reform was expected to be the road to the realization of three general and at the same time most important goals: (1) Enhance the education level of Polish society by widening the availability of secondary and higher education; (2) equalize educational opportunities; and (3) support the improvement of education quality as an integral process of education and upbringing (Reforma systemu edukacji. Projekt, 1998: 10).

Those were strategic goals, but they did not specify other required objectives based on European educational trends or the tasks of Polish education and sociopolitical transformation. It was not until 2000 that the Education Ministry managed to present the concept of post-gymnasium (post–lower secondary) education, and the appropriate Law on Higher Education was forced through the Polish Parliament as late as 2005 (Banach, 2005: 60).

The observed delays in the work on the reform make it necessary to emphasize various risks determined by the lack of a long-term programme for development of the whole Polish educational system and by its small share of the gross domestic product (GDP). No wonder that the three authors of *Education in the Process of Educational Transformations*—Bogaj, Kwiatkowski and Szymański—signal three most important risk areas in the process of reforms and transformations of the Polish educational system. In their view, the first area is the social and educational policy (predominance of debates on financial problems over substantive issues, connected with the concept of educational system reform and the fundamental vagueness and at the same time variability of positions on axiological issues). The second area comprises the effects of social reforms carried out in Poland (the slow pace of democratization and self-government processes in the educational system, the declining quality of teaching and the degradation of schools in rural areas, poor financial conditions of teachers, as well as the insufficient development of university teachers and rising costs of education in family budgets). The third area of difficulties lies in the social consciousness of the Poles and is determined by fear of commercialization of the school system, which may impede the chances of gaining good education (Bogaj, Kwiatkowski and Szymański, 1998: 211–13).

Although the fairly significant development of education at the secondary and university levels is rated as a success, the authors warn at the same time that its quality and standards are declining (Banach, 2005: 60). The reform education as a whole should after all be designed and assessed in two dimensions: institutional—from kindergarten to universities and adult education institutions, and problem-based—from teaching curricula and objectives; to the democratization of the school system; to teacher education, needs of the labour market and pedagogical research; to working conditions as compared with other EU member states.

Reformers from the Education Ministry and bureaucrats should, however, remember that the implementation of the foregoing objectives of education reform is a multifaceted process and requires sufficiently large spending as well as proper organization and forecasting in the coming years. Positive effects were accompanied first of all by a decline of preschool education; reduction of expenditure on the school system and university education in Poland; a decrease in teachers' salaries; and constant amendments to the content of the existing Teacher's Charter, continuing modifications of the core curriculum, teaching curricula and standards of examination requirements; and a decline in the childcare system and in the field of welfare and health benefits to primary and secondary school students and college students (Banach, 2005: 61).

While carrying out the first objective of Poland's educational reform—raising its standards by increasing the secondary and university education coverage, it became possible to achieve quantitative indicators approaching those in the developed European countries, that is, 80 per cent and 47 per cent of the population, respectively. It should be stressed at the same time that modern educational systems are oriented towards general education, and the Polish reformed system responds to this idea. The same applies to teaching curricula and textbooks, and to modifications of vocational education.

However, the issue of provision of equal educational opportunities for Polish children and teenagers looks far worse: the reformers should focus more on the matter of efficiency of the educational system. That is why it is necessary to counteract the decline in preschool education, lower the age of compulsory education, and seek to actually provide equal opportunities, which has already been achieved in the kindergarten and primary school.

The gymnasium (lower secondary school), on the other hand, should develop the interests and personality of the students to a far greater degree and prepare them for their personal ways of getting an education, finding an occupation and accomplishing their life goals. In this field, gymnasiums should be supported by parents, educational and non-governmental institutions, and by the Ministry of Justice. At this point, the period of population decline should be utilized to improve the learning and working conditions of school students and teachers. It is also necessary to increase the role and status of local governments in providing funds for the implementation of the reform at schools and for assistance to students (Kwiatkowski, 2006: 10–19).

When the educational reform in Poland began, closer attention should have been paid to the implementation of the third objective of the organizational and curricular measures, that is, to supporting the improvement of the quality of education itself. It was therefore necessary to conduct work on developing teaching curricula and plans. An absolute priority should be to reform the system of teacher training and improve their professional qualifications, and to improve the provision of suitable equipment to individual schools (Banach, 2005: 62, 63).

Many representatives of pedagogical science maintain that every educational system is determined by a large number of factors. One of the most significant determinants in Poland is the demographic forecast concerning the number of school students in 2015. It explicitly shows that between 1999 and 2015, the number of children and teenagers aged 7 to 18 will have decreased from 7,274,000 in 1999 to 5,474,000 in 2007 and to 4,734,000 in 2015. The reform therefore requires drawing up a long-term plan of educational policy and taking into account the subsidy percentage for the school system and university education at 6 per cent of GDP, and in 2020 at ca. 7 per cent of GDP.

Important educational barriers and misunderstandings to progress in Poland

The pedagogical community, not only in Poland, often optimistically assumes that the twenty-first century person as an educated one has a chance of becoming a qualitatively new individual. If this assumption is not erroneous, one can hope for further social and occupational advancement of both individuals and groups in intellectual, cultural and moral-ethical terms, rather than only in an instrumental context. In this sense, a person has chances of complete advancement/promotion not only when he works differently and in a different place and receives remuneration for this work but also when he himself becomes different. An eminent Polish pedagogue Mikołaj Kozakiewicz says that this will be a person who will perceive and implement a wide range of values: he will organize his scale of values through his own consciousness, via wide cultural contexts and social relations; his sensitivity will comprise a wide range of feelings, and in the course of his life he will show and develop the maximum of what determines the conceptual content of being a human (Kozakiewicz, 1973).

However, every person, in particular a young one, may encounter various obstacles in the process of personal socialization, education, upbringing and training. These impediments can be *inter alia* the economic conditions of the family and whole social classes, demographic specificity of one's own country or region, civilizational and spatial conditions, gender related and involving the educational situation of a country or region (Kawula, 1997: 54–55).

There is also a subjective dimension to someone's particular life circumstances. It is formed in the person's mind and is reflected as opinions, views, attitudes, aspirations, and in orientations, life plans or behaviour in specific circumstances. Here, psychological, ideological and cultural barriers also appear, which are linked to the range and quality of an individual's participation in culture. Within this scope, the barriers are assumed to appear in the life of every person, and they can be interpreted as a range of social inequalities. They allow an individual to increase her life chances, or they destroy them (Kawula, 1997: 55).

These are the phenomena, events and social relations created by individuals or groups of people. We usually are their subjects but are sometimes perpetrators and even victims. We have an influence on their rise, and hence stems their social and pattern-making importance in our personal and social life. Some define them as external determinants that restrict the freedom of choosing specific behaviours by individuals and groups. They may also be barriers to the development of human personality. These can be poverty, scarcity of goods and values, violence, social inequalities, excessive external control, deviation from the truth, instability of the law, bureaucracy, standards of behaviour, rivalry, indoctrination and intolerance towards otherness (Kawula,1997: 55).

The consequences of the phenomena in question are generally suitably 'organized' by political and administrative bureaucrats. Śliwerski rightly said that when the much-coveted freedom finally came in 1989, 'reforming of education was initiated under the influence of the radical change of Poland's sociopolitical system, achieving different development stages ... during successive phases of the political-system transformations' (Śliwerski, 2010: 443). Thus, for the last twenty-five years this country has been dealing with a political universe which changes every two or four years, its carrier being the ruling class with enough material and spiritual force to also decide about the scope and quality of education. After coming to power, they take measures that eliminate the solutions introduced by their predecessors and treat the sphere of education as a particularistic political interest rather than a public concern (Śliwerski, 2010: 444). Close observation of these measures leads to a sad conclusion that it will take a long time before this particularism starts losing it political significance. There is no doubt, on the other hand, that it is possible and necessary to demand that this Herculean task be attempted in order to thoroughly change the Polish ministerial reform of education begun in 1998.

Final conclusions

In 2014, Poland, as a medium-size European country, is still a European Union member state. Its population is 38,512,000 citizens, most of them Roman Catholic. There are 18,644, 000 men and 19,868,000 women, the difference remaining at a similar level for many years. The country has 13,550 six-year primary schools and 7,371 three-year gymnasiums (lower secondary schools). These are the schools that provide compulsory education to children and teenagers. Moreover, there are 2,352 upper secondary schools of general education (*liceum*), 288 specialized upper secondary schools and 453 higher education institutions with almost 1,900,000 college students; these schools are public and private. Furthermore, there are almost 17,000 kindergartens and preschool education centres, both public and private, for almost 700,000 children. The tasks of instruction, care and upbringing are performed at all education levels by 380,000 teachers (Rocznik Statystyczny Rzeczpospolitej Polskiej 2013. Rozdział: Edukacja; Encyklopedia Pedagogiczna XXI wieku, vol. 4: 1028–32).

Efficient management of the foregoing structure of the national education system, particularly with so many bureaucratic obstacles and barriers, is limited, and in many cases it is even prevented by the bureaucratic system and the people heading its agencies. In view of the foregoing, several conclusions arise, formulated by one of the most eminent experts on the problems of the education reform, Prof. Czesław Kupisiewicz:

1. There is an urgent need to re-reform the school system and higher education in Poland. The reform should be comprehensive, taking into account not only the current structure of the system but also the teaching content, organizational forms, methods and means of training.

2. It is necessary to analyse and assess the manner of preparation and execution of the reform because only those reforms can be effective that are designed and implemented with the participation of educational authorities and teachers as rightful partners.

3. The starting point for every education reform should be the restructuring of the teacher-training system(s) in order to prepare them for the constantly changing social and economic needs.

4. The reform should be supported and fully approved by all levels of the country's political and administrative authorities.

5. The reform should be carefully thought out, coordinated and supported financially, organizationally and structurally. Representatives of pedagogical science should be included in its implementation, which ought to be done by the authorities, who have so far not always remembered their rank and importance.

6. The pressing problems of pedagogy and education are therefore extremely urgent and require swift identification. The absence of appropriate response, omission or postponement of decisions causes damage with long-lasting social and political consequences. If one wants to solve this problem, one should react not to the process, but to the symptom, because that is the time of optimal response. If 'such will be the Commonwealths as the upbringing of their youth (as Chancellor Jan Zamoyski said several centuries ago)', let us rise to the occasion and take up the work of far-sighted and far-reaching reform (Kupisiewicz, 2006a: 149–50).

References

Books

Banach, C. (1992). *Edukacja szkolna wobec polskich wyzwań cywilizacyjnych. Budowa środków zaufania międzynarodowego zadaniem kultury.* Opole: WSP.

Banach, C. (2005). *Szkoła naszych oczekiwań i marzeń, potrzeb, projekcji i działań od A do Ż.* Poznań: eMPi².

Bogaj, A., Kwiatkowski, S. M. and Szymański, M. J. (1998). *Edukacja w procesie przemian społecznych.* Warszawa: IBE.

Encyklopedia Pedagogiczna XXI wieku. (ed.) Prof. Dr Hab. Tadeusz Pilch. Warszawa 2005, volume IV, Wydawnictwo Akademickie 'Żak', 1020–39.

Komitet Prognoz przy Prezydium PAN 'Polska 2000 Plus' (1998). *Społeczeństwo polskie wobec wyzwań transformacji systemowej.* Warszawa: PWN.

Kozakiewicz, M. (1973). *Bariery awansu przez wykształcenie.* Warszawa: PWN.

Krukowski, J. (1995). 'Źródła współczesnych przemian oświatowych w Europie', in A. Zając (ed.), *Oświata w nowej rzeczywistości.* Przemyśl: WOM Printers, 18–31.

Kupisiewicz, C. (2006a). *Projekty reform edukacyjnych w Polsce.* Warszawa: PWN.

Kupisiewicz, C. (2006b). *Szkoła w XX wieku.* Warszawa: PWN.

Kupisiewicz, C. (ed.) (1990). *Edukacja w warunkach zagrożenia.* Warszawa–Kraków: PWN.

Kupisiewicz, C. (ed.). (1989). *Edukacja narodowym priorytetem. Raport o stanie i kierunkach rozwoju edukacji w PRL.* Warszawa–Kraków: PWN.

Kwiatkowski, S. M. (2006). *Edukacja polska w jednoczącej się Europie.* Warszawa: ZNP.

Kwieciński, Z. (1990). *Pedagogika i edukacja wobec wyzwania kryzysu i gwałtownej zmiany społecznej. Ku pedagogii pogranicza.* Toruń: Edytor.

Kwieciński, Z. (1994). 'Mimikra czy sternik? Dramat pedagogiki w sytuacji przesilenia formacyjnego', in H. Kwiatkowska (ed.), *Ewolucja tożsamości pedagogiki.* Warszawa: WSiP, 15–35.

Łomny, Z. (1995). *Człowiek i edukacja wobec przemian globalnych.* Opole: WSP.

Muszyński, H. (1994). 'Pedagogika polska na przełomie dwóch formacji społecznych', in H. Kwiatkowska (ed.), *Ewolucja tożsamości pedagogiki.* Warszawa: WSiP, 36–46.

Reforma systemu edukacji. Projekt (1998). Warszawa: WSiP, 228 + 4 nlb.

Rocznik Statystyczny Rzeczpospolitej Polskiej, Rozdział: Edukacja (2013). Warszawa: GUS.

Suchodolski, B. (ed.) (1979), *Ekspertyza dotycząca sytuacji i rozwoju oświaty w PRL.* Warszawa: PAN.

Szczepański, J. (ed.) (1973). *Raport o stanie oświaty w PRL.* Warszawa: PWN.

Szołtysek, A.E. (1995). 'Spór o formułę edukacji w świetle ustrojowych transformacji', in E. Holona and E. Nycz (eds), *Edukacja w procesie przemian cywilizacyjnych i kulturowych,* part 3. Opole: Uniwersytet Opolski., 101–15.

Śliwerski, B. (2010). 'Oświatowa zdrada ideałów i wartości nauczycielskiej Solidarności', in E. Gorloff, R. Grzybowski and A. Kołakowski (eds), *Edukacja w warunkach zniewolenia i autonomii (1945–2009).* Kraków: Impuls, 435–56.

Journals

Frąckowiak, T. (1997). 'Refleksje o szansach życiowych człowieka w czasach młodej demokracji.' *Chowanna,* 1 (8), Katowice, 15–27.

Górnikowska-Zwolak, E. and Radziewicz-Winnicki, A. (1997). 'Instytucjonalne przemiany w polskiej oświacie—Przeszkody i ograniczenia.' *Chowanna,* 1(8), Katowice: 28–38.

Hamilton, D. (1994). 'Educational Research, Policy and Practice, Lararutbildning och Forskning I Umea.' *Teacher Education and Research in Umea,* 4: 5–11.

Kawula, S. (1997). 'Bliskie bariery w edukacji.' *Chowanna*, 1(8), Katowice: 54–66.

Krąpiec, M. A. (1993). 'O ludzką politykę?' *Tolek* (b. m. w.).

Kucha, R. (1997). 'Niektóre uwarunkowania demokratycznych przemian edukacyjnych w Polsce po roku 1989.' *Chowanna*, 1(8), Katowice: 8–14.

Kucha, R. and Misiak, J. (1996). 'The Issue of the Private Schools Development in Poland in 1989–1995, Lararutbildning och Forskning i Umea.' Teacher Education and Research in Umea, 2: 49–54.

Lawn, M. (1994). 'The Collapse of the Modern Teacher and the Rise of the Differentiated Classroom Worker?, Lararutbildning och Forskning i Umea.' Teacher Education and Research in Umea, 4: 13–20.

Mańka, A. and Roter, A. (1997). 'Monocentryczno—Pluralistyczne oblicza nowej edukacji.' *Chowanna*, 1(8), Katowice: 39–47.

Further Reading

Banach, C. (2007). 'O prognozowaniu i reformowaniu polskiego systemu edukacji w latach 1989–2006', in M. Chepil and R. Kucha (eds), *Europejska wspólna przestrzeń edukacyjna, a przeobrażenia oświatowe w Polsce i na Ukrainie 1989–2006. Nadzieje i zagrożenia.* Drohobycz–Lublin: Drohobycz Printers, 58–67.

Kucha, R. (1998). 'Obstacles and barriers to democratic educational transformations in Poland after 1989 and their main determinants', in D. K. Marzec, A. Radziewicz-Winnicki (eds), *Educational Democratization in Poland: Tradition and Post—Communist Transformation.* Częstochowa–Katowice: WSP, 31–37.

11

Romania: Transitions to a European Framework, 2000–2014

Carmen Novac and Danut Dumitrascu

Introduction

Sitting at the top of the peninsula that from the eighteenth and nineteenth centuries became increasingly referred to as 'the Balkans', Romania became part of a group of countries—Greece, Bulgaria and Serbia—that, as the power of the Ottoman Empire fell away, started to contend with Turkey, arguing that they were more a part of Europe than Asia. With Bucharest being seen as 'the Paris of Wallachia' and the fusion of the two Danubian principalities of Moldovia and Walachia, Romania gradually came into existence in the period 1859–78; in the first half of the twentieth century, Romania grew from 50 to 120 million square miles and more than doubled its predominantly agrarian population, which either chose emigration to the American continent or found an impoverished life in farming. During the Soviet times, when Ceausescu's police state became an instrument of forcing the shift from agrarian to urban life in the concrete agro-towns, the scope for any intellectual or cultural freedom became almost non-existent. During this Cold War era, when Romania became noted for the repression on its own population, it did not foresee that its national educational system was destined to be reformed according to the new requests derived from its status as member of the European Union and from its functioning in a global context in the present era (Mazower, 2000).

The modern development of the national education system in Romania has been directed towards balancing the historical precedents of organizing and functioning with the European standards of reference and with the international examples of good practice in the field; ensuring wide access and equality of chances to education without discrimination; promoting and guaranteeing the cultural identity of all Romanian citizens and also the inter-cultural dialogue;

fostering decentralization and transparency in both decision making and obtained results; upholding the 'education–research–innovation' knowledge trinomial as the basis of a higher education system; and promoting excellence both in universities and research centres.

Since the 1970s, Romania has reduced the number of enrolments in the classical high schools in favour of technical and vocational schools, with the goal of becoming an industrial power. By the end of the Ceausescu period, less than 8 per cent of secondary school students were enrolled in the classical course, and by 1990 the distribution of students enrolled in theoretical and technical high schools was 71 per cent and in vocational schools, 20 per cent. Firms and cooperatives have played an important role in vocational education and training (VET), even to the extent of guaranteeing employment at the end of the training period (Kogan et al., 2008).

The past two decades represented for Romania a period of continuous changes at political, economic, social, cultural and especially educational levels. Education was and still is a major priority for the Romanian government; starting with the revolution in 1989, it has been an important key field for developing Romanian society (Westberg, 2013). The National Reform Program 2011–13 (Romanian Government, 2011) represented the guide for defining and applying Romanian economic development according to EU politics, having as a priority accomplishing an intelligent economy, durable and favourable to inclusion, with high occupational labour levels, productivity and social cohesion. This programme also addressed educational development and set goals Romanian educational bodies have tried, and partially succeeded in, completing.

Recent reforms in education

The recent reforms and changes within the Romanian educational system are aimed at adapting education to the permanent changes and requirements of the society, in balance with Romania's adhering to the European Union, and consisted in

- Changing the curriculum;
- Evaluating pupils and students;
- Training staff, professors and teachers;
- Changing the financial management; and
- Improving the administrative management.

At the same time, education in Romania had to face the changes imposed by the Bologna Process, globalization, internationalization, the growing number of pupils and students, and restrictions and limitations due to both financial and legislative issues, and recently impacted by the economic and financial crisis.

The educational system has attempted to achieve these goals by following a series of main objectives such as these: increasing the quality of the educational exercise; training both pupils and students from a permanent (lifelong) education perspective; ensuring as a right a modern training for all human resources within the educational system—both teaching and administrative staff; developing social cohesion; and growing the number of participants in economic and social development programmes. These are but a few of the many issues the educational system in Romania had to face in the process of becoming a 'European' educational system within the European Union guidelines; this process continues to evolve and change into the present time.

An overview of the Romanian educational system

The right to education in Romania is a natural right for all citizens, without discrimination (National Education Law, 2011). Under this law, all Romanian citizens are thus entitled to equal rights and chances to education, without social or material, sexual, racial, ethical, religious or political discrimination; this is also a guarantee of personal development, of help in achieving a professional culture and qualification, and of a diverse education, as recorded in each individual's final educational results. According to the main Romanian educational law— Law no. 1/2011, most education in Romania is organized by the state, through the Minister of National Education; this ensures the organizing and functioning of all educational institutions, of all grades, profiles, specializations and forms, in all its structures, of teaching, trainings and evaluating.

According to the Romanian Constitution and Educational Law, education in Romania is taught in the Romanian language, as an official language. Respecting the international standards of education, as a European country, the Romanian state provides individuals—pupils, students and adults seeking permanent education—the possibility of studying and training in the language of the national minorities and also other international languages, depending on the request. Particularly at higher education levels, the Erasmus, Tempus and other exchange programmes provide opportunities for comparing the achievement of students across countries.

As regards early education, the Educational Law creates the premises for a unitary approach at early ages, emphasizing the importance of this phase in predicting the child's future development. So, this is the first approach of real education, and not just childcare, for children aged 3. The preparation class is another innovative instrument for helping children gradually pass, in a unitary, organized educational context, from preschool and family-based learning towards the more scholarly experience of formal schooling, namely from kindergarten to the first grade of basic school. The four-year gymnasium phase (grades 5–8) provides continuity, as it usually takes place in the same school. A new instrument for evaluating pupils is being introduced so that an educational history can be developed, with emphasis on pupils' skills, hobbies and educational performances in various activities. Such evaluations are performed at the end of second grade, fourth grade and eighth grade, and are conducted with the end goal of establishing an educational portfolio. Eighth-graders graduate after passing a national test. Obligatory education ends at 10th grade or at age 16, the legal age at which an individual can enter the Romanian labour force, in common with many other countries of the European Union (National Educational Law, 2011). High school is completed in two more years, and graduates receive a certificate of graduation, whilst those choosing to complete four years of high school enter the Baccalaureate Diploma examination.

A significant proportion of high school graduates (twelfth-graders) chose to go to a university, college or a faculty, or to continue their studies and complete tertiary education (see Figure 11.1). Whilst having a tertiary education is not an absolute requirement for professional employment, it has become valuable to graduates trying to find their first job. It is important to note that until the completion of the gymnasium educational level, there are no costs for public kindergartens, public schools or public high schools; increasingly, tertiary education implies costs or fees which depend on both the institution and the faculty of study. According to Romanian educational statistics (National Statistics

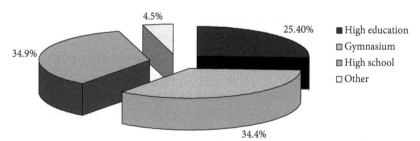

Figure 11.1 Distribution of graduates in Romania in 2011/2012 educational year.

Institute, 2013), at the end of the educational year 2011/12 there were 536,700 graduates from all educational levels, distributed as indicated in Figure 11.1.

The Romanian educational mode, in common with many of the former Eastern European systems, has begun to follow much the same pattern as many of the Western European countries. It is structured into two main parts: compulsory and pre-university stages, and pre-graduate/postgraduate university education; the pre-university stage comprises four levels: preschool level, primary level, secondary level (gymnasium, high school or school of arts and trades) and post–high school. The university education level comprises three levels: licenta university study (BA), master university study (MA) and doctorate university study (PhD).

On the basis of the new educational law, higher education institutions in Romania are now classified on the basis of an evaluation procedure into three categories: universities of education; universities of education, scientific research and artistic creation; and universities of advanced research and education. Universities are the main providers of a highly qualified labour force as well as providers of knowledge. Some important developments have taken place in universities. During the 1980s, the vast majority of students were enrolled in technical specialist fields, whereas only a few matriculated in artistic and legal areas. Technical studies have declined noticeably during the 1990s, whilst students pursuing degrees in the areas of pedagogy and economics have increased. The proportion of women enrolled increased from about 50 to 55 per cent overall, with pedagogy, pharmacy and economics being particularly over-represented, and the sciences and technical fields remaining relatively unpopular (Kogan et al., 2008). The future of the universities is ensured in *Carta Universitara* and sustained in each university through an evaluation process for the quality of study programmes, as well as institutional evaluation. Romanian universities have discovered several important missions, including education for cultural and technological citizenship, research, economic development, and politics, as well as creating and recreating knowledge.

In the economic crisis of 2007–13, the goals of Romanian universities concerned the transfer of research results to industry and society so the results could be transformed into innovative products and services leading to economic growth and wealth creation; this process is referred to as the dynamics of university-industry-government relation (Etzkowitz and Leydesdorff, 1995). The government agrees with these priorities and assists in this knowledge transfer through partially funding (the basic funding of the university comes from the Ministry) and facilitating legal and political assistance and conditions. The funds allocated by the state are chronically insufficient and do not allow the Romanian universities to enter into a real competition with other European universities (Novac, Dumitrascu, 2011). The financing of Romanian higher education is mainly based on a contract between the universities and the Ministry of Education.

Thus the public universities have the following basic funding:

- An institutional contract that establishes the support, or basic, funding for scholarship allowance and the social protection of students, which is the main document that directs negotiations between the Minister and the universities;
- A complementary contract that establishes the support funding for the research activities, capital repairs, investment expenses, allowances for accommodation and a student cafeteria.

Other additional sources of income can be considered to be: own income, which derives from students, administrative and other fees; non-reimbursable external funding, meaning all the income that enters the university through the help of eligible projects within the operational programs ('Lucian Blaga' University of Sibiu, Romania, a public Romanian university classified in 2011 as university of education and scientific research, can be taken as an example of a public Romanian university that develops more than thirty such projects with a funding value of almost 20 million Euros); incomes in the form of taxes paid for accommodation and students' meals (plus the state allowance); income from 'auto-financed' activities such as a publishing department or laboratories.

The main idea for public universities as tertiary-level education providers is to identify a structure for the financial resources that should ensure maximum efficiency financial resources both in terms of time and unit cost. Allocating these financial resources should practically support an activity in conditions of continuity and sustainability. This academia, business and community interaction is being promoted as the source of such an additional income for all the Romanian educational institutions.

Principles and development of Romanian education

In close correlation with the Universal Declaration of Human Rights, the Romanian Constitution and the Education Law, the Romanian education applies the principle of freedom of conscience, thought and opinion, as well as that of the right to a particular faith and religion, which cannot be restricted under any circumstances. This principle implies a spirit of tolerance, understanding and mutual respect so that no one may be compelled to a religious belief contrary to his own, the religious, atheist and agnostic citizens being able to live together peacefully and constructively.

It is in this context that Romanian education attempts to provide both training of young people in accordance with the latest achievements of science, technology and culture, and their religious education through teaching religion in schools and high schools—as a separate subject, according to the pupil's preference for a specific religion, in accordance with the law. Religious proselytizing is prohibited in schools. In order to achieve a thorough and high general education, an appropriate school guidance, relatively equal chances for the young people to enter high school and training schools, and also a social integration in the socially useful work area, the law provides a general and compulsory ten-year education, including four grades for primary school, four for grammar school and two for high school. To achieve an effective, high-quality compulsory education, both educators and the learners must make serious efforts, motivating the good and the best students to get good results; thus, the phenomenon of school failure should disappear in the case of students who do not want to continue their studies. Students who, with all the help they were provided, do not get proper results, may repeat the year. Hence, by the age of 16, children will have been required to attend general education, the law stating that the parents and the legal guardians are required to make sure children undertake the ten-year compulsory education.

To help students graduate from the general, compulsory, ten-year education, and also support attendance at other levels of education, the state ensures that educational provision is free, not demanding any school fees, but covering the cost of tuition from the government central budget. The state provides various facilities for all levels of education by grants from the budget, from which also come funds for building education centres, for technically and materially endowing the schools, and for training and paying the teachers. The state also provides scholarships for deserving students, for those lacking financial means, for orphans and for survivors of those who died in the dramatic revolution on December 1989, when President Ceausescu was ousted, and related events. Fees were introduced for a certain number of students, especially in higher education. In private education schools, fees are charged, taking into account that this education is organized and operates on its own financial resources, and in certain areas of public education where students admitted over the planned quota of subsidized places are required to pay fees at a similar level as that of private education.

In the future, it is possible that, subject to the required growth of economic development, the accredited private educational institutions could be materially and financially supported by the state, possibly along the same lines it is done in some Western countries. Moreover, to accomplish their goals as effectively as possible, both public and private forms of education need to be funded from local budgets and by companies and various private institutions as well as sponsors, taking into consideration that they are all beneficiaries of education—the workforce and the specialists. Therefore, the private universities might receive students from the disadvantaged categories, without making them pay fees.

To ensure equal opportunities for training and competence, all schools of the same level, profile and structure are organized and operated through a *unitary educational concept* (National Educational Law, 2011). This principle applies to private education too, because its objective is to grant the same diplomas as the public education. The unitary character of the education is given mainly by a comprehensive means of organization and functioning and by unified content of education, reflected in common syllabi and curricula. Fair competition is possible through various ways of selecting contents and interpreting the educational act, in which the professionalism, competence and mastery of the teachers, as well as their reliability, plays an important role. Matched by the capacity and the effort of learners, this ensures the acquisition of higher skills in training young people. Moreover, competition has a place not only in educational activity but also in the professional world students will enter after leaving school or college, when they will properly appreciate the achieved values and scientific, professional and civic skills.

Thanks to *democratic education*, the law and equal opportunities of learning in Romania, it is theoretically possible for any young person who obtains proper results in education and gains the appropriate educational level to be offered the opportunity to graduate from primary education to higher education, and possibly to obtain a doctorate, without discrimination. Accessibility to all levels of education is also provided by the nature of the ten-year compulsory education, by its gratuity and by the financial aid given to studious youth through scholarships and tax exemptions. The availability of education at all levels sometimes involves competition; placements are determined by the certain number of positions established according to social division of labour and level and competence of training, in order for the most deserving young people to enter a higher education level.

Ensuring equal opportunities to students as they pass from one level of education to another requires removing educational disparities between different levels of education so that transition can occur without shock or failure. In conjunction with providing equal opportunities for youth training, it is necessary to develop an elite education, one that provides gifted young people with creativity training and the possibility to achieve high performance, which is not only good for them but also for society. In Romanian education, gifted young people are allowed to advance their schooling at their own pace, and it is possible to complete two years of study in one school year. The open nature of education requires sustained efforts for high learning results; that diplomas awarded on completion of each level of education should reliably represent intellectual and professional competence in order to be acknowledged nationally and internationally, and so that graduates have the necessary skills and knowledge to face professional competitions in the schools and universities they will attend. Public pre-university education is coordinated by the Ministry of Education and Research and forty-three relevant county inspectorates, in cooperation with the beneficiary organizations and the local authorities, and in terms of the process of school decentralization (National Educational Law, 2011).

In order to increase accountability and the role of school management, pre-university education is provided with autonomy through decentralization, schools' having their own budgets and other measures. The structure of the education system in Romania objectifies organizing education systems on levels (degrees), sections and forms of school institutions in a coherent and unified ensemble. It creatively combines the traditions and the achievements of the Romanian school with the educational achievements at the European and international level. The forms of education are *day, part time and long distance.* Experimental and application pilot units also operate in the education system.

Higher education is autonomous, giving the academic community the right to conduct its own programmes, and the universities the ability to exercise their rights without ideological, political or religious interference, and the ability to assume legal rights and obligations. The rights of the university to autonomy are stipulated in the University Charter (*Carta Universitara*), drafted by each higher education institution, according to the valid regulations. University autonomy ensures the real democratization of higher education, the decentralization of management and the achievement of an effective self-management for the higher education institutions.

During the 1980s, Romania faced a major discrepancy within its educational system: high enrolment rates at the pre-tertiary level (98 per cent in primary, 83 per cent in secondary in 1989), but one of the lowest rates at the tertiary level. Although free and universally accessible in theory, tertiary education development was inhibited by economic constraints during the twentieth century. Another problem that Romania inherited from the communist period was the gap between rural and urban areas; schools in rural areas were poorly endowed in terms of infrastructure and human resources. Teachers in the rural areas were those with the lowest job performance and often were 'required' to teach in rural areas before being eligible to apply for jobs in the urban areas (Mocanu, Romania, 2008).

The system of education

Preschool education for three (four) years

Preschool education aims to supplement family education and includes children aged 3 to 6 (7) years, providing them with both the proper training and development required for their age, as well as the preparation they need for entering primary school. Including for this purpose are children 6–7 years of age, thus contributing to the formation and improvement of their physical, intellectual, emotional and social development, especially through teaching games, but also through whole-group activities. The low student/teacher ratio of 1/5 in preschool education allows for individual attention and helps prepare children for primary school. Activities take place in kindergartens under the guidance of an educator who is a graduate from a teacher training college (high school or pedagogical college).

Primary four-year education, grades 1 to 4, for 7- to 11-year-old children

Primary education is organized on the basis of daily attendance. At enrolment in first grade, children are tested for disabilities so that they can, if necessary, be enrolled in special education. Children aged 6–7 years old may attend primary school by meeting certain psychological, physiological and pedagogical requirements and criteria, according to proper personality development. Primary education is part of compulsory education. Primary education has the following objectives: students should acquire the basic knowledge, capabilities and intellectual skills regarding reading, writing, mathematics (arithmetic calculation), and speaking a foreign, internationally used language, as well as acquire skills for civilized behaviour, orientation and action in the surrounding natural geographic and socio-human environment. The main teaching factor in primary education is the teacher, a graduate of a teaching training college (high school or pedagogical college). Graduates from higher education may also be educators and schoolteachers, under the name 'instructors' and are paid according to their higher educational training.

Gymnasium four-year education, grades 5 to 8, for 11- to 15-year-old children

The gymnasium is part of the ten-year compulsory general education. Gymnasium, or secondary, education is organized on the basis of daily attendance, but it can be also organized as evening classes and part-time or distance learning. Secondary education has the following objectives: learning the fundamentals of science and general knowledge; learning at least one foreign language of international circulation; acquiring general capabilities and technological abilities; forming skills necessary for a practical activity (pre-specializing) established in an assessments of needed trained gymnasium graduates; and providing civic education to achieve a civilized behaviour and appropriate action in the socio-human environment. The knowledge acquired in the secondary education is evaluated through single topic written papers, undertaken by students in the seventh and eighth grades. Secondary school graduates can attend college or vocational schools. Teachers in secondary schools are generally graduates from university three-year colleges, but also graduates from universities, all bearing the title of teachers. After passing national exams and test, gymnasium graduates are admitted to high school education.

High school education

High schools are organized on multiple profiles: theoretical, real and humanistic, informatics, technical, economic, administrative, logistics, agriculture, forestry, agro-highlands, pedagogical (teacher training college), art, sports, military and theological. High schools have the following objectives: enriching and deepening knowledge in science and general knowledge; developing intellectual capacities, especially of thinking; outlining a practical dimension of the acquired knowledge, the understanding of the elements and methods of research; learning at least one foreign language; forming a proper civic and moral behaviour; and preparation for further study. Specialized high schools also provide career guidance. At the end of their course of studies, pupils present a practical work, and graduates are given a certificate of qualification. On graduating from high school, pupils must sit for a baccalaureate exam, and those who pass it get a Baccalaureate Diploma. High school graduates with a baccalaureate degree can continue their studies in higher education, according to admission criteria set by the university. High school graduates who do not attend higher education can pursue a post-secondary school or can be hired in a socially useful activity, perfecting their qualifications at their workplace. Teachers in high schools are university graduates who have obtained their bachelor's and master's degrees.

High school graduates, who have passed all grades with an average mark of 9.50 and get the average mark of 10 at the baccalaureate exam, will receive certificates of merit. However, universities may set criteria which, starting with the eleventh grade, provide students with the possibility to take some university courses; in such cases, the classes attended are recognized and accredited after the student obtains a Baccalaureate Diploma and university admission. Also, high-performing high school graduates, should they wish, may compete to obtain the International Baccalaureate, a diploma recognized throughout Europe.

Vocational education: 1–3 years

The *vocational education* is accessible, according to the limited number of placements, to gymnasium graduates. Vocational education is conducted in two modules:

a) *Arts and crafts schools* with grades 9 and 10, which are concluded with a Certification of Professional Competence Exam for level 1, and
b) Completion year for the eleventh grade, which ends with a Certification of professional competence exam for level 2. Graduates from vocational education have the right to continue high school, in twelfth and thirteenth grades.

Post–high school education: 1–3 years

Post-secondary education includes *post-secondary schools* and *foreman schools*. Both types of school end with graduation exams, with the graduate being awarded a certificate of professional competence.

Post-secondary schools: 1–3 years

Post-secondary schools prepare technicians for various economic and social sectors such as industry, agriculture, education and health.

Foreman education: 1–3 years

College graduates can enter foreman schools, by examination or interview, if applicable, after conducting a production internship and receiving recommendations from, for example, someone in economic, industrial or construction fields.

Higher (university) education

Higher (university) education is designed to prepare highly qualified specialists in all fields of knowledge, for example science, culture, education, arts, economy (industry, agriculture, commerce, finance, banks), public order, national defence, sports, tourism, justice, politics and management. Higher education work can be accomplished in the following types of institutions: universities, institutes and academies. *State university education* is free for the number of placements approved by the government, and for a tuition fee, according to the law. Free state higher education charges certain fees, such as those for exceeding the tuition period, admissions, registration, repeating examinations and other forms of assessment, and for activities not included in the curriculum, according to the criteria established by the university senates.

High school graduates with a baccalaureate diploma may gain admission to higher education, according to the regulations of each university, established under the general criteria provided by the Ministry of Education and Research. Those who were awarded certificates during the past two years in local or international Olympics, or in sports or artistic competitions at a continental, world or Olympic level, can be admitted without sitting for an entrance examination.

University education is offered in the following teaching forms: daily, evening, part time and distance learning. The duration and organization of each cycle of university studies comes under the competence of each university with the approval of the Ministry of Education and Research. The offer of placement takes into account the needs of the labour market and the development of social life and is established by the Ministry of Education and Research in collaboration with the universities and social partners. The duration of each cycle of studies tends to reflect the number of transferable university credits according to the European system of transferable credits (ECTS).

Undergraduate studies

Undergraduate studies cover the range of 180–240 ECTS credits. With full-time, daily attendance, the duration of studies is, in principle, three years, corresponding to attaining 180 credits. Faculties in technical and juridical education have a duration of four years (240 credit hours), whilst medical and architecture education can take six years (360 credit hours). For part-time students taking evening classes, the duration of studies is longer by one year. Prior work experience and study are recognized, as is the use of distance learning; the duration of such studies is regulated by the government. Undergraduate studies provide general and specialized theoretical and practical training, adequate to the performance of a profession, according to labour market demands. Graduates with a bachelor's degree can practice professions in accordance with the skills and rights proven by the diploma and have the opportunity to pursue master studies. The bachelor's degree certifies that its holder has acquired the general and professional skills needed for conducting a certain career.

Master's-level studies

Admission to a master's program is granted only to those who hold a bachelor's degree. In full-time daily attendance, the duration of study is two years and normally corresponds to ECTS 120 credits. Thus, the student who pursues an undergraduate degree and then undertakes master's studies must accrue a number of 300 transferable credits to be recognized. For academic studies with a duration of five and six years of daily attendance, diplomas are equivalent to the title of master. Master's-level studies are organized in several modes—as education requiring daily attendance, reduced-frequency education or distance learning—their duration being established by government ordinance. Master's-level studies are required to provide deeper training than undergraduate studies in a related field, as well as the development of scientific research capabilities, and they can also provide a basis for preparing for doctoral studies.

Master's degrees certify that the holders acquired the general and speciality skills necessary for exercising a certain profession. Graduates with a bachelor's degree (from a three-year university) may occupy teaching positions in primary and secondary education, provided they have acquired pedagogical and methodical training in the Department of Teacher Training (DTT) module (30 credits) certified by a teacher certificate. Graduates with a master's degree can occupy teaching positions in high schools as well as post-secondary and university institutions, on condition that they acquire a pedagogical and methodical training within the second module conducted by the DTT (30 credits), which is completed with a teacher certificate.

Doctoral studies

Admission to doctoral study programmes is competitive and based on the demonstrated quality of the PhD candidate. Only specialists with a master's degree or equivalent may apply to a doctoral programme, according to the law. Doctoral studies normally last for three years, though in special cases, due to the need for longer periods of research and experimentation, the duration may be extended by one or two years at the request of the doctoral thesis coordinator and with the approval of the Senate or the university which organizes the PhD. After passing certain exams and supporting a number of papers, the student develops a doctoral topic based on documentation and experimentation. The thesis is supported within the academic (scientific) council of the institution that organizes the PhD. The approved thesis is then endorsed by the University Senate (or the Scientific Council of the scientific institution) and forwarded to the Ministry of Education and Research; the national council for scientific and academic titles approves the PhD Diploma in the field evidenced by the doctoral thesis, and it is awarded by order of the Minister of Education and Research. The title of the thesis in some specific (and usually scientific) fields provides the holder with certain rights to occupy academic or professional positions, as well as some financial benefits. The regulations specific to the doctoral studies are established by the Ministry of Education and Research and approved by the government.

Teacher education

In-service education for teachers is provided after the initial training in college, where the holder can earned bachelor's and master's degrees as well as the teacher certificate by DTT; other forms of training for teachers also exist in undergraduate education: Teacher improvement and training is conducted on three levels: (1) permanent teaching certification after two years of teaching practice; (2) teacher certification level II; (3) teacher certification level I. These forms of training are conducted through specialized psycho-pedagogical and methodological training and are completed with an exam. By promoting these forms of training, teachers are ensured certain rights, including financial ones. Professional development is conducted every five years within ninety transferable credits from approved programmes. This development is done on three forms of thirty credits for each unit: (1) professional improvement, (2) pedagogical improvement and (3) IT e-learning.

Continuous training is offered for specialist professors in higher education and is done by documentary and exchange programmes at national and international levels; specialization and university cooperation programmes in the country and abroad; scientific research programmes carried out in the country or abroad through international cooperation; and educational innovation, scientific, technical or artistic creation.

Permanent education

Permanent education (lifelong learning) provides access to science, culture, modern technologies and computerization for all citizens, so they can adapt their general and professional training to the changes occurring in all spheres of social and professional life. Courses are organized by the Ministry of Education in cooperation with the regional ministries, as well as by companies, popular universities and media, either together with the schools or separately. Permanent education is conducted in various forms such as courses, seminars, debates, conferences and round tables, which aim to contribute to the improvement of general, scientific, professional, legal, ethical, managerial, cultural and artistic training of the adults at all levels and all profiles of training.

Special education

The Romanian educational system comprises a network of special schools for children and students with mental, physical, sensory, socio-emotional and behavioural deficiencies or with associated impairments. These special schools are meant for training and educating students with disabilities according to the type and degree of disability established by the board of special expertise. Special education is conducted according to school documents and teaching strategies appropriate to the type of disability, ensuring both intellectual and practical training in order to integrate these children in the general or special education network, and help them find socially useful work. This more contemporary approach to inclusive education is meant to accelerate the rate of change within special education.

Romanian education and investment in Romanian education has always required proportionally high levels of investment in public sector education institutions, especially higher education which requires significant financial resources. Providing these resources, at least in recent years, has proved to be an extremely sensitive, often critical issue for the economic system. The Romanian labour market suffered from the economic restructuring process. Overall unemployment rates have been moderate, but the labour maker did not provide sufficient employment opportunities despite achieving reasonable economic growth. A high number of people were engaged in the agricultural sector and, unlike other Central and Eastern European (CEE) countries, Romania did not embark on retrenchment of social policies until the late 1990s. Investment in education as a whole has been hard to satisfy, and in higher education, particularly difficult to develop whilst social poverty rates have continued to remain some of the highest in Europe (Mocanu, 2008).

National minorities and their recognition

About 10 per cent of the Romanian population is represented by minorities, the largest number and most regionally compact being Hungarians (Magyars and Settlers) in the north-west regions or Transylvania. Germans, who also are mostly to be found in the Transylvanian region, continuously settled there from the twelfth century onwards; many Germans have emigrated to Germany in recent years, and the number remaining within the country has halved in the past twenty years, to around sixty thousand. Perhaps the largest minority are the Roma, who can be found throughout Romania with estimates of their numbers varying from half a million to 1.5 million; many do not necessarily declare their origins for fear of discrimination. In May 1990, the government issued a regulation expanding minority-language education and, with considerable international support, provided minority-language television and radio broadcasts, along with the establishment of a Council of National Minorities in 1993. Further legal and political guarantees for minorities followed in 2003 and were significantly further improved in the run up to the country's accession to the European Union (full membership was gained in January 2007).

Conclusions

This chapter gives a brief overview of the general aspects that concern the Romanian educational system and some of its recent reform programmes, as seen through the eyes of the main legal instruments that regulate the Romanian education system. Although the most recent reforms have paid attention to gifted managers or talented pupils and students, it remains the case that there are not sufficient conditions for developing Romanian education for all, and concerns remain about the relatively slow developments in providing education for minorities for whom unemployment can be especially severe. There is a wide external recognition that higher performing teachers are needed and that teacher education is inadequate and will require further development. Further demands have also been called for in the new politics with regard to taking measures to align Romanian education to both European and international reforms.

References

Etzkowitz, H. and Leydesdorff, L. (1995). 'The Triple Helix: University, Industry, Government Relations. A laboratory for knowledge based economic development'. EASST Review, European Society for the Study of Science and Technology, 14(1): 18–36.

Kogan, I., Gebel, G. and Noelke, C. (2008). Europe Enlarged: A Handbook of Education, Labour and Welfare Regimes in Central and Eastern Europe. Polity Press, 295–305.

Lucian Blaga University of Sibiu, section *PhD Programs in Lucian Blaga University.* Online at http://doctorate.ulbsibiu.ro/en/ (accessed on June 2013).

Lucian Blaga University of Sibiu, at http://international.ulbsibiu.ro/#&slider1=1

Novac, C. and Dumitrascu, D. D. (2011). 'Pros and cons for the Entrepreneurial University', International Conference *European Integration, New Challenge,* 5th Edition, University of Oradea, Romania, Conference Proceedings, ISSN: 1844–5519, 101.

Mazower, M. (2000). 'The Balkans: From the end of Byzantium to the Present Day.' Weidenfeld and Nicolson, 118–28.

Mocanu, C., 'Romania' in Kogan et al., op cit., 295–308.

Ministry of Education, 'Romanian Educational Structure', at www.edu.ro (accessed in August and November 2013; accessed on 9 September 2013, section *International Relations Department*).

National Statistics Institute of Romania (2013). 'Press Release', no 154, Bucharest, 2013, 1–4.

Romanian Government (2011). 'National Reform Program', Bucharest, 105–15.

Romanian Government, Ministry of Education (2011). 'National Education Law', Bucharest.

Westberg, T. B. (2013). Norway Ambassador in Romania, 'Discourse at the Civil Society Conference, Bucharest, 14 October 2013.

12

Slovakia: Issues in Pedagogy and Language Education, 1989–2014

Eva Tandlichová

Introduction

Since 1994, the Slovak system of education has undergone substantial changes which are still in the process of being amended. Therefore, this chapter deals with the historical background and impetus for those changes, as well as the current situation. It will also provide an overview of possible future development. The chapter reviews the implementation of the current reform in primary and secondary education and, with this in mind, analyse the situation at universities, namely the process of teacher training. As a teacher trainer and educator of English teachers for many years, the author will devote special attention to the development and current issues within the conception of foreign language teaching in Slovakia. An in-service teacher training project focusing on the improvement of foreign language teaching from the primary level (pupils aged 6) up to school-leaving exams (students aged 19) is analysed, looking at the pros and cons of that project experience as far as the improvement of the participants' pedagogical, psychological and [foreign] language knowledge and skills are concerned.

Current changes in the Slovak education system can be considered as a climax of former reforms. Since the end of the Second World War, the (Czecho) Slovak education system has manifested several important reforms. The first reform was connected with the idea of a 'unified school which was specified in 1944 by the Slovak National Council's decree. All types of schools became state schools. The unified school principle was respected till the year 1990. The school reform of 1948 introduced nine year compulsory education which was shortened in 1953 into eight years and in 1960 it was changed again into nine year compulsory school attendance'(Humajová et al., 2008). In 1976, the document 'Further Development of the Czechoslovak Education System (*Ďalší rozvoj československej výchovnovzdelávacej sústavy*)' was published. Its main goal was to speed up the development of the school system and also the after-school institutions in order to meet the then-current needs of the society as well as the requirements of the scientific-technical revolution. That document was an impulse for another reform during which there were new syllabi and new course books written and published. The State Research Institute invited scholars to join the project in order to test the new syllabi and new course books for all school subjects; I was one of the invitees. We tested new course books for secondary school learners of English as a foreign language. And it was then that I also started my career as a course book writer. It was an intensive research which has brought me to foreign language teaching and learning new methods for such, especially the communicative method in teaching English built on real-life situations.

The reform in the content of education in other subjects seemed to have a good conception and was based on significant theoretical resources (from a Russian psychological school closely connected with L. Vygotsky's research), but the outcome resulted in the routine acceleration of course content difficulty in textbooks. Pupils were overloaded with facts and a large amount of information which was sometimes acquired by memorization. The strategies which would lead to learning comprehension were minimized (Humajová et al., 2008).

Challenges after 1989

The education system in Slovakia has undergone substantial changes since 1993. The first amendment of the school law brought more legal subjectivity to secondary schools. Primary school attendance was extended to nine years again, and compulsory school attendance was shortened to nine years. The possibility of establishing private and ecclesiastical schools brought a new challenge. In this way, the idea of a unified school system was pushed into the background, and room for variability in education for pupils, students and parents was opened. The reform created more latitude for respecting pupils with special needs and special difficulties. In the 1990s, an intensive discussion took place about the implementation of new approaches and challenges in education, and their effects. Compulsory school attendance was extended to ten years. We can agree with Humajová that the nine amendments to the 1984 law brought positive changes, but only partial improvement. It was not then possible to apply or develop systemic changes in education, and there was not even enough time (until 1989) to develop gradual continuity in education.

But there were some positive changes started inside the educational system, due to the initiative of schools and even of creative teachers. For example, the foreign languages (Russian, English, German and French) were part of the curriculum for many years but in the 1970s and 1980s there were primary schools (not many in number) where English, German and French (Russian was compulsory from the age of 10) were taught either from the age of 8 or 9 or in the fourth grade at the age of 10. The only problem was that there was no continuity; there were many new pupils in the beginner classes at secondary schools, and the teachers there had 'an extra job' to look for more activities for those students in order for them to make any progress in foreign language proficiency.

During those years, the Pedagogical Research Institute invited several experts in foreign language methodology and best language teachers to join teams for writing course books. The six-volume English course for primary schools (pupils aged 8–15) was written by the team which I led, and there was another team led by Prof. R. Repka which wrote a four-volume set for secondary schools. Both our teams tried to create modern and communicative course books in order to make teaching and learning of English more real-life oriented and creative.

The 1990s manifested a boom of changes in methods and techniques. In many cases, those changes were born as bottom-up initiatives from creative teachers or school managers. Teachers and school principals tried to apply democracy in teaching and school management in order to make teaching more learner friendly and learner centred. It is said that more than 40 per cent of primary schools offered extended study in math, foreign languages, sport or music. Some schools were able to respect the parents and pupils' interests and offer special options. Experts considered these attempts at reform to be a not very systemic strategy.

With respect to foreign language teaching, Russian was excluded from the curriculum. Since the end of the Second World War, it had been a compulsory first foreign language in Czechoslovakia. Pupils started learning Russian from the age of 10 (fifth grade of primary school) and continued at secondary school. Russian, together with Slovak (the mother tongue) and maths were compulsory subjects in the *Maturita* (school-leaving) exam. Looking at the role of Russian in schools, it was not taught as a foreign language because pupils dealt with Russian literature and learned Russian poems by heart. Competitions in reading Russian poetry, called Pushkin's Memorial, took place. Some lessons were given in

Russian grammar, which was very difficult for learners to remember because the grammar translation method, including memorization, was used. This approach resulted in very few school graduates who could speak Russian well.

After 1989, the Ministry of Education decided to drop Russian and give more lessons in other foreign languages—English, German, French, Spanish and Italian—which were taught even before 1989. Although a welcome idea, there were not many qualified teachers to teach those languages. Therefore, the Ministry of Education decided to re-qualify the original teachers of Russian in intensive language courses in order for them to be able to teach English, German, French, Spanish and Italian. Twenty years later, the situation has changed, and there is a revival in interest in learning Russian, whilst the statistics illustrate that an increasing number of learners choose Russian from among the foreign languages offered in the curriculum.

The 1990s brought further reforms: in 1994 the Ministry of Education published the first complex conception known as *Projekt Konštantín—Národný Program Výchovy a Vzdelávania* (Constantine Project—The National Progamme of Education and Training), but due to a change of minister, that project was not brought to fruition. In 1998, the new minister appointed a group of experts who created *Koncepciu rozvoja výchovy a vzdelávania v SR s horizontom na najbližších 10–15 rokov* (New Conception of the Development of Education and Training within 10–15 years), entitled *Milénium*. Written by Prof. M. Zelina, an outstanding psychologist, it highlighted the importance of education (upbringing) and the importance of productive emotional experience as well as the importance of the development of non-cognitive features of personality; thus the *Milénium* emphasized the statement that education is more than training (Zelina, 2005). The changes which took place by the year 2001 were done without any deeper analysis when the National Programme of Education and Training Milénium was approved by the Slovak government. One of Slovak's outstanding pedagogues (and later one of the *Milénium* project authors) Prof. Ivan Turek called for reforms in education because of the immense amount of information that learners had to absorb in limited time. Therefore, for Turek it was important to consider the teaching-learning process a never-ending process, with school attendance just the start of a lifelong education and training process. He also highlighted the demand for a curriculum which would include not just knowledge but would also put an emphasis on practical skills, that is, the importance of competences acquisition (Turek, 1997).

What has been done since 2001 when *Milénium* first came to the Slovak educational stage? What has been put into practice? First, the decentralization of education took place (including both positive and negative outcomes); and finances were distributed in a more transparent way, although no more money was put into education. The state school-leaving exam (*Maturita*) has been changed according to recommendations of the *Milénium*, though the students continued to fail PISA tests in reading and problem-solving tasks. The experts explained the failure by saying that the school system does not allow for the development of creative thinking, creativity, (self-)evaluation and concurrent non-cognitive functions, such as self-esteem or curiosity. Attempts were also made to include changes in higher education and universities and their study programmes, but without much success.

Zelina was sceptical in saying that 'in [the] case of foreign language teaching and learning the progress was slow and we lacked (and still do in a way) enough qualified teachers' (Zelina, 2005: 6). But other research done by experts in the field under the auspices of the National Institute for Education concluded:

[T]eaching foreign languages has become one of the priority requirements for education in the European milieu. The year 2001 was declared the European Year of Languages, and foreign languages have been receiving increasing attention ever since then—not merely from the part of teachers and pupils, but also from the Government policy actors. [...] We no longer require from primary school leavers and secondary school graduates a mere solid basis of their knowledge and skills, but an increasingly individualized attitude to the performance of their activities, autonomy, and responsibility, all of these based on the principles of competitive advantages, mobility, and initiative. [...] In respect of the above set of issues, it appears inevitable to reconsider the following:

- Assess the present state in teaching of foreign languages at all types of schools,
- Map the qualification structure of teachers of foreign languages,
- Reconsider time allocation and suitability of choice of the foreign-language textbooks employed,
- Reconsider, modify or eventually amend the curricula for training the prospective teachers of foreign languages,
- Arrange postgraduate education of teachers of foreign languages and devote increasing attention to lifelong education of teachers of foreign languages.' (Butašová et al., 2009)

Then the National Institute for Education started a series of arrangements to improve the teaching and learning of foreign languages in the Slovak Republic. They have invited methodologists, experts and teachers to participate. Two projects took place: the ESF project *Improving the Effectiveness of Teaching of Foreign Languages in the Light of the Accession of Slovakia into the EU*, and the KEGA project *Draft Conception of the Language Policy of Teaching of Foreign Languages at Primary and Secondary Schools*. In 2001, extensive research was carried out to find out about the real language competences of pupils in the ninth grade of primary school (15-year-old pupils).

Zelina also highlighted the fact that very little has been done to improve the status of teachers. The task has been with us since then, and the teachers' trade union representatives have been in constant dialogue with the Ministry of Education to do something about the unacceptable situation.

According to various EU documents and namely the Common European Framework for Languages: Learning, Teaching, Assessment (CEF) (2001) transformation and amendments in curricula should enable learner-centred teaching and learning; and support learner-autonomy development and education based on the development of general and communicative competences. Key competences have been defined, and these were taken into account when the State Educational Programme was prepared for all school subjects in Slovakia. The State Educational Programme together with School Educational Programmes followed not only recommendations of PISA and TIMSS but also predominantly the Slovak Education Act, valid for all schools and educational institutions in Slovakia.

The New Conception of Foreign Language Teaching and Learning in Primary and Secondary Schools, in accordance with CEF, highlights the fact that *general competences* are not typical for the language(s) only; they are inseparable from various other activities and the use of language, and include the following:

1. *Declarative knowledge*, that is, *knowledge of the world*, which has been built up in childhood and developed through education and experience during adolescence and throughout adult life;
2. *Sociocultural knowledge*, which includes knowledge of the society and culture of the given community, that is, it may relate to everyday living, interpersonal relations, values, beliefs and attitudes, body language, social conventions and *intercultural awareness*, which covers how each community appears from the perspective of the other.
3. *Skills and know-how*, that is, *social skills*, which require the ability to act in accordance with the corresponding types of conventions; *living skills*, which are based on the ability to carry out effectively the routine actions required for daily life; *vocational and professional skills*, which cover the ability to

perform specialized actions (mental and physical) required to carry out the duties of employment; *leisure skills*, which entail the ability to carry out effectively the actions required for leisure activities; *intercultural skills and know-how*, which involve the ability to bring the culture of origin and the foreign culture into relation with each other, cultural sensitivity, the capacity to fulfil the role of cultural intermediary between one's own culture and foreign culture, and the ability to overcome stereotyped relationships.

4. *'Existential' competence*, that is, that a person's activity is affected also by his or her attitudes, motivation, values, beliefs and personality factors.

5. *Ability to learn*, that is, the ability to observe and participate in new experiences and to incorporate new knowledge into existing knowledge, modifying the latter where necessary.

6. *Study skills*, that is, the ability to make effective use of the learning opportunities created by teaching situations.

7. *Heuristic skills*, that is, the ability of the learner to come to terms with new experience and to bring other competences to bear in the specific learning situation; the ability of the learner to find, understand and if necessary convey a new situation; the ability to use new technologies.

Communicative competence in the narrower sense has the following components:

- *Linguistic competence* is concerned with knowledge of the language itself, that is, knowledge of and ability to use spelling, pronunciation, vocabulary, word formation, morphology, syntax, stylistics and semantics.
- *Sociolinguistic competence* is concerned with the knowledge and skills required to deal with social dimension of language use. The matters treated are those specifically relating to language use: linguistic markers of social relations, politeness conventions, expressions of folk wisdom, and the ability to register differences, that is, differences between varieties of language used in different contexts, dialect and accent.
- *Pragmatic competence* is concerned with the learner's knowledge of the principles according to which messages are organized, structured and arranged (discourse competence); used to perform communicative functions (functional competence); and sequenced according to international and transactional schemata (design competence).

The above-mentioned competences have also been included in the document which was prepared by the experts in 2007, following the requirements and recommendations of the *Common European Framework for Languages: Learning, Teaching, Assessment* (CEF). It also states that teaching and learning foreign languages is a priority in any modern European society for better understanding among nations and greater mobility and work within international companies facilitated through use of foreign languages. The Conception stressed the idea that the teaching of foreign languages reflects the need for the establishment of effective conditions for lifelong education. Therefore, the basic tenet of the language policy reforms calls for the support of a multicultural European society which presupposes the acquisition of the above-mentioned competences in (at least) two foreign languages. According to this document, the general aim is to guarantee the B1/B2 level (according to CEF) in the first foreign language and the A2/B1 level in the second foreign language in all school graduates in the Slovak Republic.

The National Institute for Education conducted a longitudinal research project in order to support the idea of changes and improvements in teaching and learning foreign languages in Slovak schools. And so the Conception follows current needs and offers real effective solutions, but it also calls for overall changes in the Slovak education system. The authors have dealt with the problem within a wider context, with the team focusing their attention on general aims and content changes in the school subject 'foreign languages'. Therefore, the Conception should be considered as one of the possible ways to integrate language learning into a curriculum more orientated towards European and international demands.

This Conception has been elaborated using the results of an ESF project *Prehĺbenie efektívnosti vyučovania cudzích jazykov v súvislosti so vstupom Slovenska do EÚ* (The Improvement in the Effectiveness of Foreign Language Teaching and Learning, at the time when Slovakia joined the European Union). The team for this project was led by A. Butašová from the Pedagogical Faculty of Comenius University in Bratislava Slovakia, and the team members came from the Faculty of Arts, Constantine the Philosopher University in Nitra, Slovakia. Those experts are the authors of the above-mentioned document, which was published under the auspices of the National Institute for Education. The team has done serious research into the Slovak Republic's language policy and have offered a perspective on the current state in teaching foreign languages, as well as an analysis of the situation in pupils and teachers' preparation in selected European countries. The study also documents results of the empirical research about the language competences the fifteen-year-olds have presented. and offers research results in the situation of continuity in foreign language teaching and learning between primary and secondary school curricula. Using those results, the authors suggest possible solutions for improvement in foreign language teaching and an optimal and alternative model of the school curriculum for the school subject 'foreign language' at primary and secondary schools. This model has been created for English, German, Russian, French, Spanish and Italian languages. The syllabi, elaborated for those languages, have been based on that Conception for A1, A2, B1 and B2 levels according to the Common European Framework for Languages.

Let us have a look at the reasons why it was necessary to start the reform. First of all, there were various syllabi for foreign language teaching and learning but no unified model for effective foreign language teaching. It was impossible to define standard communicative skills which should have been achieved after having finished a certain period of education, so there was no possibility of an equal chance for the pupils' further progression. Secondly, when pupils finished primary education, their knowledge and skills in foreign language acquisition were very different, and it was almost impossible for them to continue at a higher level at secondary schools (i.e. there was discontinuity). Thirdly, high variety in basic pedagogic documents and the absence of general aims in foreign language education resulted in ineffective foreign language teaching, so there was no unity in defining the education content, and consequently there were limitations in education policy planning. Finally, no philosophy in language policy planning resulted in big differences in content and goals among individual foreign languages.

Another very significant problem (which still exists, although it has been minimized a little) is that there are many unqualified foreign language teachers, especially at primary level. Most of them are teachers of English, which is at the moment a lingua franca, that is, a global language of international communication. Such a situation results in big differences in the quality of foreign language education and instruction among schools, which seems to be in contrast with the *National Programme of Education and Training in 15–20 years*, the *Milénium*.

As the language policy in Slovakia had not been a priority in previous years, and there was not a body which would have dealt with the problems of language education, the implementation of modern trends in foreign language teaching and learning was slow, and fluctuation of foreign language teachers in schools increased. Low salaries and underpayment of language teachers was (and is) the result for their lack of motivation to stay in schools. As the authors suggested, those goals and intentions could have been fulfilled only under the following conditions, which are still under the development and have not been fully applied:

- To reconsider and put limits to a high variety of syllabus content for foreign languages and create one with well-defined communicative levels;
- To define the individual communicative competences according to the Common European Framework for Languages in pupils at particular levels of proficiency;
- To guarantee the continuum in language development from the very beginning up to the school-leaving exam;
- To introduce compulsory foreign language teaching and learning of two foreign languages (from the primary up to the secondary education);
- To write national course books with the Slovak authors and native speakers of the foreign language in teams;
- To define the status of the teachers and foreign language teachers in society;
- To make the teaching profession more attractive, including the salaries or other material stimuli;
- To help those learners who want to have more schooling in foreign languages study at language schools or other institutions;
- To introduce a study programme for primary schoolteachers at the universities, which would offer the study of foreign language and its methodology as well;
- To make amendments of this programme and school curricula for pupils with special differences;
- To reconsider the number of pupils in the group;
- To include Content and Language Integrated Learning (CLIL) into foreign language education;
- To adapt foreign language syllabi for secondary vocational schools and apprentice centres;
- As regards bilingual schools, to prepare learners in the foreign language so that they are able to pass school-leaving exams in that particular EU country (i.e. those students will be at a C1 level of that particular foreign language). (Adapted after the Conception, 2007)

In 2008, another significant reform step was passed—the complex law on education and training (the so-called School Law). The focus was put on the content of education in order to guarantee the skills and quality of acquired knowledge. The law introduced *the state and school educational programme.* The educational standards, which specify knowledge, skills and abilities the learners should acquire for the continuity in education, have also been defined in the law. Compulsory school attendance lasts ten years. Teaching and learning of foreign languages and information communicative technologies have also been intensified by the law. Kríž highlights the fact that the framework curriculum guarantees the acquisition of the same minimum teaching material needed from the achievement of a certain level of education which equips school learners to access a wider range of future courses and jobs (Humajová et al., 2008). To ease the start of the first school year, the law made the last year in nursery compulsory for all children. By 2009, a law on vocational training and education passed which invited employers and the private sector to join the system of vocation education; in the same year, the Ministry issued the principles for professional career development of pedagogues and other pedagogic professionals.

Also in 2008, experts in foreign language methodology from several Slovak universities (Advisory Board of the Slovak National Institute for Education under the auspices of the Ministry of Education) initiated the five-year national project devoted to the improvement of foreign language proficiency in primary schoolteachers so that foreign languages could be taught by qualified teachers to students from the age of 8 on. This has been stated in the Conception and also confirmed by the Slovak government in the amendments of the Educational Law. According to that decision, school principals should introduce the foreign language as a compulsory subject in the third grade, that is, at the age of 8 or 9. The aim of this project (financed by the European Union budget) has been to guarantee that foreign language teaching in the third grade will be done by qualified teachers in the long term. To fulfil that aim, close cooperation with universities and teacher training colleges was needed because only universities can guarantee qualified in-service teacher training; the universities have had a long tradition of in-service courses for non-teachers (of foreign languages), and so their services in this project have been indispensable. The universities were involved in the preparation of the Conception of the Teaching and Learning of Foreign Languages at Primary and Secondary Schools from the very beginning. Not only Slovak universities but also other institutions helped the project to start and continue, including the Council of Europe, the British Council Slovakia, Goethe Institute in Bratislava, ECML (European Centre of Modern Languages) and CIEP (Centre International d'Études Pédagogiques) France, and their participation was invaluable, There were two teams established to guarantee the fulfilment of the goals and expectations under the management and running of the project by the managing team—its members had been employees of the

State Pedagogic Institute and also external participants from the educational institutions. Those members were responsible for recruiting the participants, that is, teachers, and the administration of all the activities, including the monitoring and web page. The teachers who wanted to take part in the training stated which language they wanted to study and what level of proficiency they had (there were participants from A0 to B1 levels). Therefore, they were divided into beginner, intermediate and upper intermediate levels in order to improve their foreign language proficiency. The programme for the four-year training has been different for those teachers who started from the A0 level; they started with general English, German, French, Spanish, Italian and Russian, and after four semesters the foreign language methodology for primary school and intercultural communication were added. The programme for teachers whose foreign language proficiency was better, that is, at the intermediate or upper intermediate level, included fewer practical foreign language lessons, and these teachers started earlier with foreign language methodology and intercultural communication.

A special group of teachers were those teachers of foreign languages (English, French, German, Italian, Spanish and Russian) at secondary schools (i.e. ISCED 2) who wanted to help teach foreign languages at the primary level, (i.e. ISCED 1). Their programme was much shorter as it included just lectures and seminars from foreign language methodology for primary school (ages 8–11) and intercultural communication. Summer schools during the schooling were also appreciated by the participants as they were two-week intensive courses mostly in the particular foreign language in Slovakia run by native speakers and Slovak foreign language speakers. In 2013, the participants appreciated the opportunity to take part in summer schools abroad in England, France, Spain, Italy and Russia. For some of them, it was the first time they could take part in such a course abroad. At the end of the schooling, the participants wrote a final thesis based on the foreign language methodology and practical application of that theory in action research or school practice. The theses were examined by two reviewers, and the participants sat the exam, following which the certificate and qualification were confirmed. This project was completed at the end of 2013.

Experts in foreign language methodology and teacher training for primary education have been members of the expert team that was responsible for the content of the programme, for the selection and recruiting of lecturers and seminar leaders and also for the preparation of the proposal of the new study programme: foreign language; primary and elementary education. Regular meetings of the team took place, as well as constant monitoring of the quality of participants' schooling and training. Some of the team members took an active part in lectures and seminars for the teachers, as all of them are university professors and lecturers and experts in foreign language methodology, linguistics and culture studies. In April 2013, a conference was held under the auspices of the Ministry of Education, and representatives from the Council of Europe as well as those from Slovakia took part. After very fruitful presentations, papers and discussion, the participants (teachers, university representatives and representatives of the Ministry and the National Institute for Education) agreed on the following resolutions, which were passed to the Minister of Education:

- To change the description of the study programme for primary education teachers-to-be and include the foreign language so that they can start their careers as qualified foreign language teachers at primary schools;
- To secure the application of the principle of multilingualism (therefore, it is recommended to help even the learners with special differences to learn the foreign language) and to ensure that there is a special pedagogue in each school;
- To guarantee that a second, foreign language is in the curriculum from the age of 11.

The schooling and training of fifteen teachers of foreign languages in order to create experts in testing was the most positive achievement of the project: these teachers were trained by experts from Slovak Comenius University and the Centre International d'Études Pédagogiques in France, which is under the French Ministry of Education. That institution has been appointed by the Council of Europe to write tests and testing tasks in accordance with the Common European Framework of Languages: Learning, Teaching, Assessment. This has enabled the Slovak Republic to have experts for the creation of testing tools in accordance with the Common European Framework for Languages. That cooperation has also helped the project to test the participants during the project at A1/A2 and B1/B2 levels and to create a database of tasks for oral and written tests, all of which have been piloted in the project.

While working on the Project testing problems and issues connected with test formation, the National Institute for Certified Educational Measurements (NÚCEM) developed its professional status in foreign language testing (which has been with us for some time as there were experts involved in creating tests for school graduates at the ages of 18 or 19 in foreign languages and mother tongue) and other school subjects. This introduction of certified measurements after a certain period of schooling has been *a great innovative event* in the Slovak educational system and offers some positive results, though there is still space for improvement and changes.

The NÚCEM is a state-budgeted legal organization founded by the Ministry of Education of the Slovak Republic. It was established on 1 September 2008 as a part of changes made in the educational system that were introduced by the new Education Act in the Slovak Republic. The basic mission of NÚCEM includes:

- Providing the external part and a written form of the internal part of the school-leaving examination assigned by the Ministry of Education,
- Providing external testing of pupils at primary school pupils, and
- Preparing international measurements in accordance with programmes where the Slovak Republic participates according to their rules.

NÚCEM carries out important international assessments of the outcomes and content of education that fulfil criteria of comparative pedagogical research. The aim of the international assessments is not to evaluate the achievement of individual students or schools, but to observe the achievements of educational systems of participating countries and their changes in time; to discover their strengths and weaknesses; and to find out possibilities for improvement. Recently, we acknowledge five international studies, mainly *OECD PISA* and *TALIS* and studies of *IEA PIRLS, TIMSS* and *ICCS*.

The Department of International Measurements (OMM) at NÚCEM, which works as a national coordination centre for international studies in Slovakia, realizes development and adaptation of evaluative frameworks of these studies and tools for measurement of educational achievements; it also prepares and organizes data collection of participating schools and handles data processing and analysis of the outcomes. The Department of International Measurements also provides national reports and constructs the outcomes for application research in the field of education and educational policy. In the Slovak Republic, there is no other working department with comparable experience in this field.

External testing of ninth-grade pupils at primary schools is carried out each year in order to detect individual levels of pupils' knowledge of mathematics and the national language. The results of the tests can be used by headmasters of secondary schools as one of the criteria for accepting pupils to study. The preparation and implementation of testing lies in the competence of the Department of Evaluation Tools Development for Lower Secondary Education, which continues in the school year 2011/12 in accordance with Law No. 245/2008 on education (School Act) and amending acts, and the Regulation of Ministry of Education No. 320/2008 on primary schools.

The *Maturita* is a school-leaving exam for the upper secondary education (ISCED 3) and it is obligatory for all students of secondary grammar schools, schools of art and vocational schools. This school-leaving exam consists of two parts—external and internal. The internal written part includes an essay on a given topic in the Slovak language, foreign language at B2/B1 levels, Hungarian language or Ukrainian language. The internal oral part includes the above-mentioned languages, one optional subject (either science or humanities) and another optional subject according to the student's choice, whilst the external part includes tests in foreign languages, Slovak language, Hungarian language or Ukrainian language and mathematics.

The written form of the internal part entails an essay to be written in the mother tongue and/or a foreign language. The essay themes are announced by NÚCEM. Each school, in cooperation with the regional school authority, provides the oral form of the internal part of the school-leaving examination. Before, for a period of about nine years, NÚCEM's staff had had intense experience with the evaluation processes within the Slovak educational system, as a part of the National Institute of Education. The main aims were as follows:

- To implement certified educational measurements at the national level;
- To prepare international measurements in accordance with the programmes, where the Slovak Republic participates and fully complies with the rules of individual programmes;
- To do the research and development in the area of measurements and evaluation of the quality of education;
- To carry out continuous monitoring of the results of education, conditions and development of education at the national level as well as their international comparisons; and
- To evaluate the quality of education at primary and secondary schools at the level of national educational programmes. (Adapted from www.nucem.sk)

Contemporary issues

In 2013, the Ministry of Education, science, research and sport of the Slovak Republic presented a report on the state of education in Slovakia for general discussion. The report characterizes the current state of the Slovak school system and presents strategic goals for its future development. There are twenty-two steps for further development of primary and secondary schools and higher education that have been identified.

Public discussion and comments from experts were closed at 30 June 2013. Using those recommendations, the Ministry adapted the original material and made it public for further discussion and comments until the end of October 2013, and now the Ministry is working on it. The Ministry of Education is also concerned about the recent PISA measurements, which have disclosed weak achievements of Slovak pupils in mathematics and reading. The Ministry will invite experts and teachers to look for better methods and techniques in teaching maths and in improving reading comprehension in order for learners to be able to link previous knowledge and skills with the new ones embedded in the text.

Further current issues have been dealt with at the National Institute for Education through its *predmetové komisie* (advisory boards for individual schools subjects). There are twenty-seven of them: twenty-five boards for individual school subjects and two professional boards. Their key current research is in the improvement of school curricula. As concerns foreign languages, we deal with the analysis of the Documents for level A1–B2. This analysis has been done after some time has been given to piloting the original documents. Such analyses have been in progress in all other boards. This Advisory Board had also its say in the amendments of individual curricula and the amount of lessons per week.

In January 2012, the Slovak government passed the *Národnú stratégiu pre globálne vzdelávanie na obdobie 2012–2016* (National strategy for global education in the years 2012–2016). According to that document, the Slovak government respects the role of global issues in education. Therefore, the role of global education is to motivate pupils and students towards the acquisition and development of competences (knowledge, skills and attitudes) needed for creative and positive solutions to global issues. The state pedagogic institute is planning to prepare a methodological document for teachers on the methods and techniques recommended for the development of global education.

Another event in the school year 2013/14 will be to test the effectiveness of the experimental version of the European language portfolio for seven- to ten-year-olds. This document helps the development of pupils' awareness about multilingualism, language competences, the role of learning, their contacts with other languages and intercultural experiences.

As far as foreign languages are concerned, there is another project taking place 'Metodika CLIL v nižšom sekundárnom vzdelávaní' (CLIL in Lower Secondary Education). This project follows the experimental *evaluatio ofn Didaktická efektívnosť metódy CLIL na 1. stupni ZŠ vo vyučovaní cudzích jazykov* (Didactic Effectiveness of CLIL method in Teaching Foreign Languages in Elementary Schools: 2008–2012). Its aim is to test the influence of the CLIL method in lower secondary education upon pupils' education results. This project is to be conducted until 2019.

Conclusion

This chapter has presented the current situation in Slovak education system and current issues which are inseparable from the effort of the government, teachers and education experts to improve the teaching and learning processes. It is not an easy goal, but worth the effort because education and the development of general and specific competences in pupils and students is seen to be a priority. The improvement of methods and techniques used by the teachers and educators should help learners develop their creativity, self-esteem and autonomy in learning in order for them to understand that taking over the responsibility for how much and how well they learn opens the way to lifelong education and constant development of their personalities. The systemic development of in-service teacher education also needs constant attention in order for teachers to keep in touch with modern methods and techniques for the improvement of the teaching-learning process. An ongoing discussion continues about vocational schools and apprentice centres. Even though much has been done, there are still gaps, especially in foreign language teaching and in the case of pupils with special differences. Some partial research has been done (namely, through PhD theses) in early foreign language teaching and learning, that is, teaching foreign languages in kindergartens.

References

Butašová, A. et al. (2009). Conception of Teaching Foreign Languages at Primary Schools and Secondary Schools Increasing the Effectiveness of Teaching Foreign Languages National Institute for Education Bratislava, ISBN 978-80-89225-72-9.

Common European Framework of Reference for Languages: Learning, Teaching, Assessment. (2001). Cambridge: CUP, ISBN 0-521-80313-6.

Humajová, Z., Kríž, M., Zajac, P., Pupala, B. (2008). Vzdelávanie pre život reforma školstva v súvislostiach. M.R. Štefánik Conservative Institute, ISBN 978-80-89121-12-0.

Milénium, Národný program výchovy a vzdelávania v SR na najbližších 15–20 rokov. (1998).

Turek, I. (1997). Zvyšovanie efektívnosti vyučovania. Metodické centrum Bratislava.

Zelina, M., Milénium v roku. (2005). In Veda, škola, život. Metodicko-pedagogické centrum Bratislava, 2005, ISBN 80-8052-237-5, EAN 9788080522377.

Web pages

www.eurydice.org
www.globalnevzdelavanie.sk
www.government.gov.sk
www.learningandteaching.com
www.minedu.sk
www.nucem.sk
www.schoolchoices.org
www.statpedu.sk
www.cpk.sk/web/dokumenty/npvv.pdf

13

Slovenia: An Overview

Mojca Peček

Introduction

In 1918, after almost six hundred years under Habsburg rule, Slovenia joined the Kingdom of Serbs, Croats and Slovenes, later named the Kingdom of Yugoslavia. Within the Socialist Federal Republic of Yugoslavia, established after World War II, Slovenia was one of six socialist republics under the federal Parliament and government in Belgrade. Its independence was enhanced in the federal constitution of 1974. However, because of inter-ethnic conflicts, deepening Yugoslavia's economic crisis and disintegration that later evolved into a ten-day war, Slovenia inevitably gained its independence. Slovenia became an independent state in 1991 and a member state of the European Union in 2004. In terms of land area (20.273 km^2) and population (2.06 million in 2013), Slovenia is among the smaller European countries. As part of Yugoslavia, Slovenia had succeeded in maintaining close economic, cultural and other relations with Central and Western European countries. Later, two important factors also influenced Slovenia's development in the 1990s: first, a relatively homogenous ethnic structure (88 per cent Slovenes) and, second, Slovenia's position in Central Europe in the extreme north-western part of the former Yugoslavia. This favourable position enabled Slovenia to largely avoid fratricidal Balkan wars and facilitated its re-approximation with other European countries (Natek et al., 2000).

In this chapter, the way in which the contemporary Slovenian education system arose is discussed, and the structure of the contemporary education system in its current state of development is presented. Additionally, this chapter also outlines how the existing education system succeeded in realising its principles, especially with vulnerable pupil groups such as pupils with special educational needs (SEN) and immigrant pupils.

Foundations of the educational system

The education system in present-day Slovenian territory has a long tradition. It can be said to have originally began in the form of rural and urban church schools in the thirteenth century. The state organization of primary schools was launched in 1774 by an Austrian legislative act called the General School Ordinance, but it was in the 1990s, when Slovenia became an independent state, that the turning point in contemporary development of the educational system occurred. In 1995, the *White Paper on Education in the Republic of Slovenia* was introduced, stating the core principles of the current Slovenian school system, and this was followed by a package of new school acts. New legislation regulating the entire education system, from preschool to university education, came into force. It enabled considerable changes for decision makers and decision-making processes and established basic governance and a regulatory framework for school operations. Acts and regulations have been amended several times, but the reform was based on the following principles: the right to education; equal opportunities and non-discrimination; freedom of choice; fostering of excellence; education quality; increases in teacher and school autonomy and professional responsibility; cultural plurality, values and knowledge; and lifelong learning (Krek, 1996).

According to this legislation, children begin schooling in primary schools at age 6, and compulsory basic education lasts nine years, whilst also allowing for the possibility of educating children at home. The *Matura* was introduced as a general requirement for entry into higher education curricula, and for the first time, legislation enabled the establishment of private schools. The Constitution protects the status of, and gives special rights to, members of the Roma community who live in Slovenia. Children of immigrants have the right to compulsory primary education under the same conditions as other citizens of the Republic of Slovenia. Italian and Hungarians, ethnic minorities living in Slovenia, have the right to an education in their own language (Eurypedia, 2013a).

A substantial part of the formerly centralized administrative powers were devolved to the head principles, but detailed criteria were simultaneously prescribed for school governance and management. The principle of autonomy is realized by preserving secular schools and by separation of church and state (school), as well as by protecting the individuality and privacy of pupils and teachers, with tighter control over personal data collection and use (Peček, 2008). In the management of public education institutions, the Ministry of

Education, Science and Sport plays several roles: as regulator, founder, main finance contributor and supervisor.

The education system in Slovenia is almost fully financed by the state budget; local authorities only contribute a small share of its finances. The state finances state schools, accredited private schools and, to the extent determined by law, also other private schools. However, the majority of basic and upper secondary school pupils attend public schools (99.1 per cent) (Eurypedia, 2013a). The total public expenditure for formal education in Slovenia in 2010 exceeded 2 billion Euros; in comparison with 2009, its share in gross domestic product remained the same (5.66 per cent) (Jablanović, 2012).

The educational level of Slovenia's population is improving, with almost all teenagers now continuing their studies into the upper secondary level. The development of a network of tertiary education institutions, along with young people's increasingly difficult entry into the labour market, has also led to the increased enrolment in tertiary education. On 1 January 2011, one in two residents had upper secondary education, one in four had basic education and one in six had tertiary education or better. Typically, women are better educated than men. One of the objectives of the European Union's (EU) education growth strategy for 2020 is to increase the population share aged 30–34 who have tertiary education to at least 40 per cent. In Slovenia, this goal has already been partly achieved: 41.5 per cent of women in this age group already have tertiary education. However, the benchmark among men with tertiary education has only reached approximately half the total population (22.9 per cent) (Dolenc et al., 2013).

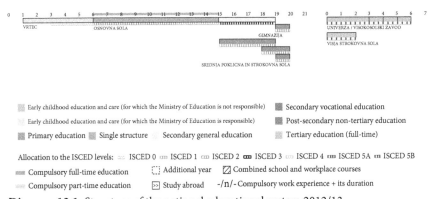

Diagram 13.1 Structure of the national educational system 2012/13 (Eurypedia, 2013a).

Preschool education

Preschool education is part of the education system as a separate level and is not compulsory. It is delivered by public or private preschool institutions which children can attend from the age of eleven months until they enter compulsory education at age 6. Preschool education combines education, play and care, meals, rest and sleep, and various educational programmes. Public preschool programmes emphasize the child's right to choose, which is related to the right to play and the right to creative expression. Much attention is paid to equal progress opportunities, which apply to all preschoolers—SEN children, immigrant children, Romani children and children from socially disadvantaged families. The curriculum is divided into two cycles (for children aged 1–3 years and for children 3–6 years old). It defines six areas: movement, language, art, nature, society and mathematics. The goals set in individual fields provide the framework for the teachers' selection of contents and activities (Bahovec et al., 1999; Kobolt et al., 2010a).

In the school year 2012–13, almost 90 per cent of children in the older age group (3–6) and more than half of children in the younger age group (1–3) attended preschool institutions. Public preschool institutions are founded and financed by municipalities. Parents cover from 0 to 80 per cent of preschool education costs, depending on their income and assets (Eurypedia, 2013a).

Compulsory basic education

Compulsory basic education is organized in a single-structure, nine-year basic school attended by pupils aged 6 to 15 and is free for all children. Parents have a statutory duty and a right to choose a public or private school, or they may educate their child at home. Basic education is divided into three 3-year cycles. In the first cycle, pupils have the same teacher for most subjects. Subject teachers may participate in cooperative teaching with the class teacher in physical education, music, drawing and languages in the ethnically mixed areas. The first year is jointly taught by two teachers, with the second teacher being either a preschool teacher or a class teacher (the second teacher participates in teaching half of the periods). In the second cycle, specialist teachers are gradually introduced in education. During the third cycle (from seventh to ninth grade), pupils are taught exclusively by specialist subject teachers. From the school year 2006/7 onwards, some subjects (e.g. mother tongue lectures, mathematics, foreign language in eighth and ninth grades) may be taught either by two teachers, or teaching may involve in-class grouping or subject streaming; it is up to the school to decide among these three options.

The law stipulates a maximum of twenty-eight pupils per class. This requirement is lower for classes that include SEN pupils or pupils from the Roma community. The average class size in 2012/13 was 19.3. Classes normally consist of pupils of the same age. However, in small schools, pupils of different ages may be taught together (multi-grade classes) (Eurydice, 2008; Statistical Office of the Republic of Slovenia, 2013). The main primary school objectives include the following: enabling pupils to acquire knowledge and skills in accordance with their abilities and interests; supporting personal development; developing abilities for lifelong learning and further education; developing awareness of belonging to the nation, national identity and cultural heritage and nurturing general cultural values; developing respect for human rights, tolerance and acceptance of diversity; developing communication skills in the Slovenian language and foreign languages; facilitating sustainable development and taking responsibility for one's actions, one's health, other people and the environment; and developing entrepreneurial skills, innovation and creativity. Outcomes for specific subjects and knowledge standards are explained in the curricula (Eurypedia, 2013a).

The National Curriculum Document, adopted by the National Council of Experts for General Education, comprises general content of compulsory subjects and general objectives that all pupils should achieve. Within this framework, schools and teachers specify actual subject content; they choose their own teaching methods and have the freedom to select textbooks and exercise books (although textbooks must be selected from a list of approved materials adopted by the Council of Experts). Basic school activities include the compulsory curriculum and optional extracurricular activities. Compulsory school subjects in basic education are mother tongue lessons (Slovenian; Hungarian and Italian in their area of residence), one foreign language from ages 9 to 14, mathematics, geography, history, civic and patriotic education and ethics, environmental studies, physics, chemistry, biology, social studies, music, visual arts, technologies (ICT included), home economics and sports. In the last cycle, schools must offer optional compulsory subjects in the field of social sciences and humanities and in the field of natural sciences and technology. Pupils in the last cycle choose two periods of optional subject/s per week. If parents agree, pupils can take three hours of optional study but must select at least two optional subjects. The extracurricular activities consist of preschool and after-school classes and other forms of pupil care, such as supplementary lessons (for underachievers), additional lessons (for talented pupils) and out-of-school classes. In after-school classes, pupils study, complete their homework and participate in cultural or artistic activities and sports (Peček, 2008; Eurydice, 2008; Eurypedia, 2013a).

Teachers assess pupils on the basis of the curriculum's learning objectives and the assessment procedure regulations. Learning outcomes are assessed continuously in written, oral and practical forms. Teachers use descriptive grades in the first two grades and numerical grades thereafter. Pupils and parents regularly receive information about pupils' progress throughout the school year. At the end of each school year, they receive a report that contains the grades awarded in individual subjects. At the end of the second and the third cycles, national assessment is organized. The purpose of external assessments is to give feedback about each pupil's achievements (Eurydice, 2008; Eurypedia, 2013a).

Successful completion of basic education enables pupils to proceed to an education programme at a selected upper secondary school. Pupils who fulfil the compulsory education requirements and successfully complete at least seven of the nine years can proceed to a short vocational upper secondary education. Pupils who fail to successfully complete basic schooling in nine years have a statutory right to stay in basic school for another two years, and SEN pupils can stay for three more years. Under special circumstances, this period can be extended for up to six years. In the school year 2011/12, 1.5 per cent of pupils failed to complete basic education within the legal time limit (Statistical Office of the Republic of Slovenia, 2013).

Upper secondary education

Table 13.1 Structure of upper secondary education (Eurydice, 2008)

General upper secondary education—*gimnazija*—gymnasium	15–18 years of age (four years)
Technical upper secondary education	15–18 years of age (four years)
Vocational-technical upper secondary education	18–19 years of age (two years after completion of three-year vocational education)
Medium-length vocational upper secondary education	15–17 years of age (three years)
Short vocational upper secondary education	15–17 years of age (two and a half years or three years)
Preparatory classes for the *Matura* examination	(one year)
Vocational courses	(one year)

Upper secondary education takes 2–5 years and caters to young people between 15 and 19 years of age. It is free and divided into general upper secondary education (*gimnazija*), technical upper secondary education and vocational upper secondary education. The transition from basic compulsory to upper secondary education is regulated at the national level through the national joint application system. Schools with a limited number of places consider the final grades from basic compulsory subjects in the last three years of compulsory education (Eurydice, 2008).

At the end of 2010/11, 79,830 full-time students and 15,518 adult students were enrolled in upper secondary schools. Of these students, 41 per cent were enrolled in a general upper secondary programme (*gimnazija*). In the same year, 19,190 full-time students and 4,592 adult students completed upper secondary education; among them, more than half of the pupils (52 per cent) finished upper secondary education from general programme fields and from social science, business and law. In the beginning of 2011/12, 79,901 students were enrolled in upper secondary schools, mostly in general (*gimnazija*) and technical upper secondary schools. Only 16 per cent of them were enrolled in short-term vocational and other vocational programmes (Eurypedia, 2013b). The main objectives of upper secondary education in Slovenia are as follows: to provide general education to the entire population; to enable the highest possible population share to obtain the highest possible education level and develop and attain the highest possible level of creativity; and to enable inclusion in the European integration processes (Eurypedia, 2013a).

Decisions about the founding and financing of upper secondary schools and the distribution of education programmes are adopted at national level. However, schools and teachers are rather autonomous in their implementation of teaching content, teaching methods, recruitment and management of employment relationships, and new student enrolment (Eurypedia, 2013a). Pupils move to a higher grade if they have received positive assessment in all subjects and if they fulfil other requirements, as specified by the programme. They can take re-examination tests in a maximum of three subjects. The school year is divided into two assessment periods; teachers are responsible for assessment.

General secondary programmes (*gimnazija*) prepare students for further studies and are divided into two groups: 'general' (which also includes classical *gimnazija*) and professionally oriented (technical, economical and art *gimnazija*). Syllabi differ slightly for specific types of *gimnazija* programmes; however, they all have a basic structure of compulsory and elective parts. The compulsory part comprises 81 per cent (in general *gimnazija*) to 93 per cent (in some options of art *gimnazija*) of all hours; students may decide on the rest. In all *gimnazija* programmes, students learn at least two foreign languages (Eurypedia, 2013a). *Gimnazija* programmes last four years and end with an external examination called the *Matura* examination, which grants students access to all types of higher education. Those *gimnazija* students who, for various reasons, do not wish to continue their education can enter the labour market by attending a vocational course and gaining a vocational qualification at the corresponding level of secondary vocational and technical programmes. On the other hand, students who have completed vocational and technical programmes can enrol in a *Matura* course and take the *Matura* examination. Vocational courses and *Matura* courses bridge the gap between general and vocational education (Pavlič Možina and Preseren, 2011).

The planning, programming and provision of vocational and technical education are the joint responsibility of social partners (i.e. employers and trade unions) and the state. The common aims and goals of secondary vocational and technical education were defined in a common curricular document. This document stresses attainment targets in interdisciplinary fields and interest activities (Jeznik 2007; Skubic Ermenc and Jeznik, 2007).

Short-term vocational programmes should last a year and a half for students who have completed their basic education, and two and a half years for those who have not. The programmes end in a final vocational *Matura* examination. The final examination certificate enables students to enter the labour market or the first year of any other (upper) secondary vocational programme (Pavlič Možina and Preseren, 2011). Pupils who have successfully completed basic school can enrol in three-year secondary vocational programmes. The final examination certificate enables students to enter the labour market or to continue education in two-year vocational-technical programmes, which have been developed to increase the quality of vocational education.

The aims of vocational-technical programmes are the same as those of technical education programmes and lead to educational qualifications, also called technical qualifications, at the secondary technical programme level in a specific field. Graduates who find a job immediately after completing a three-year vocational programme can re-enter education after at least three years of employment, to obtain a qualification at the level of a secondary technical school by passing examinations. If they also pass examinations in the general subjects of the vocational *Matura* examination, they can continue their studies at the tertiary vocational education (Pavlič Možina and Preseren, 2011).

Technical education is designed primarily as preparation for vocational and professional colleges, although it also leads to jobs with a broad set of qualifications. Secondary technical programmes last four years and end with the vocational *Matura* examination, which enables students to enter the labour market or to continue education at vocational colleges or professionally oriented higher education programmes. There is also an option to take additional subjects in the *Matura* examination, which qualify an individual to enrol in academic higher education programmes (Pavlič Možina and Prešeren, 2011).

Tertiary education

Tertiary education includes short-cycle higher vocational education and higher education study programmes. Over the past fifteen years, it has undergone several legislative and structural changes, rapid institutional development and a significant increase in student numbers. Higher vocational education is provided by higher vocational colleges, which were introduced in 1996, and is institutionally separate from traditional higher education offered by public or private universities and single higher education institutions. Although faculties and art academies can offer both academic and professional courses, professional colleges can offer only professional study programmes. After legislative changes in 2004, professional colleges may also be accredited for second-cycle study programmes if they meet academic standards regarding staff and equipment.

Like some other EU countries, Slovenia opted for a gradual implementation of the Bologna reform, and since the academic year 2009/10, only so-called 'post-reform' programmes have been offered. All programmes accredited after April 2004 are measured in credit points according to the ECTS (European Credit Transfer System). One credit point represents 25–30 student work hours; one academic year can include 1,500 to 1,800 student work hours, or 60 CP. In addition to teaching, higher education institutions also conduct research and host art activities. Higher education reform in 2004 introduced a three-cycle structure, with the first cycle as a binary system of academic and professional study programmes (180–240 CP; 3–4years), leading to the first-cycle degree. The second cycle offers master's courses (60–120 CP; 1–2 years), and the third cycle comprises doctoral studies (180 CP; 3 years). Long non-structured master's programmes are allowed as an exception (e.g. EU-regulated professions) (Pavlič Možina and Prešeren, 2011).

In 2011/12, 104,003 students were enrolled in tertiary education programmes, of which 13.7 per cent were enrolled in short-cycle higher education courses and

86.3 per cent in higher education courses. Moreover, 76 per cent were full-time students, and 82 per cent of higher education students were involved in Bologna programmes. In the academic year 2011/12, there were 15,079 students enrolled in master's degree programmes (Bologna level 2). Of those master's students, 12,712 were enrolled in full-time master's degree programmes. In 2011, the number of new graduates on the tertiary level exceeded 20,000: 4,832 graduated from short-cycle higher education programmes; 3,179 from level 1 graduate programmes; 5,341 from level 2; and almost 1,200 from level 3. In Bologna-based programmes, 4,860 graduated from level 1; 914 from level 2; and 66 from level 3. The proportion of students who have graduated from Bologna-based programmes is 37 per cent (Eurypedia, 2013b).

The general admission criteria for access to higher education are defined by law, although specific access requirements are defined in study programmes. The admission requirements include the following: a general *Matura* certificate or a vocational *Matura* examination and an additional exam for university first-cycle study programmes; a vocational *Matura* or a general *Matura* certificate for professional first-cycle programmes; a first-cycle degree from a corresponding field of studies (and additional exams in other cases) for master's studies; a second-cycle degree for doctoral studies; and additional test results if special abilities (e.g. artistic talents, and physical skills) are required for certain study programmes. Additionally, this transition (as is the transition to upper secondary education) is arranged on the national level. The number of places available is fixed for all study programmes. The places available for new applicants are announced each year by higher education institutions in a pre-enrolment announcement, which is filed separately for undergraduate and postgraduate study programmes (Pavlič Možina and Prešeren, 2011).

In public higher education institutions, Slovenian students and students from EU member states pay tuition fees for part-time studies, whereas full-time studies are free. For postgraduate pre-reform and third-cycle post-reform studies, tuition fees are paid by students. Under certain conditions, these studies can be subsidized by public funds; thus, the tuition fee is correspondingly lower.

Private education

Legislation enabled the establishment of private schools which acquire public validity when a proper professional council ascertains equal educational standards or when schools can ensure the minimum knowledge required for successful education completion. To encourage the establishment of private schools during this transitional period, the state has granted the same funds for salaries and material costs that public schools receive. Otherwise, private schools, when they implement a publicly valid program, are entitled to 85 per cent of funds per pupil, and thus fees for pupils can only amount to maximum of 15 per cent of state funds per pupil (Šimenc, 2007; Kobolt et al., 2010a). Currently, there are two private basic Waldorf schools and one Catholic school; on the secondary school level, there are four Catholic gymnasiums, Eurošola and Waldorf secondary schools.

Education of vulnerable groups of pupils

Children with SEN, immigrant children, Romani children, children from minority ethnic groups (e.g. Italian and Hungarian) and children from lower socio-economic backgrounds are considered to be the most vulnerable pupil groups. Particular educational criteria are applied to shaping individualized programmes of assistance, support and interventions for those children.

SEN education provisions follow a multi-track approach, which means that a variety of services between mainstream education and special needs institutions are offered. Legislation for SEN children requires that they may be integrated into regular classes if they can perform the standards prescribed by the school's educational programme. If mainstream preschool institutions or schools cannot ensure the assistance and adjustments the child needs, the placement procedure assesses the needs of individual children and places them into an adequately adjusted programme in special schools, institutions for SEN education or related departments within mainstream preschool institutions and schools. An SEN Guidance Commission coordinates professional and administrative activities that qualify a child for placement in an appropriate educational setting (Eurydice, 2008; Eurypedia, 2013a).

Education in preschool institutions and schools in ethnically and linguistically mixed areas is provided in accordance with the Constitution of the Republic of Slovenia, educational legislation and laws regulating special educational rights of Italian and Hungarian ethnic minorities. In the Hungarian-speaking area, bilingual instruction in Hungarian and Slovenian is compulsory. The Italian-speaking area hosts Italian schools that have Slovenian as a compulsory subject and Slovenian schools that have Italian as a compulsory subject.

Special privileges are granted to children of the Roma community, which enjoys a special status in accordance with the Constitution of the Republic of

Slovenia. Preschool institutions and schools may reduce the number of children in groups when these groups include Romani children. Schools also provide a wide range of additional learning assistance that is directed towards Romani pupils or towards all pupils who need extra help: complementary classes, work method adaptations, individual and group assistance, additional teaching assistance and Romani assistance.

When immigrant children are included in preschool education, there are no special measures prescribed for their inclusion. However, the preschool education curriculum contains a provision specifying that special attention can be devoted to children. All children—foreign citizens or children without citizenship, refugees and asylum seekers—residing in Slovenia have the right to basic compulsory school education under the same conditions as Slovene citizens. At higher levels of education, there are no special systemic measures that support the integration of immigrant children. Immigrant children with insufficient knowledge and mastery of the Slovene language have the right to an additional support in Slovene language acquisition—a total of forty hours per year, but only for the first year of integration (Kobolt et al 2010a; Zakon o spremembah in dopolnitvah zakona o osnovni šoli, 2011). Schools decide to provide this support individually or in groups, usually outside regular classes, but the funds for its provision are allocated by the Ministry of Education and Sport. Immigrant children are also encouraged to use regular learning support systems that are intended for all pupils who need them (e.g. supplementary classes, individual and group support). With the acquisition of refugee status, child refugees also acquire the right to free participation in a Slovene language and culture course for three hundred hours, as well as the right to reimbursement for public transportation costs to and from the course location, which are paid for by the Ministry of the Interior. The course must be organized within six months of the acquisition date for refugee status. The curriculum for Slovene as a foreign language is still under preparation. Following parental approval, adjustments in assessment and evaluation forms and deadlines, the number of grades and similar adjustments can be offered to immigrant children. Foreign pupils' knowledge is assessed according to their progress in learning standard attainment, as defined in the curricula. The Council of Teachers adopts adjustment decisions. Assessment and evaluation adjustments can be enacted for up to two school years (Kobolt et al., 2010a).

Immigrant children who have just arrived in Slovenia, as well as those who were born in Slovenia and belong to the second or even third generation of immigrants, have the right to mother tongue instruction and education about their culture. Such education is provided in accordance with international treaties with immigrants' originating states (Zakon o spremembah in dopolnitvah zakona o osnovni šoli, 2011). In other cases, mother tongue instruction is organized through the national community's initiative. Mother tongue instruction is rarely organized in schools; however, initiatives for the organization of mother tongue instruction increasingly come from schools and teachers working with immigrant children. Mother tongue instruction is provided outside regular classes and takes the form of an extracurricular activity (Kobolt et al. 2010a). For pupils from socially deprived environments, legislation provides complementary and supplementary lessons and enables them to acquire various subventions (e.g. for meals).

Realization of principles and policies—The case of vulnerable pupil groups

To answer the question of how legislated principles and policies are realized in practice, vulnerable pupil groups will be the test subjects. Special attention will be put on the two biggest groups of vulnerable pupils: SEN pupils and immigrant pupils from countries within the former Yugoslavia, from which 88 per cent of foreign citizens come. Almost 417,000 residents of Slovenia (one in five) are first-, second- or third-generation immigrants. More than half of immigrants are first-generation immigrants, that is, people whose first residence was outside Slovenia (Statistical Office of the Republic of Slovenia, 2013). Among the basic school population, there are 6.2 per cent of SEN children who are integrated in basic school programmes with regular curricula (Dolenc et al., 2013; Statistical Office of the Republic of Slovenia, 2013).

As the previously referenced *White Paper* (the main document providing strategic guidelines on education in Slovenia) claims, 'We have to establish a democratic education system incorporating the principle of equal opportunity together with the requirement to make provisions for differences (individual differences, group differences and differences in the rate and pace of development): the right to choose and be different' (Krek, 1996, p. 39). Let us see how this principle is defined in school legislation and realized in practice.

As was already mentioned, SEN children can be integrated into the regular school system only if they can, with regards to type and rate of deficiency, deficit or disorder, achieve educational programme standards. In regular school classes, the child can receive additional professional help and follow an adjusted educational program. School enrolment criteria require that a pupil with a type of deficiency is able to achieve educational standards that are expected of the rest of the pupils. The emphasis seems to be on the disability/impairment, its level and the standardization of the ability, all of which clearly show that this act's basis is medical discourse, which primarily considers disorders and difficulties related to learning success and school progress (Peček, Lesar, 2006). According to Kobolt et al. (2010b), the current legislative solution offers no systemic foundations for shaping inclusive schools in Slovenia. Ten years of hard work and significant material costs have been dedicated to put a categorical system based on medical paradigms into force: assistance is prescribed by experts—doctors from different disciplines, such as psychologists and special professionals, who assess the child in ambulant circumstances and are not familiar with child's social functioning in home or school environments. Their decisions are most likely legitimate for pupils with motor, hearing, cognitive and other medical or special learning disabilities, disorders and problems. However, these medical decisions are not legitimate and fair for those children whose problems, disorders and deficiencies lie predominately in relational, social and motivational dimensions, and which are expressed only as long-term frustrations or as accumulated traumatic experiences that lead to unsuccessful learning experiences. With this kind of placement, according to Kobolt et al. (2010b), children are treated as a set of mutually independent segments or areas—learning is separated from experience, motivations, expectations, habits and stimulations; it is separated from a child's social experience. It is not acknowledged that every child, including those who are physically handicapped or those who have specific cognitive deficiencies, has social needs—for affiliation on the one hand and autonomy on the other, and for social recognition, acceptance by peers and comparison with others where he or she will not always finish last. However, the key criterion of regular education is to meet the knowledge standard instead of social inclusion; this approach focuses on knowledge achievements, and other aspects of individual development and the social context of educational environment fade into the background (Kobolt et al. 2010a). Thus the aim of the school system is assimilation—not inclusion (Peček, Lesar 2006).

How does the system take care of the descendants of immigrants from the former Yugoslavia? These individuals migrated to Slovenia in several waves as economic immigrants after the Second World War, at that time travelling across a joint country, and later as refugees during wars in the former Yugoslavia.

Recently, Slovenian basic and secondary schools have encountered children of economic immigrants, mostly emigrating from countries of the former Yugoslavia. Political and demographic changes caused by war and the former Yugoslavia's disintegration have significantly affected the identity of many growing up in the 1990s. These changes have brought new uncertainties in their identity search and have negatively affected their social position, which was often already unprivileged (Kobolt et al., 2010a). Moreover, 44 per cent of foreign citizens who came from countries of the former Yugoslavia had only a basic education or less, and only 4 per cent had tertiary education. Their most common education level was vocational upper secondary (Dolenc et al., 2013). Thus, on average, these individuals are less educated than Slovene citizens. All of these systems negatively affect the school performance of immigrants' descendants: lower grades in primary school; transitions to less demanding (often two- or three-year) secondary schools and seldom to gymnasiums (grammar school); and more frequent placement in residential care homes or correctional homes (Dekleva and Razpotnik, 2002). We can certainly ascribe part of the blame for this unacceptable performance to the educational system.

The objectives of the basic school education, for example, are concerned with the optimal development for each individual and with teaching children about tolerance and human rights; nevertheless, pupils seem to be expected to accept the Slovenian language as their language of expression and to develop an awareness of their belonging in the Slovenian nation. These objectives do not mention the development of one's 'native language', but specifically refer to 'Slovenian'; there is no mention of any other ethnicity except Italian and Hungarian; all other Slovenian citizens seem to be expected to accept, develop and promote their 'Slovenian' ethnicity. The status of the Slovenian ethnic group is a privileged one, which means that children of non-Slovenian backgrounds, except Italians and Hungarians, are not given enough opportunities to develop their own cultures and identities; their own cultures and identities do not seem to be recognized (Peček and Lesar 2006).

In basic school, immigrant children have the right to extra hours of Slovenian language during their first year of integration, but they have no such rights or possibilities in secondary schools. Because one year of extra Slovenian language hours is usually not enough, both basic and secondary schools are left to their own devices for how they will communicate with these pupils (Kobolt et al 2010a). Another problem is the lack of Slovenian language competency in immigrant pupils who have been in Slovenia for some time. More attention needs to be given to developing their language competencies so that they can be successful in school. Because such language development is rare, immigrant children are frequently classified as SEN pupils, based on their linguistic and cultural differences, as this classification secures the school additional funding for extra Slovenian language classes (Skubic Ermenc 2004; Peček and Lesar 2006); occasionally, these students are even sent to schools with adjusted programmes (Barle et al., 2004).

The research also indicates that some teachers are not willing to accept children with SEN or immigrant children in their classrooms and that they do not recognize the teaching profession as an important factor in those pupils' social inclusion. Therefore, these teachers do not search for constructive solutions that would enable children to overcome serious obstacles in knowledge acquisition or purely objective barriers (i.e. language barriers) (Novljan et al. 2004; Peček, Čuk and Lesar 2008). Moreover, these teachers seek solutions by lowering learning demands, which is unacceptable from the perspective of school legislation. Additionally, they often transfer the responsibility for inclusion and achieving curriculum objectives to the parents, the pupils themselves and/or the experts (Peček and Lesar, 2006; Kobolt et al., 2010a). According to research, teachers show no obvious preparedness to develop inclusive practices, and they themselves often express that they do not have enough knowledge and are not adequately trained to work with vulnerable pupil groups (Novljan et al. 2004; Magajna et al. 2005). These teaching practices, however, cannot be understood outside the context of the entire educational system, for the system contains inclusive tendencies in principle, but does not deliver them in reality, that is, in the education legislation, rules and regulations (Peček and Lesar 2006). Results from the extant research also challenge the teacher education system, demonstrating that similar attitudes towards vulnerable pupil groups are found among student teachers (Peček and Macura-Milovanović, 2012; Macura-Milovanović and Peček 2013)

On the whole, the Slovenian educational system is geared towards productivity, and pupils' academic achievements and teacher efficacy are measured in terms of the knowledge pupils retain, which highlights the cognitive dimension of pupils' development and dismisses other dimensions as insignificant (Peček et al. 2008). This system is also one of the reasons why teachers seem to assume that vulnerable pupils are responsible for adjusting to the school system, not the other way around, and that parents, not teachers, are primarily responsible for helping their children do their school work.

Conclusion

The Slovenian educational system has seen many changes in recent years; a framework has been established, and its basic premises are known. However, the system is constantly changing and striving to find solutions that address current demands. This constant change is why the new White Paper on Education in the Republic of Slovenia was written in 2011 (Krek and Metljak, 2011), which surveyed the current state of educational system, analysed numerous individual changes in the school system, evaluation studies, research projects and appraisals, and proposed solutions for the further development of the educational system. In light of certain White Paper solutions and public discussion commentary, the Ministry developed the Amendment to the Basic School Act, which was adopted by the National Assembly; the Fiscal Balance Act, which intervened in the provisions of the Basic School Act, was also adopted. The solutions introduced were organizational and material in nature. For example, this legislation introduced the first mandatory foreign language subject in grade 2 of the basic school. The new regulation will apply gradually; in the school year 2014/15, 15 per cent of basic schools will take part, and in 2016/17, the first mandatory foreign language subject will apply to all pupils in grade 2. The basic school will provide first-grade pupils with the non-mandatory foreign language subject, starting in 2015/16. These Basic School Act changes introduced non-mandatory elective subjects—a second foreign language, arts, computer science, sports and technics—to pupils in grades 4 through 6, along with non-mandatory second foreign language electives to pupils in grades 7 through 9. The amendments will be applied for pupils in grades 4 and 7 in the school year 2014/15, for pupils in grades 5 and 8 in 2015/16 and for pupils in grades 6 and 9 in 2016/17 (Eurypedia, 2013a).

Additionally, curricula objectives and contents for basic education have been revised, and the Council of Experts for General Education have accepted new and revised subject curricula. Schools started gradual curricula implementation in 2011. According to new and revised curricula, pupils are expected to memorize less data, and teachers will have more time to teach them to understand the fundamental knowledge; teachers are expected to use more active teaching approaches, for example experimentation and problem solving.

Due to their high educational requirements already at the basic school level, those parents who can afford private tutors are hiring them for their children. For the Slovenian school system, tutoring is nothing extraordinary; what is perhaps a bit unusual is that lower-class children are receiving tutoring at the basic school level, and tutoring is available for those who are striving for a sufficient assessment and those who are trying to obtain excellent grades; this fact speaks to families having high expectations and oriented towards high productivity. We can also conclude that some wealthier parents hire tutors not only for educational purposes but also to assist in a child's social and moral development (Kobolt et al., 2010a). The expectation is that the new and revised curricula will address this problem.

Additionally, a general reform of *gimnazija* programmes was initiated in early 2006. In February 2008, the National Council of Experts for General Education adopted 'Starting Points for the *Gimnazija* Curricular Reform' for implementation. The new approaches increase teacher autonomy and student responsibility. The earlier knowledge standards were replaced by desired outcome results. Individualization and personalization of learning is prioritized. This move shifted focus from knowledge content towards the development of student learning strategies and knowledge application in diverse situations. The scope of learning options increased, and the cross-curricular connections were strengthened. The foreign languages are based on the Common European Framework of reference for languages (Eurydice, 2008; Eurypedia, 2013a).

Even though interest and enrolment in vocational education programmes is in decline, labour market analyses show remarkable demand for subjects with secondary vocational education. Therefore, to cement vocational training's appeal, it is important to further increase its selectiveness, ensure the widest possible conceptual base (e.g. training for working in the entire professional area or field is planned instead of ensuring only one vocational qualification) and develop transversal competencies. Vocational education reform (2008–11) already caused adaptations of old educational programmes to meet new job market demands. The new educational programmes are based on consideration of technological and societal changes in the economy. These programmes are modularly based and evaluated in terms of credit; practical training through work for employers is increased, and schools and their social partners, particularly local companies, create 20 per cent of the curriculum (Eurypedia, 2013a).

It can be argued that fundamental directions of Slovenian schools fall in line with contemporary developmental trends in other European countries; however, some legislative frameworks have to be changed, and there are obstacles to the realization of written principles in everyday school practice. To realize these educational ideals, political consensus and stable economic situations are needed, which are currently lacking in Slovenia.

References

Bahovec, E. D., Bregar, G. K., Čas, M., Domicelj, M., Saje-Hribar, N., Japelj, B., Jontes, B. et al. (1999). *Kurikulum za vrtce (Curriculum for kindergartens)*. Ljubljana: Ministrstvo za šolstvo in šport.

Barle Lakota, A., Brezić, P., Gajgar, M., Gašperšič, M., Horvat-Muc, J., Jazbec, M., Jukić, O. et al. (2004). *Strategija vzgoje in izobraževanja Romov v Republiki Sloveniji (Strategy for educating Roma in Republic of Slovenia)*. Ljubljana: Ministrstvo za šolstvo, znanost in šport RS.

Dekleva, B. and Razpotnik, Š. (2002). *Čefurji so bili rojeni tu: Življenje mladih priseljencev druge generacije v Ljubljani (Yugoslav immigrants were born here: Life of young immigrants of second generation in Ljubljana)*. Ljubljana: Pedagoška fakulteta: Inštitut za kriminologijo pri Pravni fakulteti.

Dolenc, D., Miklič, E., Razpotnik, B., Šter, D. and Žnidaršič, T. (2013). *People, families, dwellings*. Ljubljana: Statistical office of the Republic of Slovenia.

Eurydice. (2008). *National summary sheets on education systems in Europe and ongoing reforms, Slovenia*. European Commission. http://www.eurydice.si/images/stories/ slovenski_izobrazevalni_sistem/SI_EN_national_summary_sheet.pdf (accessed on 20 June 2013).

Eurypedia. (2013a). *Slovenia, Overview*. https://webgate.ec.europa.eu/fpfis/mwikis/ eurydice/index.php/Slovenia:Overview (accessed on 9 November 2013).

Eurypedia. (2013b). *Slovenia, Statistics on Organisation and Governance*. https:// webgate.ec.europa.eu/fpfis/mwikis/eurydice/index.php/Slovenia: Statistics_on_ Organisation_and_Governance#Pre-school_education (accessed on 19 June 2013).

Jablanović, B. (2012). 'Education'. *Rapid reports*, 29 November 2012 (16). Ljubljana: Statistical office of the republic of Slovenia.

Jeznik, K. (2007). *Krepitev avtonomne vloge šol in učitelja pri prenovi poklicnega in strokovnega izobraževanja v Sloveniji (Strengthening the autonomous role of school and teacher in the reform of vocational and technical education in Slovenia)*. Ljubljana: Center za poklicno izobraževanje.

Kobolt, A., Ule, M., Dekleva, M., Peček Čuk, M., Rapuš Pavel, J., Razpotnik, Š. and Živoder, A. (2010a). *Slovenia*. Goete work package II: Country Report. Governance of Educational Trajectories in Europe. Ljubljana: Faculty of Education and Faculty of Social Science.

Kobolt, A., Caf, B., Brenčič, I., Lesar, I., Rapuš-Pavel, J., Pelc Zupančič, K., Peček Čuk, M. et al. (2010b). *Izstopajoče vedenje in pedagoški odzivi (Disturbing behaviour and pedagogical responses)*. Ljubljana: Pedagoška fakulteta.

Krek, J. (ed.) (1996). *White Paper on Education in the Republic of Slovenia*. Ljubljana: Ministry of Education and Sport.

Krek, J. and Metljak, M. (eds) (2011). *Bela knjiga o vzgoji in izobraževanju v Republiki Sloveniji (White Paper on Education in the Republic of Slovenia)*. Ljubljana: Zavod RS za šolstvo.

Macura Milovanović, S. and Peček, M. (2013). 'Attitudes of Serbian and Slovenian student teachers towards causes of learning underachievement amongst Roma pupils'. *International Journal of Inclusive Education*, 17(6), 629–45.

Magajna, L., Pečjak, S., Bregar, K. G., Čačinovič Vogrinčič, G., Kavkler, M. and Tancig, S. (2005). *Učenci z učnimi težavami v osnovni šoli—Razvoj celovitega sistema učinkovite pomoči. Children with learning difficulties in primary school: The development of the support system.* Ljubljana: Razvojno-raziskovalni inštitut Svetovalnega centra.

Natek, M., Natek, K., Šimec, R., Gabrovec, M., Pavlin, B. and Klasinc, S. (2000). *Portrait of the Fegions, Volume 9, Slovenia.* Luxemburg: Eurostat, European Commission.

Novljan, E., Jelenc, D., Kastelic, L., Kogovšek, D., Lipec-Stopar, M., Pulec Lah, S., Vrhovski-Mohorić, M. and Žolgar, I. (2004). *Uvajanje pogojev za inkluzivno šolanje otrok s posebnimi vzgojno izobraževalnimi potrebami—Analiza stanja in predlogi (Introduction of requirements for inclusive schooling of children with special educational needs: Analysis of situation and recommendations).* Ljubljana: Pedagoška fakulteta.

Pavlič Možina, S. and Prešeren, P. (eds) (2011). *Facts about Slovenia* (8th edn). Ljubljana: Government Communication Office.

Peček, M. (2008). *Responsibilities and autonomy of teachers: Slovenia.* http://www.mszs.si/eurydice/pub/avtonomija/Respon_Autonomy_Slovenia.pdf (accessed on 19 June 2013).

Peček, M. and Lesar, I. (2006). *Pravičnost slovenske šole: Mit ali realnost (Justice of Slovenian school: Myth or reality).* Ljubljana: Sophia.

Peček, M. and Macura-Milovanović, S. (2012). 'Who is responsible for vulnerable pupils? The attitudes of teacher candidates in Serbia and Slovenia'. *European Journal of Teacher Education*, 35(3), 327–46.

Peček, M., Čuk, I. and Lesar, I. (2008). 'Teachers' perceptions of the inclusion of marginalised groups'. *Educational Studies*, 34(3), 223–37.

Peček, M., Valenčič Zuljan, M., Čuk, I. and Lesar, I. (2008). 'Should assessment reflect only pupils' knowledge?', *Educational Studies*, 34(2), 73–82.

Šimenc, M. (ed.) (2007). *Prikaz ureditve zasebnega šolstva v državah Evropske unije (Review of regulation of private education in countries of European Union).* Ljubljana: SVIZ; Ceps.

Skubic Ermenc, K. (2004). 'Prispevek k razpravi o posebnih potrebah z vidika učencev priseljencev'. (Contribution to a discussion about special need from the perspective of immigrant pupils) *Vzgoja in izobraževanje*, 6, 53–56.

Skubic Ermenc, K. and Jeznik, K. (2007). *Kurikul in avtonomija v slovenskem začetnem poklicnem izobraževanju (Curriculum and autonomy in Slovenian initial vocational education).* Ljubljana: Center za poklicno izobraževanje.

Statistical office of the Republic of Slovenia. (2013). *Basic education for youth and adults in Slovenia at the end of the school year 2011/12 and at the beginning of the school year 2012/13.* http://www.stat.si/eng/novica_prikazi.aspx?ID=5427 (accessed on 9 November 2013).

'Zakon o spremembah in dopolnitvah zakona o osnovni šoli'. (2011). Uradni list RS (87), 11317.

Index

Lightning Source UK Ltd.
Milton Keynes UK
UKHW02f0111260318
320031UK00002B/11/P